NURSING LAW

SÍLE P. O'KELLY

B.A. (Mod), Barrister-at-law, King's Inns and the Inns of Court N.I.

and

JOHANNA RONAN

R.G.N, R.M., B.A., Barrister at-law, Kings Inns.

With a foreword by The Hon. Mr Justice Hugh O'Flaherty
of the Supreme Court

BUTTERWORTHS
1994

Republic of Ireland	Butterworth (Ireland) Ltd, 26 Upper Ormond Quay, DUBLIN 7
United Kingdom	Butterworth & Co (Publishers) Ltd, Halsbury House, 35 Chancery Lane, LONDON WC2A 1EL and 4 Hill Street, EDINBURGH EH2 3JZ
Australia	Butterworths Pty Ltd, SYDNEY, MELBOURNE, BRISBANE, ADELAIDE, PERTH, CANBERRA and HOBART
Canada	Butterworths Canada Ltd, TORONTO and VANCOUVER
Malaysia	Malayan Law Journal Sdn Bhd, KUALA LUMPUR
New Zealand	Butterworths of New Zealand Ltd, WELLINGTON and AUCKLAND
Puerto Rico	Butterworth of Puerto Rico, Inc, SAN JUAN.
Singapore	Butterworths Asia, SINGAPORE
South Africa	Butterworths Publishers (Pty) Ltd, DURBAN
USA	Butterworth Legal Publishers, Carlsbad, CALIFORNIA and Salem, NEW HAMPSHIRE

© Butterworth Ireland Ltd

A CIP Catalogue record for this book is available from the British Library.

ISBN 1 85475 3150

Typeset in Ireland by
Typeform Ltd, Newtown Industrial Estate, Clonshaugh, DUBLIN 17.

Printed in Ireland by Sciprint Ltd, SHANNON

To my mother Claire, my daughter Claire, my sons and Robin

and

to my parents and Denis.

TABLE OF CONTENTS

FOREWORD

Nursing Law provides for the Irish nurse a full and clear account on how the law affects the nursing profession. Although nursing as a profession is as old as the sicknesses which have afflicted mankind at all times it was only through the progressive regulation of nursing since the mid 19th century that we have the organised, respected and life-saving profession we know today. Any caring profession must be bound up with ethics. Earl Warren, one time Chief Justice of the United States said:

> "In civilised life law floats in a sea of ethics. Each is indispensable to civilisation. Without law we should be at the mercy of the least scrupulous, without ethics law could not exist".

This book provides invaluable information for the nurse and student nurse as to how the law impinges upon the profession. It traces the history of the regulation of nursing in Ireland from earliest times. It emphasises the role played by Ireland in the evolution of modern medical care. In 19th century Dublin - which was the golden age of Irish medicine in all its manifestations - there were many outstanding women who pioneered the idea of the voluntary hospital, one of whom, Catherine McAuley who founded Dublin's famed Mater Hospital is depicted on our five pound note. As the authors point out, Florence Nightingale applied for nursing training in 1852 to St. Vincent's Hospital, Dublin though she did not see the matter through.

We are afforded a full analysis of the Nurses Act 1985 - now the bedrock legislation covering the nursing profession. It established An Bord Altranais which has as its general concern "the promotion of high standards of professional education and professional conduct among nurses". But the book ranges far and wide on all aspects of the law that impinge on the nurse: labour law, tort law and, in particular, medical malpractice suits.

The proliferation of malpractice actions against medical personnel is something that must be of concern to both the medial and legal professions. Even the very sound of the word "malpractice" has an ugly ring about it. We know that these suits have brought about in other jurisdictions prohibitive insurance premiums, reluctance of doctors to attend accident scenes, for example, and unnecessary procedures in obstetrics.

The development of medical science and the supreme importance of that development to humanity makes it particularly undesirable and inconsistent with the common good that doctors should be obliged to carry out in their professional duties under frequent threat of unsustainable legal claims. So the Supreme Court held in the case of *Dunne, an infant v The National Maternity Hospital*.[1] On the

---

[1] [1989] IR 91.

other hand, the complete dependence of patients upon the skill and care of their medical and nursing attendants, and the gravity from their point of view of a failure in such care, makes it undesirable and unjustifiable to accept as a of law a lax or permissive standard of care for the purpose of assessing of what is and is not medical negligence.

The next matter that is worthy of comment is related to this. I refer to the "disaster" cases. The State is funding much of the cost of insurance premiums in any event. Is there a case to be made for having a fund to compensate - not necessarily to the level of a full-blown civil action - but at least to a significant degree those thus afflicted? I am convinced that the costs saved in defending claims against hospitals, doctors, nurses and regional health boards would make it an economical proposition. It would also provide a just solution for the rare cases where there is a total disaster.

It was my high privilege, when at the bar, to count as my colleagues both authors, Johanna Ronan and Síle O'Kelly, the former who, of course, as well as being a nurse is also a barrister at law. In any popularity poll I suppose it would be safe to bet that nurses would come on top whereas the advocates' profession would tend to languish at the bottom. But is this fair? Many barristers, probably the bulk of the profession, act for the poor and oppressed and often at a low rate of remuneration.

Lord Devlin who was the judge who presided at the *Bodkin Adams* trial, where, incidentally, the matter of the accuracy of nurses' notebooks was very crucial[2] characterised the role of the defence advocate *to be one of the champions picked from the law's army of mercenaries, trained to defend the abandoned and to work for pay.*

That surely was noble calling, too!

Before commending this book to both professions as well as the general public I better comply with the modern requirements concerning "declaration of interests" and say that my wife, Kathleen, is a Mater and Coombe nurse as were previous generations of her family.

That declaration made, however, it is my high honour and great privilege to recommend this book as one that will prove a treasure to both the nursing and legal professions and one that should also be of great interest to members of the general public.

Hugh O'Flaherty

The Supreme Court,
Four Courts,
Dublin 7.
21 July 1994.

---

[2] See *Easing the Passing* (The trial of Doctor John Bodkin Adams) by Patrick Devlin The Bodley Head London, 1985.

PREFACE

Nursing has existed since pre-Christian times and there was a reference to nursing in the Brehon Law which contained basic provisions for "sick maintenance". However, nursing as we know it today evolved from the mid-nineteenth century, but despite the rapid development of hospitals from that time, the first statutory regulation of nurses in Ireland were the Midwives (Ireland) Act 1918 and the Nurses Registration (Ireland) Act 1919. This statutory position was radically changed by the Nurses Act 1985 which regulates the training, discipline and the fitness to practice of nurses. The role of the nurse has evolved from that of a voluntary person caring for the sick to that of a highly qualified professional person with quite identifiable duties and responsibilities. An Bord Altranais recently published "The Future of Nurse Education and Training in Ireland" which contains numerous recommendations relating to the future development of the education of nurses and to the maintenance of the high reputation which Irish nurses hold world-wide.

The authors, over the last number of years, have given lectures in law both to student and qualified nurses. In this book, the first in Ireland, we cover the various areas of law which impinge upon a nurse both as a student and as a fully qualified registered nurse. Johanna Ronan is a nurse and midwife and also a barrister and she was encouraged by her friend Paddy Whelan to write a book on Nursing Law in Ireland. This did not become possible until she met Síle O'Kelly, a colleague at the Bar, and both agreed to join as co-authors in this venture. Our thanks are due to a number of people who have helped in the preparation of this book. We are extremely grateful to Mr Justice O'Flaherty for agreeing to write a foreword. We also wish to express our thanks to our colleagues in the legal, nursing and medical professions who have given us careful and constructive suggestions. Thanks are also due to the staff of Butterworths for their patience and help at all stages of production. Finally, a very special word of thanks to both Denis and Robin for their constant encouragement and tolerance over the past three years. Responsibility for any errors belongs to us both.

The law is as stated as of 30 June 1994.

Síle O'Kelly and Johanna Ronan,
The Law Library,
The Four Courts,
Dublin 7.

30 July 1994

ABBREVIATIONS

Art: Article
ch: chapter
EC: European Community.
EEC: European Economic Community
EU: European Union.
para: paragraph.
s: section.
ss: sections.
SI: statutory instrument.
subs: subsection.

TABLE OF CASES

TABLE OF STATUTES

CHAPTER 1

HISTORY OF NURSING

INTRODUCTION

[1.01] Nursing has existed since pre-Christian times in Ireland. Princess Macha founded the first hospital in or about 252 BC[1] within the precincts of the royal residence in Ulster. This was used by the Red Branch Knights until its destruction in 332 AD.[2]

[1.02] The prevailing law in Ireland at this time was the Brehon Law which required that:

"... it was the custom that provision for "sick maintenance"- including curative treatment, attendance and nourishing food - was required to be made for all who needed it. The persons on whom the responsibility of providing it devolved were clearly defined in every case. It might be a man who had made himself responsible by having, either with or without criminal intention, inflicted injury on another. It might be the "next of kin" whose duty it was to take charge of an orphan child or a sick imbecile of his kindred, for whose sick maintenance securities had to be given by him, or proper provision made."[3]

[1.03] It was a requirement of the Brehon Law that, within each area, the homes of the physicians (who were regarded as special families) be available on the terms mentioned below to the wounded and the sick.

"The care and maintenance under the Law of Sick Maintenance is documented clearly in the Book of Aicill as follows "There is a stay also for providing him [the sick man] with proper bed furniture," says the text, "i.e. plaids and bolsters, i.e. a suitable bed-for providing him with a proper house, i.e. that it be not a dirty snail-besmeared house, or that it be not one of the three inferior houses - i.e. that there be four doors out of it, in order that the sick man may be seen from every side, and water must run across the middle of it - for providing also against the things prohibited by the physician, i.e. that the sick man may not be injured, i.e. by women or dogs - i.e. that fools or female scolds be not let into the house to him, or that he be not injured by forbidden food: And he is a person whose death is not probable, and the stay is one day.[4]"

---

[1] Sophia Bryant *"Liberty Order and Law"* at p 306.

[2] *Rosary Magazine*, March 1920.

[3] Sophia Bryant *"Liberty Order and Law"*.

[4] *Book of Aicill* at p 289.

With the advent of Christianity, care of the sick was generally taken over by religious houses. Within the infirmaries nursing care was carried out by both male and female members of these communities. The evolution of nursing was discussed in *The Working Party on General Nursing Report*[5] which stated that:

"As far back as the 16th century the title *Matron* was in use. Matron was usually a married woman or a widow and functioned as a housekeeper. As nursing evolved mainly through the work done by the religious orders who attended the sick and saw that the physicians' orders were carried out, the title *Sister* came into use and continues to be used. *Nurses* were rarely promoted and were regarded as domestic servants. After the Reformation the monasteries were suppressed. The Elizabethan Poor Laws (1601) which influenced society in Great Britain did not apply to Ireland. No provision was made in this country for the relief of the poor or the sick pauper until the beginning of the 18th century.

The growth of Irish hospitals in the 18th century was dependent on socially minded philanthropic individuals who founded *hospitals* for the free treatment of the sick poor. This development occurred only in the cities and mainly in Dublin. Some of the voluntary hospitals founded in the early decades of the 18th century such as the Charitable Infirmary Jervis Street,[6] Dr. Steevens Hospital[7] and the Rotunda Hospital are still in existence and playing a valuable role in the health services. Similar hospitals were opened in Cork and Waterford. These hospitals formed the nucleus of what are now described as voluntary hospitals."

EARLY HOSPITALS

[1.04] The following are extracts from a lecture given by Dr. T. Percy Kirkpatrick delivered at the Bicentenary Congress of the Rotunda Hospital in 1945:

"Some few Irishmen studied midwifery at the Hotel Dieu in Paris, but before 1718 there was not a single civil hospital in Dublin for the treatment of the sick, or for the teaching of doctors. In that year six surgeons opened a small hospital in Cook Street for the reception of surgical patients: this is now known as Jervis Street Hospital. In 1733, in pursuance of the will of Dr. Richard Steevens, who died in 1710, Steeven's Hospital was opened, "for the maintenance and curing such sick and wounded persons whose disease and wounds are curable."

"Neither of these institutions, nor Mercer's Hospital, opened in 1734, made any provision for the care of lying-in women. Both rich and poor alike suffered from the want of skilled assistance at childbirth, but the hardships of the poor at that time were almost indescribable. Side by side with the wealthy citizens of Georgian Dublin many people existed in the greatest poverty and squalor. The care of the sick poor had no place either in the King's Government nor in the municipal administration. The plea put forward in 1725 by John Murbary (d.1739) for the establishment of a maternity hospital in London had not met with any response, and it was not till the year 1739 that

---

[5] Published by the Department of Health in March 1980.

[6] This Hospital has now been amalgamated with Beaumont Hospital.

[7] Dr Steeven's Hospital has been amalgamated with St James.

Sir Richard Manningham (1690-1759) opened a few beds for lying-in women in a house in Jermyn Street, the forerunner of the present Queen Charlotte's Hospital."

[1.05] Dr. Kirkpatrick then referred to Bartholomew Mosse, the noted surgeon and founder of the Rotunda Hospital:

"On May 22, 1742, he was admitted as a Licentiate in Midwifery in the King's and Queen's College of physicians, after which, we are told, "he quit the practice of surgery", and devoted himself to midwifery. On October 6, 1743, he married his cousin, Miss Jane Whittingham, at St. Bride's Church, Dublin. Mosse could not have been long in practice before he realised the folly of expecting to get good results in midwifery practice amongst the poor under the conditions that prevailed in Dublin at the time, but there did not seem to be any prospect of improvement in those conditions, nor did there seem to be any desire amongst those in authority to make the necessary effort. The provision of hospital accommodation for poor lying-in women was at the time a new idea, and it presented difficulties so great that they might well have daunted the most enthusiastic philanthropist. For a young surgeon who had recently started a practice by which he hoped to support himself and his newly married wife, to attempt to solve this problem must have seemed to many to be the act of a madman. Mosse, however, was a young man who saw visions, and having seen them was determined to make them realities. All through his life difficulties seemed rather to stimulate him to greater effort than to depress him. As soon as he realised the urgency of the need he determined to provide the means to alleviate it, and his mind having been made up he started to interest his friends in his proposals."

[1.06] Dr Kirkpatrick further described how Bartholomew Mosse set about setting up his midwifery hospitals:

"In March, 1743, we find him collecting subscriptions, and he tells us that he had got together "a union of a number of persons of different occupations, most of whom subscribed four shillings and four pence yearly, to be paid quarterly, for the support of the intended hospital." A committee of four or five well known charitable men was formed, and with this limited support, but with unbounded faith and confidence, a house in George's Lane, now South Great George's Street, was rented for the hospital. The house had previously been used as a theatre, in which Peg Woffington had made her first appearance on the stage. There was barely sufficient money to fit up a few beds, but Mosse felt that there should be no delay in making a start. He was confident that an actual hospital in being would attract more public sympathy than the mere promise to build one in the future. On March 15, 1745 (O.S.), the hospital was opened, with all that pomp and ceremony, the advertisement value of which Mosse knew so well; the first patient - Judith Rochford - was admitted, and there on March 20th "she was safely delivered of a son." The beds at first were few in number, but the committee, inspired by Mosse, hoped that there would be at least twenty-four available in the house.

The great adventure had started, the Hospital was in being, women were being delivered in it, but it is probable that not a single person, except Mosse, thought that its life would be long. Mosse had realised his vision: we wonder did he ever glimpse the great future before his foundation, or did he die to young to "dream dreams"?

Few details of the medical practice in the Hospital have come down to us. We are told that constant attendance will be given at the Hospital by Mr Mosse "until assisted by the rest of the gentlemen of the faculty." Opposition rather than assistance was what was given by the faculty, and Mosse was left to bear the whole burden. "Every woman admitted to the house is to have a warm decent bed to herself, and shall be provided with all manner of necessaries, and the greatest care imaginable will be taken of her and her new born infant until she will be able to leave the hospital without danger, and all without the least expense to her." From March 25, 1745, to July 1, 1746, two hundred and nine women were admitted to the house, of whom two hundred and four were delivered of two hundred and eight children."

[1.07] Bartholomew Mosse then set about realising his more ambitious scheme for a larger hospital which he fulfilled when he acquired the premises now known as the Rotunda in March 1748, which was incorporated by Royal Charter in 1756. The importance of this recognition was described as follows:

"This Charter was of the greatest importance, for not only did it give an official sanction to the work that had been done, but it laid down the general principles on which the House was to be managed. Not only was the Hospital to be for the treatment of poor lying-in women, but it was to afford a place for the study of obstetrics and for the teaching of midwives. Mosse was appointed Master for life, but after him "no person however deserving shall be capable of being elected to the said hospital who has been Master for seven years, either successively or at different times, but amounting in the whole to seven years." In making choice of a Master preference should be given to those who had served as Assistant Masters, so that although the Masters changed continuity in the teaching and practice was maintained."

[1.08] Another speaker at the Congress, William Doolin MBFRCSI, referred to the contribution made by Dublin philanthropy to medicine "and the birth of a voluntary hospital" in Dublin at this time:

"Looking back over that past whose story he has told so often and so well, were some visitor to Dublin this week to put me the question: "What has been Dublin's chief contribution to medicine?" my reply would be "the idea of the voluntary hospital." At the opening of the 18th century all British hospitals were under Royal or State control. Here, in a much neglected British dependency, neither State nor monarch showed any evidence of charitable concern for the sick poor; it needed all the *saeva indignatio* of a Swift to sting the ruling classes to some sense, however dim, of their responsibilities as rulers. The example of Richard Steevens and of Mary Mercer in this city was speedily followed by Dr John Addenbrooke at Cambridge and by Thomas Guy at London, an example which resulted in the establishment of a principle which is very dear to us in both islands today - the principle of the voluntary hospital. As an outstanding instance of that practical form of private Christian charity we celebrate this week - belatedly, but none the less proudly- the bicentenary of the foundation of the oldest voluntary institution in the world for the care of women in childbirth. Wherever the history of obstetrics is read or written the name of Bartholomew Mosse must stand imperishable in such records."

As can be seen from the above extracts, Dublin was foremost in providing care and attention to the poor and sick on a voluntary basis.

FLORENCE NIGHTINGALE

[1.09] While it is a commonly held belief that Florence Nightingale was the pioneer of nursing, she was in fact among the forefront of those involved in the formal training in nursing schools. Prior to the establishment of the Nightingale Training School for nurses at St. Thomas' Hospital in 1860, St. John's Sisterhood in 1856 took over the training in both Kings College Hospital and Charing Cross Hospital, which are still in existence today. In Ireland, St. Vincent's Hospital had a training arrangement for nurses as far back as 1835 and in 1852 Florence Nightingale applied to be admitted there for training though she did not attend. The Working Party Report[8] described the nurses around this period as follows:

"Before formal nurse training was introduced, nurses could be broadly divided into four categories -

(i) inmates nursing the sick poor in poor houses,

(ii) nurses working in voluntary hospitals who were of a slightly higher social level,

(iii) sisters in charge of wards, and

(iv) matrons who were of a superior class to the others and who had some degree of administrative and management function.

It is interesting to note that all these grades were regarded as being exclusively female although in earlier history reference can be found to both male and female nurses."

[1.10] Early efforts towards the systematic training of nurses failed and while there is evidence of training efforts in some of the voluntary hospitals, their example was not followed elsewhere. Plans for the instruction of nurses were outlined as early as 1817. However, no general pattern emerged and it was not until the 1890's that formal training programmes were established and hospital authorities seeing the value of probationers, from the services point of view, accepted them for training. Thus emerged the system, that still exists today, of a heavy dependency on probationer/student nurses for service. Matrons were responsible for training nurses for their own hospitals though often they delegated this function to suitable ward sisters and thus originated the role of the nurse tutor.

---

[8] Published by The Department of Health March 1980.

The same basic system is in existence today except it is now governed by statute, the Department of Health and EU regulations.

LEGISLATION

[1.11] While there was English legislation governing the area of nursing, the first Irish Acts were the Midwives (Ireland) Act 1918 and the Nurses Registration (Ireland) Act 1919. Midwives were the first branch of nursing to be regulated by statute both in England and Ireland. When Bartholomew Mosse founded the Rotunda Hospital in 1748, there were only two licensed midwives in Ireland. In England in 1902 a Midwives Act was passed "to secure the better training of midwives and to regulate their practice." The provisions relating to training, discipline and malpractice in the 1918 and 1919 Acts were similar to those contained in the Nurses Act 1985.

Midwives (Ireland) Act 1918

[1.12] This Act came into being in order to regulate and secure better training for midwives. The Act established the Central Midwives Board, the first nursing register in Ireland and this was called the Roll of Midwives and was published annually by the Board. Under its provisions the Board was empowered to:

1. Issue and cancel certificates.

2. Make rules and regulations regarding the issue of these certificates.

3. Train and examine a midwife for re-admission to the Roll of Midwives.

4. Regulate, supervise and restrict, within due limits, the practice of midwifery.

5. Remove a midwife for disobeying the Rules and Regulations laid down in the Act or for misconduct.

6. Restore a midwife to the Roll.

The above rules were only valid if approved by the Privy Council. Provision was also made regarding the falsification of the register, the penalty for which was a fine of £5.00 and/or one year in prison.

Nurses Registration (Ireland) Act 1919

[1.13] Section 1 of this Act established the General Nursing Council of Ireland. Section 2 obliged the Council to form and keep a register of nurses. This was to consist of the following parts:

2(2) (*a*) a general part containing the names of all the nurses who satisfy the conditions of admission to that part of the register;

(*b*) a supplementary part containing the names of male nurses;

(*c*) a supplementary part containing the names of nurses trained in the nursing and care of persons suffering from mental diseases;

(*d*) a supplementary part containing the names of nurses trained in the nursing of sick children;

(*e*) any other prescribed part.

Where any person satisfies the conditions of admission to any supplementary or prescribed part of the register, his name may be included in that part of the register notwithstanding that it is also included in the general part.

[1.14] Section 3(1)(*a*) empowered the Council to make rules and regulations regarding the formation, maintenance and publication of the register of nurses. Section 3 also dealt with the education and discipline of nurses. Both the conditions for removal and restoration are set out in subs 3(1)(*d*). Under s 5(*a*) fees were payable for application and retention to the register, in the sum not exceeding one guinea and two shillings and sixpence respectively. Section 7(1) dealt with the right of appeal to the High Court from a decision of the Council to remove a nurse from the register. Unlawful assumption of title or falsification of the register carried a penalty of £10 for the first offence and £50 for any subsequent offences.

Midwives Act 1944

[1.15] This Act established "a Board to be styled or known as the Central Midwives Board." The Rules regarding the training, examination and registration of midwives were contained in this Act. The Minister for Health appointed members of the Board, four of which were midwives. Section 9(2) provides that:

9(2) Where an appointment is made under this section of persons to be members of the Board -

(*a*) four of such persons shall be midwives ordinarily resident within the State appointed by the Minister after consultation with such representative nursing organisations as he thinks proper to consult, and

(*b*) one at least of the remaining three of such persons shall be a registered medical practitioner.

Nurses Act 1950

[1.16] The purpose of this Act was to make further and better provision for the registration, certification, control and training of nurses and for other matters relating to nurses and the practice of nursing. Section 6 of this Act dissolved the General Midwives Council and s 7 established An Bord Altranais (the Board). Section 6(1) provided for the dissolution of the General Nursing Council and the Central Midwives Board. Within An Bord Altranais a Midwives Committee was established in accordance with s 26 under the authority of the Board. At this stage the midwives had lost their independent board and any recommendations midwives put forward had to be put to An Bord Altranais for its approval. The Midwifery Register now has a division contained within the nursing register. The Midwifery Committee consisted of eight members, five of which were appointed by the Minister and four were obliged to be midwives. This Act contained disciplinary powers and the Midwives Statutory Committee had to approve of any sanction against a midwife. Although the midwives retained their independent training schools, the Board had the power to approve them under s 53 and also to approve hostel accommodation for them in training.

[l.17] "Nurse" was defined in the Act as "a person registered in the register of nurses and includes a midwife and the word *nursing* includes midwifery." This definition has been amended with the addition of "man" by the Nurses Act 1985.

Nurses Act 1985

[1.18] As a result of representations from various interested bodies concerning the changing role of the nurse, the Minister for Health in 1975 established the Working Party on General Nursing with the following terms of reference:-

> "To examine and report on the role of nurses other than psychiatric nurses in the health services, on the education, training and grading structures appropriate for that role in the future, and to make recommendations. In regard to training to examine, in consultation with such persons and bodies as are considered appropriate, the recommendations for a common basic training course for all nurses to be followed by specialisation in particular fields which were made by the Commission of Inquiry on Mental Illness in 1966 and by the Working Party on Psychiatric Nursing Services in 1972."

[1.19] In 1971 the Irish Nursing Organisation (I.N.O.) submitted a resolution that had been adopted at its Annual General Meeting:-

> "We recommend as a matter of urgency the setting up of a Working Party by the Minister for Health to examine nursing staff structures, with not less than two-third nursing personnel and to make a thorough analysis of the nursing structure in the hospital services (excluding the psychiatric service which have already been the subject of study). Such an examination is essential to the national development of the service and in order to decide on future structures."

[1.20] A further submission by the I.N.O. in 1974 was made in conjunction with the Irish Matrons Association (I.M.A.), setting forth the terms of reference which they considered should be established :-

> "To review the nursing and midwifery needs of the country and to establish how best to meet these requirements through the effective utilisation of professional resources."

[1.21] In 1974 An Bord Altranais arrived at their resolution having examined the report of the Committee on Nursing in England:[9]

"(i) that the Minister for Health be requested to appoint a Commission to undertake a full survey of the present nurse training facilities in Ireland and recommend whether or not need exists to extend the present training facilities;

(ii) that this Commission should take cognisance of the present utilisation of nursing services in the hospital scene - both in training and non training hospitals - and examine if a need exists in Ireland for a grade of nurse similar to the enrolled nurse in England or the Practical Nurse in America."[10]

Prior to the above representations, the Commission of Enquiry on Mental Illness (1966) was in favour of a common basic training for all nursing staff.

[1.22] As a result of the Working Party Report, the Nurses Act 1985 was enacted thus incorporating many of the Report's recommendations. The Nurses Act 1985 is very similar in content to the Medical Practitioners Act 1978 and the Dentists Act 1985. Part I deals with preliminary and general aspects in ss 1-5:
(1 - Short Title, 2 - Interpretation, 3 - Commencement, 4 - Establishment Day, 5 - Repeals) and Part V repeals the Midwifery Act 1944 and the Nurses' Acts 1950 and 1961.

[1.23] Part II deals with the provisions establishing An Bord Altranais and the dissolution of the former Board. The composition of An Bord Altranais is controlled both by appointment by the Minister for Health and the election of members by persons within the profession. It also deals with the borrowing powers and accounts of the Board. Section 26 empowers the Board, with the approval of the Minister, to make rules in order to assist the Board in carrying out its functions.

[1.24] Part IV deals with education and training which is discussed in Chapter 2. Part V deals with the fitness to practise of a nurse and is discussed in Chapters 4 and 5.

Definition of "Nurses and Nursing"

[1.25] A nurse is defined in s 2 as ".. a woman or a man whose name is entered on the register and includes a midwife and "nursing" includes "midwifery"". The difference between this definition and that in the 1919 Act is the addition of the words "or a man". This definition is also referred to in the Code of Conduct. The Working Party on General Nursing[11] adopted a comprehensive definition of a

---

9   Briggs 1972.
10   The Working Party on General Nursing.

nurse which was based on a study carried out by the International Council of Nurses and is as follows:-

"The nurse is responsible for planning, providing and evaluating nursing care in all settings, for the promotion of health, or support in death, prevention of illness, care of the sick, rehabilitation and functions as a member of the health team. In attempting to identify the nurse's role in a general sense, the Working Party examined the various definitions which have been made over the years. All of them have considerable merit and relevance for the nursing profession. The International Council of Nurses' definition of a nurse referred to above captures in essence the spirit of every other definition but it is still worth recording here the following one by the renowned American nurse, Virginia Henderson:-

"The unique function of the nurse is to assist the individual, sick or well, in the performance of those activities contributing to health or its recovery (or to peaceful death) that he would perform unaided had he the necessary strength, will or knowledge, and to do so in such a way as to help him gain independence as rapidly as possible..."

An Bord Altranais (The Board)

[1.26] An Bord Altranais is the statutory regulatory body for the nursing profession in Ireland. Its main functions relate to:

- The maintenance of a register of nurses.

- The control of the education and training of student nurses and the post-training of nurses.

- The operation of fitness to practise procedures.

- The ensuring of compliance with the EU Directives on nursing and midwifery.[12]

An Bord Altranais replaces the former Board and has as its general concern the promotion of "high standards of professional education and training and professional conduct among nurses". The Board is also obliged to fulfil its functions as defined in s 6 of the 1985 Act:-

6 (1) There shall, by virtue of this section, be established on the establishment day a body to be known as An Bord Altranais or, in the English language, as the Nursing Board (in this Act referred to as the Board) the general concern of which shall be to promote high standards of professional education and training and professional conduct among nurses, and which shall, in particular, fulfil the functions assigned to it by this Act.

---

[11] Department of Health 1980.
[12] An Bord Altranais, *The Future of Nurse Education and Training in Ireland*, (1994) p.vii.

(2) The Board shall be a body corporate with perpetual succession and power to sue and be sued in its corporate name and to acquire, hold and dispose of land.

(3) The Board may, subject to the provisions of this Act, regulate its own procedure.

[1.27] Section 7(2) dissolves the former Board and transfers the rights, liabilities and property to the new Board:

7(2) All property, whether real or personal (including choses-in-action), which immediately before the establishment day was vested in or belonged to or was held in trust or subject to conditions for the former Board, and all rights, powers, and privileges relating to or connected with any such property, shall on the establishment day, without any conveyance or assignment but subject where necessary to transfer in the books of any bank, corporation or company, become and be vested in or the property of or held in trust or subject to conditions for (as the case may require) the Board.

Membership of the Board

[1.28] Section 9 deals with membership of the Board, the majority of which are nurses elected from within their own ranks:

9(1) The Board shall consist of 29 members appointed in the following manner, that is to say-

(*a*) five nurses resident in the State and who are engaged in training nurses of whom-

(i) one shall represent nurses who are training nurses in general nursing,
(ii) one shall represent nurses who are training nurses in paediatric nursing,
(iii) one shall represent nurses who are training nurses in psychiatric nursing,
(iv) one shall represent nurses who are training nurses in the care of mentally handicapped persons, and
(v) one shall represent nurses who are training nurses in midwifery, elected by nurses;

(*b*) five nurses resident in the State and who are engaged in nursing administration of whom-

(i) one shall represent nurses who are engaged in general nursing administration,
(ii) one shall represent nurses who are engaged in the administration of public health nursing,
(iii) one shall represent nurses who are engaged in the administration of psychiatric nursing,
(iv) one shall represent nurses who are engaged in the administration of midwifery, and
(v) one shall represent nurses who are engaged in the administration of nursing of mentally handicapped persons, elected by nurses;

(*c*) seven nurses resident in the State who are engaged in clinical nursing practice of whom-

   (i) two shall represent nurses who are engaged in clinical practice in general nursing,

   (ii) two shall represent nurses who are engaged in clinical practice in psychiatric nursing,

   (iii) one shall represent nurses who are engaged in clinical practice in midwifery,

   (iv) one shall represent nurses who are engaged in clinical practice in public health nursing, and

   (v) one shall represent nurses who are engaged in clinical practice in the nursing of mentally handicapped persons, elected by nurses;

(*d*) twelve persons appointed by the Minister, after consultation with such bodies or organisations as he considers suitable to advise him, of whom-

   (i) one shall be a registered medical practitioner engaged in the practice of medicine in a hospital approved of by the Board for the training of general nurses,

   (ii) one shall be a registered medical practitioner engaged in the practice of medicine in a hospital approved of by the Board for the training of psychiatric nurses,

   (iii) one shall be a registered medical practitioner engaged in the practice of obstetrics in a hospital approved of by the Board for the training of midwifes,

   (iv) one shall be a person representative of the management of health boards,

   (v) one shall be a person representative of the management of hospitals, other than hospitals administered by health boards,

   (vi) two shall be persons representative of the Department of Health,

   (vii) one shall be a person who is experienced in the field of education,

   (viii) one shall be of the third level educational establishments which are involved in the education and training of nurses,

   (ix) one shall be a nurse, and

   (x) two shall be persons representative of the interest of the general public.

[1.29] Three of the persons whom the Minister appoints are to be registered medical practitioners. Membership of the Board is for a period of five years and no person shall remain in office for more than two consecutive terms of five years. The elections are carried out in accordance with the rules made by the Board and with the approval of the Minister under the Act. A person may vote or be nominated for election without a minimum qualifying period.

Committees of the Board

[1.30] Section 13 empowers the Board to set up various committees, at their discretion, and they shall under subs (2) establish a Fitness to Practise

Committee.[13] There are different rules for this Committee in that its members may only be drawn from members of the Board. A majority of the Committee are obliged to be nurses elected to the Board, and finally a third of the Committee must be members of the Board appointed by the Minister for Health.

13(1) The Board may, subject to the subsequent provisions of this section, from time to time establish committees to perform such, if any, functions of the Board as, in the opinion of the Board, may be better or more conveniently performed by a committee, and are assigned to a committee by the Board.

(2) In particular and without prejudice to the generality of *subsection (1)* of this section, the Board shall establish a committee in relation to its function under *Part V* of this Act.

(3) A committee established under this section, other than the committee referred to in *subsection (2)* of this section may, if the Board thinks fit, include in its membership persons who are not members of the Board.

(4) The chairman of every committee established under this section shall be a member of the Board provided that in the case of the committee referred to in *subsection (2)* of this section the chairman shall be a member of the Board other than the President or the Vice-President of the Board.

(5) Every member of the committee established under *subsection (2)* of this section shall be a member of the Board.

(6) A majority of the members of the committee referred to in *subsection (2)* of this section shall be persons who have been appointed by election to the Board and at least one-third of the members of that committee shall be persons other than persons who have been appointed by election to the Board.

(7) The acts of a committee established under this section shall be subject to confirmation by the Board unless the Board, at any time, dispenses with the necessity for such confirmation.

(8) The Board may, subject to the provisions of this Act, regulate the procedure of committees established under this section, but, subject to any such regulation, committees established under this section may regulate their own procedure.

Removal of the Board

[1.31] Section 15 provides for the removal of the Board in the event of it failing, refusing or neglecting to perform the functions assigned to it. There is also provision for the appointment, by the Board, of a Chief Executive Officer and other officers and servants by the Board subject to the consent of the Minister for

---

[13] See chapters 4 and 5.

Health.[14] Retirement age is sixty-five years for permanent officers of the Board.[15] Superannuation as it applies to Board and its officers is dealt with in s 19. In the event of either an officer or a servant of the Board being elected to either House of the Oireachtas or the Assembly of the European Communities or filling a vacancy in the Assembly he shall stand seconded from employment of the Board.[16] The Board is also charged with the keeping of proper accounts of all income and expenditure and subject to any conditions imposed by the Minister can borrow money for capital or current purposes.[17]

Fees

[1.32] Section 25 enables the Board to have an income as it is empowered to charge fees for both the registration, retention and restoration of nurses to a "Live" Register. Registration is dealt with in Part III of the 1985 Act.

> **25** The Board may charge such fees as may, from time to time, be determined by the Board, with the consent of the Minister, for-
>
> (*a*) the registration of a person in the register,
>
> (*b*) the retention of the name of a person in the register,
>
> (*c*) the restoration in the register of the name of any person whose name has been erased or removed pursuant to the provisions of this Act from the register,
>
> (*d*) the giving to any person of a certificate of registration,
>
> (*e*) the registration of any candidate for nurse training in any register maintained by the Board,
>
> (*f*) entry into any examination conducted by the Board,
>
> (*g*) applications to undergo nurse training,
>
> (h) any other service which the Board may, from time to time, provide.

[1.33] Since a nurse is defined in the Act as a person who is on the Register, it is obligatory for her to pay a registration fee each year as provided for by s 25. The Board, with the consent of the Minister, sets the retention fee. The Board is also empowered under s 39(1)(*b*) to apply to the High Court for the removal of persons from the register who have not paid their fee:

> **39** (1) Where a nurse-

---

[14] Sections 16, 17.

[15] Section 18.

[16] Section 20(1).

[17] Sections 21(1), 22(1).

(*b*) has failed to pay a retention fee charged by the Board after the Board had, not less than two months previously by notice in writing sent by pre-paid post to the person, at his address as stated in the register, requested payment of the fee on more than one occasion,

The Board may decide that the name of such person should be erased from the register or that, during a period of specified duration, registration of that person's name in the register should not have effect.

On 12 July 1993, a successful application was made to the High Court for the removal of nurses from the Register who had not paid their retention fee.

Rules

[1.34] The Board may, with the approval of the Minister, make rules regarding committees, their membership and functions under the Act:

> **26** The Board may, with the approval of the Minister, make rules for the purpose of the operation of this Act and any such rules may, *inter alia*, provide for the establishment, membership, functions and procedures of committees to assist the Board in carrying out its functions under this Act.

As a result of the powers contained in ss 26-28, 31-33 the Board has made rules which are cited as the Nurses Rules 1988.[18]

Part III - Registration[19]

[1.35] Part III deals with the registration of names in the Register of Nurses, correction of the Register and the registration of persons in the ancillary professions. A nurse must notify the Board of any change of address. The Board is obliged to ensure that the Register is "live and accurate". Section 28 deals with the procedure for registration on the Register. The Board has to be satisfied that the prescribed conditions for registration have been complied with. Section 24(4) gives effect to EEC Directives 77/452 and 80/154 in that the State is obliged to have mutual recognition of a national of a Member State who has been awarded a qualification in nursing in another Member State. In the event of the Board under s 28(5) refusing to register a person on the grounds of the unfitness of that person to engage in the practise of nursing, there is a right of appeal to the High Court. On the hearing of the application, the High Court may:

(*a*) declare that it was proper for the Board to make the decision, or

(*b*) cancel the decision and direct the Board to register the name of the person making the application, or

---

[18] See Appendix.
[19] Sections 27, 28, 29, 30.

(*c*) cancel the decision and-

> (i) direct the Board to make a new decision, or
>
> (ii) give such other directions to the Board as the Court thinks proper.

Section 29 provides the Board with the power to correct the Register in the event of a change of address, or the death of a member, for the purpose of keeping the Register up to date.

Part VI - Miscellaneous Provisions

[1.36] Sections 48 to 59 deal with matters whereby the Board may make arrangements in which other persons may assist the Board in its functions.[20] The Act does not permit the improper use of[21] the title of nurse,[22] midwives.[23]

Midwifery

[1.37] Section 57(l) provides that a midwife who is not employed by a Health Board must notify the relevant Health Board where she practises or intends to practise midwifery:

> **57**(1) Where a midwife, who is not employed by a health board, or by a hospital authority providing maternity services or by a maternity home authority, is practising or proposes to practise midwifery, he shall notify the health board, or health boards, as the case may be, in whose functional area he practises or intends practising of such practice or proposal to practise.
>
> (2) It shall be the duty of a health board in whose functional area a midwife of the type referred to in *subsection (1)* of this section is practising or proposes to practise to exercise, in accordance with regulations made by the Minister, general supervision and control over such midwife.

[1.38] There is also a prohibition on any person *attending* a woman in childbirth unless they come within the provisions of s 58:

> **58** (1) No person shall attend a woman in childbirth unless such person is-
>
> (*a*) a midwife, or
>
> (*b*) a registered medical practitioner, or
>
> (*c*) undergoing training to be a registered medical practitioner or a midwife and gives such attention as part of a course of professional training, or

---

[20] Section 48.

[21] Section 49.

[22] Sections 50, 51, 52, 53.

[23] Section 53(3) deals with the functions of the Board.

(*d*) undergoing experience and training in obstetrics and gives such attention as part of a course of professional training, unless such attention is given, otherwise than for reward, in any case of sudden or urgent necessity where neither a midwife nor a registered medical practitioner is immediately available.

(2) Any person who acts in contravention of *subsection (1)* of this section shall be guilty of an offence and shall be liable on summary conviction to a fine not exceeding £1,000.

Except in emergency situations only a suitably qualified person may attend a woman in childbirth.

Prosecution of Offences

[**1.39**] Prosecutions may be brought under s 59 of the Nurses Act. Every offence under the Act may be prosecuted by the Board.

SUMMARY

[**1.40**] The above chapter outlines the history of nursing since early times and shows how nursing has developed from being the work of voluntary people to that of highly qualified professional persons. Today the nursing profession is legislated for by the Oireachtas. The 1985 Nurses Act gives An Bord Altranais the statutory powers to regulate the training of nurses, to maintain a "live register" of nurses and to operate a fitness to practice procedure for nurses.

CHAPTER 2

EDUCATION

[2.01] All aspects of the education and training of nurses are now legislated for by Part IV of the Nurses Act 1985 and various EU Directives which co-ordinate and expand the training schemes with an emphasis on specialised training.

EDUCATION PROGRAMMES

[2.02] An Bord Altranais provides four courses leading to a nursing qualification which entitle a nurse to be registered on the Nursing Register. This is all set out in the handbook provided by An Bord Altranais entitled *Nursing: A Career to Consider* and is as follows:

"- General nursing course leading to the qualification Registered General Nurse (R.G.N.).
- Mental Handicap nursing course leading to the qualification Registered Mental Handicap Nurse (R.M.H.N.).
- Paediatric nursing course leading to the qualification Registered Sick Children's Nurse (R.S.C.N.).
- Psychiatric nursing course leading to the qualification Registered Psychiatric Nurse (R.P.N.).

The duration of each of the courses is three years, including public holidays and annual leave. The education and training programmes have theoretical, technical and clinical instruction. Students now must have forty weeks of theoretical training. In any three year training course, not less than two-thirds of the course must consist of theory and not less than one-half must be clinical practice.

General nursing
In general hospitals, it is mostly patients with physical disorders who are catered for. The nurse is concerned with nursing back to health the sick and physically injured. Nurses in the general hospitals perform skilled bed-side nursing services, e.g., caring for a patient after surgery, or with a medical condition. Nurses have responsibility for the total nursing care of each patient. Intake for general nurse training is in Spring and Autumn of each year.

Psychiatric nursing
Psychiatric nursing involves caring for persons exhibiting abnormal behaviour e.g., an emotional or personality disorder, a nervous breakdown. Nursing care involves specific skills such as counselling and the need to be able to respond to the changes in people who at the time may not be reached by ordinary forms of logic or communication. Mental illness is like physical illness in that it may be cured, or a

19

patient can be helped to come to terms with his limitations. The future trend in this discipline of nursing is to care for the majority of patients in their homes. Some will be admitted to the psychiatric units of general hospitals for treatment. Intake for psychiatric nurse training is in Autumn each year.

Paediatric nursing
This discipline involves nursing children who are ill, from birth to early teens. The nurse must show great powers of observation particularly with the very young children who are unable to communicate verbally. Each child is an individual with his own pace of development and the sick children's nurse must plan each child's nursing care with this in mind. Children's Hospitals aim to provide care in a cheerful home-like environment. Nursing sick children is challenging and at times demanding but immensely rewarding. Intake for sick children's nurse training are Spring and Autumn each year.

Mental Handicap nursing
The nurse in the area of mental handicap plays a major role in helping to develop mentally handicapped persons to their optimum capabilities. He/she must organise and co-ordinate programmes which will help the person to develop all aspects i.e. the emotional, social, self help, vocational and recreational areas. Because of the different degrees of severity of mental handicap, the nurse must also be skilled in carrying out nursing procedures, which may be necessary if an additional handicap or physical illness is present. Intake for mental handicap training is in autumn each year."

REGISTRATION

[2.03] When a nurse is admitted for training, she is entitled to apply to the Board to have her name entered on the Candidates Register. Upon completion of the appropriate entry form on the Candidates Register, she is then issued with an identification number and a student card. When qualified as a nurse she may then seek, if she so wishes, to qualify in any other division of nursing provided she complies with the rules as set out by An Bord Altranais. Midwives and tutors are required to complete two years of training prior to entry on the Register. The rules issued by An Bord Altranais set out the educational requirements which must be complied with in order to register in the Nursing register. The educational aims of the Board are to ensure that the nurse has an understanding of the concepts upon which nursing is based.

EU DIRECTIVES

[2.04] There are two EU Directives[1] which affect both the training and regulation of nurses within the EU. These must be incorporated into the education of nurses, so as to enable them once entered on the Nursing Register, to freedom of

---

[1] Directives 77/452 and 77/453. See the Appendix.

movement of employment within the EU. The nurse is entitled to apply for registration in any of the Member States.

PROVISIONS REGARDING TRAINING AND EDUCATION CONTAINED IN THE NURSES ACT 1985

[2.05] The Nurses Act 1985 empowers the Board to make provision for the requirements regarding the training and examination standards that are necessary to enable a candidate to be placed on the "live" Register of Nurses. These requirements are made subject to the rules pursuant to s 26.

[2.06] Section 31 sets out the rules for courses of training and examinations for candidates for registration in the Register of Nurses:

31 The Board may, in accordance with the rules, provide or make provision for the courses of training and examinations to be taken by candidates for registration in the register of nurses and may prescribe the manner in which and the conditions under which training shall be provided and such rules may, in particular, provide for-

(*a*) the approval by the Board for the purposes of such rules of lecturers and teachers,

(*b*) the conditions of admission to the examinations, and

(*c*) the granting of certificates to persons taking the courses and passing the examinations.

[2.07] Section 32 sets out the rules for courses of training and examinations for nurses:

32 The Board may, in accordance with rules, provide or make provision for courses of training and examinations for nurses, and for the granting to nurses taking such courses and passing such examinations of certificates or diplomas, and may prescribe the manner in which and the conditions under which training shall be provided, ad such rules may, in particular, provide for-

(*a*) the approval by the Board for the purposes of such rules of lecturers and teachers,

(*b*) the conditions of admission to the examinations, and

(*c*) the granting of certificates to persons taking the courses and passing the examinations.

[2.08] In relation to the holding of examinations s 33 provides that:

33 (1) The Board may hold the examinations provided for by rules and may, by such rules, regulate the conduct of such examinations.

(2) The examiners (none of whom shall be a member of the Board) at every examination held under this section shall be appointed by the Board, shall hold such qualifications and have such experience in relation to nursing as the Board thinks proper, and shall be remunerated in accordance with a scale fixed by the Board with the approval of the Minister.

TRAINING INSTITUTIONS FOR GENERAL NURSING

[2.09] Section 34 requires that the Board must be satisfied as to the suitability of hospitals or institutions where the training of nurses or candidates takes place. This section empowers the Board to make rules[2] specifying the conditions of suitability in institutions and hospitals. Where the Board wishes to withdraw its approval of a training hospital or institution it is necessary to have the Minister's approval. However in the event of the Board refusing approval, the Minister may direct that the Board shall approve the institution or hospital concerned.[3]

ENTRY REQUIREMENTS FOR HOSPITALS AND INSTITUTIONS

[2.10] While the Board may determine the minimum educational entry requirements, each approved training school is at liberty to set its own requirements for entry provided it complies with the minimum standards as laid down by the Board.[4] Section 35 provides that:

> **35** (1) The Board may determine the minimum educational requirements necessary for entry for training as a nurse into a hospital or institution approved of by the Board pursuant to *section 34* of this Act.
>
> (2) The Board may, if it so determines, establish a central applications bureau to process applications from persons wishing to undertake training as a nurse.
>
> (3) If the Board establishes, pursuant to *subsection (2)* of this section, a central applications bureau, a hospital or institution approved of by the Board pursuant to *section 34* of this Act shall not, without the consent of the Board, accept for training any person who is not approved of and recommended by the Board.

MISCELLANEOUS FUNCTIONS OF THE BOARD IN RELATION TO EDUCATION AND TRAINING

[2.11] Section 36 provides that the Board, at least once every five years, must satisfy itself that the hospital or institution is suitable as a training school.[5] It further sets out the standards of theoretical and practical knowledge, clinical training and experience required for examination purposes.[6] This is set out by an approved syllabus covering each division of basic nursing training.[7] Section 36 is

---

[2] Section 26.
[3] Section 26(5).
[4] Section 35(1).
[5] Section 36(1)(*a*).
[6] Section 36(1)(*b*).
[7] Section 36(1)(*c*).

as follows:

36 (1) The Board shall, from time to time as occasion may require but, in any event, not less than once in every five years, satisfy itself as to-

(*a*) the suitability of the education and training for nurses provided by any hospital or institution approved of by the Board pursuant to *section 34* of this Act,

(*b*) the standards of theoretical and practical knowledge required for examinations,

(*c*) the clinical training and experience provided in any training programme organised by a hospital or institution approved of by the board pursuant to *section 34* of this Act, and

(*d*) the adequacy and suitability of post registration training courses for nurses provided by bodies recognised by the Board for that purpose,

(2) The Board may engage in research into the education and training of nurses, including the formulation of experimental curricula and the evaluation of existing programmes and examination and assessment procedures.

(3) The Board may maintain statistical records and make such records available for research and planning, including manpower planning purposes.

Section 37 requires the Board to ensure that the training of nurses in Ireland complies with the relevant EU Directives and Regulations.

MIDWIVES

[2.12] A midwife has been defined as:
"A person who, having been regularly admitted to a midwifery educational programme, duly recognised in the country in which it is located, has successfully completed the prescribed course of studies in midwifery and has acquired the requisite qualification to be registered and/or legally licensed to practice midwifery. She must be able to give the necessary supervision, care and advice to women during pregnancy, labour and the postpartum period, to conduct deliveries on her own responsibility and to care for the new-born and the infant. This care includes preventative measures, the detection of abnormal conditions in mother and child, the procurement of medical assistance and the execution of emergency measures in the absence of medical help. She has an important task in health counselling and education, not only for the women but also within the family and the community. The work should involve ante-natal education and preparation for parenthood and extends to certain areas of gynaecology, family planning and child care. She may practice in hospitals, health units, domiciliary conditions or in any other service."[8]

---

[8] The definition of a midwife adopted by the International Confederation of Midwives and the International Federation of Gynaecology and Obstetrics in 1972 and 1973 respectively. Amended and ratified by the International Federation of Gynaecology and Obstetrics 1991 and the WHO 1992.

The above definition of a midwife and midwifery practice highlights a complex and specialist role. The definition also highlights the degree of autonomy and independent practice afforded to the midwife.[9]

[2.13] The activities of a midwife are stated in article 4 of the European Directive 80/155/EC:

> **4** Member States shall ensure that midwives are at least entitled to take up and pursue the following activities:
>
> (*a*) to provide sound family planning information and advice,
>
> (*b*) to diagnose pregnancies and monitor normal pregnancies, to carry out examinations necessary for the monitoring of the development of normal pregnancies,
>
> (*c*) to prescribe or advise on the examinations necessary for earliest possible diagnosis of pregnancies at risk,
>
> (*d*) to provide a programme of parenthood preparation and a complete preparation for childbirth including advice on hygiene and nutrition,
>
> (*e*) to care for and assist the mother during labour and to monitor the condition of the foetus in utero by the appropriate clinical and technical means,
>
> (*f*) to conduct spontaneous deliveries including, where required, an episiotomy, and in urgent cases, a breech delivery,
>
> (*g*) to recognise the warning signs of abnormality in the mother or infant which necessitate referral to a doctor and to assist the latter where appropriate; to take the necessary emergency measures in the doctor's absence, in particular the manual removal of the placenta, possibly followed by manual examination of the uterus,
>
> (*h*) to examine and care for the new-born infant; to take all initiatives which are necessary in case of need and to carry out where necessary immediate resuscitation,
>
> (*i*) to care for and monitor progress of the mother in the post-natal period and to give all necessary advice to the mother on infant care to enable her to ensure the optimum progress of the new-born infant,
>
> (*j*) to carry out the treatment prescribed by a doctor,
>
> (*k*) to maintain all necessary records.

---

[9] See s 5 of *The Future of Nurse Education and Training in Ireland*, An Bord Altranais, July 1994.

[2.14] On completion of her general training and admittance to the Register, pursuant to the Nurses Act 1985, the nurse then applies to a recognised midwifery school. This entails a two year course with both practical and clinical training as regulated by an Bord Altranais. Having attained the required standard she is then admitted to the midwifery division of the General Registrar of Nursing. She is then entitled to practice as a midwife in either a hospital or in the community.

[2.15] Section 58 contains a prohibition on persons attending childbirth unless they come within the exempted list of which a midwife is one:

58 (1) No person shall attend a woman in childbirth unless such person is-

(*a*) a midwife, or

(*b*) a registered medical practitioner, or

(*c*) undergoing training to be a registered medical practitioner or a midwife and gives such attention as part of a course of professional training, or

(*d*) undergoing experience and training in obstetrics and gives such attention as part of a course of professional training, unless such attention is given, otherwise than for reward, in any case of sudden or urgent necessity where neither a midwife nor a registered medical practitioner is immediately available.

(2) Any person who acts in contravention of *subsection (1)* of this section shall be guilty of an offence and shall be liable on summary conviction to a fine not exceeding £1,000.

The Midwife in the Community

[2.16] A midwife is governed by the following statutes when practising midwifery in the community:

(1) Sections 57, 58 of the Nurses Act 1985.
(2) Section 62 of the Health Act 1970.
(3) Section 10 of the Misuse of Drugs Regulations 1979.[10]

[2.17] Section 62 of the Health Act 1970 provides for the medical and midwifery care for mothers:

62 (1) A health board shall make available without charge medical, surgical and midwifery services for attendance to the health, in respect of motherhood, of women who are persons with full eligibility or persons with limited eligibility.

(2) A woman entitled to receive medical services under this section may choose to receive them from any registered medical practitioner who has entered into an

---

[10] See chapter 9 at para **[9.13]**.

agreement with the Health Board for the provision of services and who is willing to accept her as a patient.

(3) When a woman avails herself of services under this section for a confinement taking place otherwise than in a hospital or maternity home, the Health board shall provide without charge obstetrical requisites to such extent as may be specified by regulations made by the Minister.

[2.18] In *Sprught v The Southern Health Board*, an action before Blayney J, pursuant to s 62, the plaintiff requested the attendance of both a medical doctor and a midwife at a homebirth. Blayney J was of the opinion that either a midwife or a medical doctor was sufficient at a delivery and the Health Board was not required to supply both.

PUBLIC HEALTH NURSE

[2.19] A public health nurse attends to the needs of the public in the community, (to those that are eligible for such services). The role of the nurse in the community has been defined as:

"In community oriented nursing, the concepts of primary health care are integrated into nursing practice at all levels: home, dispensary health centre, hospital. In providing healthcare, whether to individuals, the family or the community, the nurse is expected to employ three processes - assessment of needs, planning and implementing the measures requires, and evaluation of the effectiveness of the care provided."[11]

In order to qualify as a public health nurse, she must have completed her basic training as a general nurse and midwife. It is essential to do a one year diploma course in Public Health Nursing in order to qualify as a R.P.H.N.. She then has to complete the public health course as set out by An Bord Altranais, the Department of Health and the Health Boards. A public health nurse is employed under the Health Act 1970 and the terms and conditions of her employment are governed by that Act. The main sections which are applicable are ss 14, 17, 22.

[2.20] Section 14 deals with her appointment and confers on her the status of "officer" after the completion of a probation period, normally lasting six months:

14 (1) In addition to the chief executive officer, there shall be appointed to a health board such and so many other officers and such and so many servants as the board from time to time determines in accordance with the directions of the Minister.

(2) The appointment of an officer referred to in *subsection (1)* or of a servant of a health board shall be a function of the chief executive officer.

(3) An officer or servant of a health board appointed under this section shall hold his

---

[11] The 1986 Document on Public Health Nursing at p. 11.

office or employment on such terms and conditions and shall perform such duties as the chief executive officer from time to time determines.

(4) There shall be paid by a health board to an officer or servant appointed under this section such remuneration and allowances as the chief executive officer from time to time determines.

(5) (*a*) In making an appointment of an officer or servant, the chief executive officer shall act in accordance with the directions of the Minister, but no such direction shall be in conflict with *section 15.*

(*b*) In making a determination under *subsection (3)* or *(4)*, the chief executive officer shall act in accordance with the directions of the Minister and shall have regard to any arrangements in operation for conciliation and arbitration for persons affected by the determination.

(6) Any officer of a health board who is aggrieved by a determination under *subsection (3)* or *(4)* may apply to the Minister to issue a direction in that respect under *subsection (5).*

(7) An officer appointed under this section may arrange for his duties to be performed for a specified period by a deputy nominated by the officer, with the consent of the Minister, or with the consent of the chief executive officer given in accordance with any directions given by the Minister.

(8) A deputy nominated under *subsection (7)* shall possess the relevant qualifications approved under *section 18.*

[2.21] Section 17 deals with compliance in the performance of her duty with the decisions and directions of the chief executive officer and the Health Board:

17 (1) In the performance of their duties, the chief executive officer and the other officers of a health board shall act in accordance with such decisions and directions (whether of a general or a particular nature) as, subject to *subsection (3)*, are conveyed to or through the chief executive officer by the board, and in accordance with any such decisions and directions so conveyed of a committee to which functions have been delegated by the board.

(2) When the chief executive officer or another officer of a health board performs a duty in accordance with *subsection (1)*, he shall be deemed to act on behalf of the board.

(3) The board shall not take any decision or give any direction in relation to any matter which under this Act or any other enactment is a function of the chief executive officer or of another officer of the board.

(4) The following functions relating to the health board shall be functions of the chief executive officer of the board-

(*a*) any function specified by this Act or by any other enactment to be a function of the chief executive officer of the board,

(*b*) any function with respect to a decision as to whether or not any particular person shall be eligible to avail himself of a service (including a service for the payment of grants or allowances), or as to the extent to which, and the manner in which, a person shall avail himself of any such service,

(*c*) any function with respect to a decision as to the making or recovery of a charge, or the amount of any charge for a service for a particular person,

(*d*) any function with respect to the control, supervision, service, remuneration, privileges or superannuation of officers and servants of the board,

(*e*) such other functions as may be prescribed.

(5) Any dispute-

(*a*) as to whether or not a particular function is a function of the chief executive officer, or

(*b*) as to whether or not a particular function is a function of an officer of a health board other than the chief executive officer, shall be determined by the Minister.

NURSING CARE FOR PSYCHIATRIC PATIENTS

[2.22] The 1945 Mental Treatment Act provides for the care of the mentally ill outside of an institution. In 1992, a Green Paper on Mental Health identified a great need for the legislation to be updated and to enable the development of psychiatric services into a more comprehensive and community orientated service. Various reports have examined the evolving role of the psychiatric nurse in the context of community care. The role of the psychiatric nurse has been perceived as including:

"- Working with patients in special occupational or industrial therapy units outside the hospital.
- Acting as liaison with social workers, with the families or employers of patients and dealing with problems in the home or work situations.
- Supporting the public health nurse in her responsibility for a group of families or individuals and helping with special skills as the occasion demands.
- Assisting in running hostels, social clubs or similar centres and establishing and maintaining contact with voluntary organisations.
- Encouraging and assisting the patients in the community as required."[12]

An Bord Altranais has acknowledged the need to continue to provide psychiatric nurses with post-registration education appropriate to the evolving mental services.[13]

---

[12] The *Report on Psychiatric Nursing Services of Health Boards*, 1972.
[13] The *Future of Nurse Education and Training in Ireland*, An Bord Altranais, July 1994.

Psychiatric Patients

[2.23] People who suffer from mental illness and require treatment for same are admitted to the appropriate hospital. There are various types of admission. Patients are either voluntary or non-voluntary patients and are further classified as follows:-

    (a) Temporary patient chargeable.
    (b) Temporary patient private.
    (c) Person of unsound mind chargeable.
    (d) Person of unsound mind private.

[2.24] Any patient over the age of sixteen years can submit himself for admission to a psychiatric institution. This is usually done on medical advice. Upon acceptance by the person in charge of the institution, a written application on the statutory form is completed for a public patient whether chargeable or non-chargeable. There is no statutory form required for a private patient. When a person under the age of sixteen wishes to make an application for admission the application will have to be made by his parent or guardian. It will be necessary to produce a recommendation from a registered medical practitioner stating that he has examined the person whose admission is sought, on a specified date not more than seven days before the date of the application, and that in his opinion the patient will benefit by the proposed reception. There is no statutory form on which this recommendation has to be given.

[2.25] Where a patient is not willing to submit to voluntary treatment or "is incapable of expressing his wishes" an application may be made by a relative or any person to have him received as a temporary patient as a person of an unsound mind.

[2.26] The Act sets out the provisions for an admission order when dealing with public and private patients. Section 184 deals with the admission of public patients. Section 185 deals with the admission of private patients. The difference between these sections is that while a public patient's admittance requires that the statutory forms be signed by one doctor, the private patient's admittance form requires the signature of two doctors. In the case of an emergency, s 176 provides that a person of unsound mind who is regarded as a danger to himself and the public can be admitted to an institution.

[2.27] Mentally ill people are incapable of being in control of their own lives and the Mental Treatment Act 1945 contains some draconian provisions, particularly in regard to involuntary and emergency patients. It must be remembered that such patients have been deprived of all their civil liberties. When a nurse is taking care of such people, she must be aware of the fact that she is acting in accordance with the statutory provisions which must be strictly adhered to, and that any breach of the provisions can have far reaching consequences.

OCCUPATIONAL HEALTH NURSE

[2.28] The first industrial nurse was appointed in Ireland in 1890 and since then nurses have been employed as occupational health nurses in industries, educational establishments and hospitals. The role of the occupational health nurse has encompassed:

- The promotion of health.
- The prevention of illness and injury.
- The rehabilitation and resettlement of the ill and injured.

The provision of special training for the occupational health nurse was commenced by An Bord Altranais in 1976. In 1988 the Occupational Health Nursing course was incorporated into a multi-disciplinary Diploma in Safety, Health and Welfare at Work. An Bord Altranais acknowledges the important role of the occupational health nurse particularly arising from the emphasis being placed by employers on health and safety in the work environment through the implementation of the Safety, Health and Welfare at Work Act 1989.[14]

POST REGISTRATION COURSES

[2.29] There are a number of recognised post registration courses available for nurses which are approved by an Bord Altranais. These enable a nurse to specialise in any area of her profession. Once she has completed a course, as regulated by An Bord Altranais, she is entitled to apply for registration to the appropriate division of the Register. The following is a list of the approved courses which is constantly updated by the Board:

Accident and Emergency.
Alcoholism.
Anaesthetic Nursing.
Behaviour Modification.
Behavioural Psychotherapy.
Behavioural Therapy.
Child and Adolescent Psychiatric
Nursing Course.
Continuing Care of the Dying.
Patient and the Family.
Infection Nursing.
Intensive Care/Coronary Care.
Intensive Care.
Neonatal Intensive Care and
    Development Paediatrics.

Coronary Care.
Ear, Nose and Throat Nursing.
Forensic Psychiatric Nursing.
Gerontological Nursing
Neurological/Neurosurgical Nursing.
Operating Theatre.
Ophthalmic Nursing.
Orthopaedic Nursing.
Paediatric Nursing.
Plastic Surgical Oro-Maxillo.
Rehabilitation Nursing.
Renal Nursing.

---

[14] The *Future of Nurse Education and Training in Ireland*, An Bord Altranais, July 1994 at p. 48.

[2.30] There are also a number of third level educational courses:

Bachelor of Nursing Studies.
Diploma in Nursing, (social care and mental health).
Diploma in Nursing.
Public Health Nursing.
Stoma Care.

Where a nurse wishes to obtain further information with regard to these post graduate courses she applies to An Bord Altranais for the necessary information.

GROUND STRUCTURES WITHIN THE TRAINING HOSPITALS

Matron

[2.31] A matron in a training hospital is responsible for overseeing that the Board's standards are maintained and is at the top of the pyramidal structure in the hospital and all nursing staff are accountable to her. The range of her responsibilities may vary from hospital to hospital.

Ward Sister

[2.32] The Working Party Report[15] defined a ward sister's role as "being required to be an expert in nursing, in practical teaching and in managing people and resources". This definition would also include responsibility for the training and assessment of the students and periodic reporting to matron. The ward sister is also responsible for overseeing that all nursing duties are carried out on the ward and that a high standard is maintained.

Staff Nurse

[2.33] The staff nurse is both accountable and responsible to the ward sister for all duties undertaken by her. Student nurses are under her care regarding their practical training in liaison with the tutor. In order to perform any duties, the student nurse must be under the constant supervision of the ward sister or staff nurse in the carrying out of her ward duties. It is necessary that all members of the nursing staff work as a team.

Tutor

[2.34] Nurse tutors, midwife tutors and clinical tutors are all part of the nursing staff of the hospitals. The nursing tutor is the student's first introduction to nursing. The tutor is the person who is primarily responsible for the education and training of the student in conjunction with other members of staff. From the early 1950s there developed the new roles of both the nurse tutor and the clinical teacher. The commencement of preparation for the educational role of the nurse teacher was in 1960 in University College Dublin and this course was developed

---

[15] Department of Health 1980 at p 35.

into a three year Bachelor of Nursing Studies course in 1984. The aim of this degree course is to enable experienced registered nurses and midwives to teach in the class room and the clinical areas and to manage the education of nurses.

[2.35] Historically, developments in the nurse teacher's role demonstrate that as the demands of classroom teaching increased, nurse tutors became increasingly absorbed into the school of nursing activities. In recognition of the need for greater guidance, supervision and clinical teaching, a clinical teacher post was created. The registration of clinical teachers continued up until 1988 when the register was closed. Recent trends in nurse education have veered towards the creation of one grade of teacher who would be fully competent to teach both in the classroom and the clinical areas. This development was recommended in the Working Party Report 1980.

[2.36] All schools of nursing have two grades of tutor, a principal and a nurse teacher and the number of nurse teachers can vary depending on the size of the school and the number of student nurses in it. This multifaceted role includes classroom and clinical teaching, together with numerous other activities particularly in the areas of nurse management and administration.

[2.37] The following is a list of the functions of a tutor. She:

1. Participates in the formulation of polices of the School of Nursing.

2. Evaluates policy with the Principal Tutor and colleagues as appropriate.

3. Participates in planning the curriculum and educational programme in accordance with the syllabus of An Bord Altranais.

4. Consults and liaises with senior nursing personnel in clinical areas to ensure educational requirements are being maintained.

5. Teaches assigned subjects to all groups of students as delegated by the Principal tutor.

6. Counsels student nurses as necessary.

7. Participates in the instruction of student nurses in clinical areas as designated by the Principal Tutor.

8. Acts as examiner/assessor in:

  (a) Hospital written and oral examinations, and
  (b) State examinations, where appropriate.

[2.38] The administrative functions of a tutor include the:

1. Preparation and organisation of programmes for study blocks as designated by the Principal Tutor.

2. Submission of prepared programmes to the Principal Tutor.

3. Keeping of records of :

  (a) Study block activities.
  (b) Students progress during blocks.

4. Participation in the selection of student nurses as requested.

[2.39] A tutor is also a member of the Education Committee. She evaluates and reports on the progress of student nurses to the principal tutor and gives merit rating to outstanding students according to the accepted practice. A tutor should keep up to date on developments in nursing and nurse education by attending lectures and seminars. She also reports back to colleagues on topics discussed, relevant to changes in clinical practice or matters with implications for nurse training. The tutor attends meetings and acts on Committees as assigned by the principal tutor.

[2.40] The role of the tutor has changed over the years. These changes include:

(a) Teaching and learning activities.

(b) Clinical teaching and the preparation of open learning materials.

(c) Planning the curriculum, planning the teaching programmes and evaluation of same.

(d) Monitoring the students' progress by a variety of assessments and examinations.

(e) Monitoring and auditing clinical areas.

(f) Involvement in audit and quality circle groups.

(g) Publication of journal articles, management, educational; and professional.

THE FUTURE OF NURSE EDUCATION AND TRAINING IN IRELAND

[2.41] An Bord Altranais recently published a report on the future of nurse education and training in Ireland. The Report presents twenty-eight recommendations which relate to the organisational, educational, training and economic issues surrounding the future preparation of nurses. The recommendations when implemented will ensure the continued development of the profession and enable it to meet the expectations of the profession itself and of the health services.

SUMMARY

[2.42] This chapter has outlined the basic requirements which must be complied with before a person is entitled to call herself/himself a nurse. It also outlines the role of a nurse and her participation within her profession. The nurse is obliged to work within the confines of her professional training pursuant to the syllabus as laid down by an Bord Altranais. All nurses need a working knowledge and awareness of the relevant law and in particular, legislation emanating from the Department of Health and EU Directives.

CHAPTER 3

EMPLOYMENT

INTRODUCTION

[3.01] Today employment law is largely based on the concept of control, whereas formerly it was based on the concept of service. Hence the terminology still in use today refers to master and servant, although employer and employee is the more usual form now. This relationship has been defined by Halsbury[1] as follows:

> "Whether or not in any given case, the relationship of master and servant exists is a question of fact; but in all cases the relation imports the existence of power in the employer not only to direct what work the servant is to do, but also the manner in which the work is to be done."

This relationship has evolved over a period of time with principal rights flowing from statute, contract and the common law.

LEGISLATION

[3.02] There are many types of legislation dealing with the conditions and terms of employment, which include hours of work, days off, holidays, minimum notice, maternity leave and in certain circumstances, redundancy payments. Safety in the workplace is also governed by statute.[2] The relevant Acts that relate to the conditions of employment are as follows:

1. Unfair Dismissal Acts 1977-1993.
2. Redundancy Payments Acts 1967-1984.
3. Health Act 1970.
4. Minimum Notice and Terms of Employment Act 1973.
5. Holidays (Employees) Act 1973.
6. Anti-Discrimination (Pay) Act 1974.
7. Employment Equality Act 1977.
8. Maternity Protection of Employees Act 1981.
9. Safety, Health and Welfare at Work Act 1989.
10. Worker Protection (Regular Part-Time Employees) Act 1991.
11. Industrial Relations Act 1990.
12. Payment of Wages Act 1991.
13. Competition Act 1991.

---

[1] *Halsbury's Law of England* 1st Edition Vol. 20 at 131.
[2] Safety, Health and Welfare at Work Act 1989.

14. Acquired Rights of Employees Directive 77/187.
15. Terms of Employment (Information) Act 1994.

EMPLOYMENT CONTRACTS

[3.03] In order to be valid a contract need not be written, in other words, a contract with rights attaching can be verbal and is enforceable at law. However the more usual contract is in written form and will contain the terms and conditions of employment. A contract of employment may be entered into by an employer and employee so long as both parties possess what is known as contractual capacity, i.e., having reached the age of majority and having the mental capacity to understand the nature of the contract. When a contract is in written form it must comply with statute law and must contain the terms of employment which both parties have agreed to and are bound by. These terms must not be tainted with illegality or fraud. It is generally not possible to contract out of statutory rights (unless they are greater than the statute allows). When terms are not specified they may be implied from common law and/or custom and practice. While the law sets out the basic requirements which must be contained in the contract, any further benefits or conditions that the parties agree to may be inserted.

TYPES OF CONTRACT

[3.04] There are different types of employment relationships. It is necessary to distinguish between "contracts for services", "contracts of services", "independent contractors" and "office holders". Since the rights and duties which flow from each of these types of contracts and the methods by which they are enforced will vary, it is necessary to identify the type of contract involved.

[3.05] The relationship between the employer and employee is largely based on a contract from which protection is given to both the employer and employee along with certain duties which flow from the relationship. In order to decide what rights and duties are in this contract it is necessary to decide which type of contract has been agreed to by the parties. The courts in the past have placed great emphasis on "control" and Halsbury[3] has defined it as:

"Whether or not the employer retains the power, not only of direction what work is to be done, but also of controlling the manner of doing the work. If a person can be overlooked in regard to the manner of doing his work, such a person is not a contractor".

Contract of Services

[3.06] A contract of services occurs where the employer retains the right to discipline and control the terms and conditions of work. Consequently there is a heavy onus on the employer to protect his employees, in that he must provide a

---
[3] Halsbury's Laws of England 1st Ed. Vol. 20.

safe and proper system of work and protect his employees from any foreseeable dangers which may result in physical or mental injury.

[3.07] Most contracts of service are in writing and the terms and conditions are clearly expressed therein. These generally contain the following - a term of probation, remuneration, hours of work, holidays, sick leave, promotion, periods of notice for termination, and terms whereby summary dismissal would be justified. It is important that all contracts be carefully read before they are signed since once they are signed both parties are bound by the conditions and terms that are contained therein.

[3.08] The courts have on several occasions looked to see whether the manner in which a person is working would fall to be considered either as contract *of* service or contract *for* service. This was considered in a number of cases. Various tests have developed to determine the nature of this relationship with the most important test being the element of "control". The Supreme Court has said that while there are many ingredients in the relationship, the main ingredient would be "the fact of the master's right to direct the servant not merely as to what is to be done but as to how it is to be done".[4] However in *Massey v Crown Life Assurance Co,*[5] Lord Denning said:

> "...If the true relationship of the parties is that of master and servant under a contract of service, the parties cannot alter the truth of that relationship by putting a different label on it."

In other words the reality of the situation will be considered as well as all aspects of the relationship between the parties.

Contract for Services

[3.09] A contract for services arises where a person is employed to provide a specific service which produces a particular result. The employer has limited control over how the work is carried out and the employee is subject only to the conditions of his contract and retains a discretion as to how and when the work is done. Very often in this situation an employee will pay their own tax and decide their hours of work. In this regard Lord Denning said that:[6]

> "Under a contract of service, a man is employed as part of the business, and his work is done as an integral part of the business; whereas under a contract for services, his work, although done for the business, is not integrated into it but is only accessory to it."

[3.10] The question as to whether a surgeon works under a contract for services or contract of services was discussed in *O'Friel v The Trustees, St Michael's*

---

[4] Walsh J in *Roche v Patrick Kelly & Co Ltd* [1969] IR 100.

[5] [1978] 2 All ER 576; (1978) ICR 590.

[6] *Stephan Jordan and Harrison Ltd v MacDonald & Evans* [1952] TLR 101.

Hospital, Dun Laoghaire.[7] It was argued on behalf of the claimant, before the Employment Appeals Tribunal, that he was obliged to give a certain commitment to the respondent, including being "on call" for a twenty-four hour period every week and regular attendance in surgery and at the out-patients' clinic at times which were not set by him. This, it was argued, was characteristic of a contract of employment. Counsel for the hospital argued that the arrangement was almost completely flexible. There were none of the statutory attributes of employment such as PAYE, or PRSI. In respect of the payments made to him, it was argued that the hospital was only a conduit pipe and was not paying a salary to the surgeons. The Tribunal in their determination considered that what was at issue in this case was whether the working arrangements between the parties amounted to a "contract of service" or a "contract for services". In doing so the Tribunal looked at a number of decisions and in particular the *dictum* of Denning LJ in *Stevenson Jordan & Harrison Ltd v MacDonald & Evans*:

> "It is often easy to recognise a contract of service when you see it, but difficult to say wherein the difference lies. A ship's master, a chauffeur and a reporter on the staff of a newspaper are all employed under a contract of service, but a ship's pilot, a taxi-man and a newspaper contributor are employed under a contract for services."

[3.11] The Tribunal also referred to the earlier case of *Scanlon v Browne and Carolan Ltd.*[8] which set out the following tests:

1. The element of control.
2. The right to "hire and fire".
3. The requirement that service must be personal or may be delegated.
4. Liability in the event of a worker on the premises being injured by the negligence of a fellow worker.
5. Responsibility for custody and stamping of social welfare cards.

The Tribunal considered that "control" was the most important test. They also considered that the claimant's fees and hours of work were controlled by his colleagues and himself. The Tribunal considered that the claimant was not employed by the hospital but had a contract for services.

Office Holder

[3.12] The main feature of the office is that it can be created either by statute, charter, articles of association of a company or by a deed of trust and the holder may be removed from office if the statute or other instrument authorises this removal. However it is possible to be the holder of an office and also have a contract. Kenny J in *Glover v BLN Limited,*[9] in describing the characteristic feature of an office said:

---

[7] UD 301/1980.
[8] M60/1977.
[9] [1973] IR 388.

"The characteristic features of an office are that it is created by an Act of Parliament, charter, statutory regulation, articles of association of a company or of a body corporate formed under the authority of a statute, deed of trust, grant or by prescription; and that the holder of it may be removed if the instrument creating the office authorises this. However, the person who holds it may have a contract under which he may be entitled to retain it for a fixed period..."

The holder of an office does not hold the office under contract, but holds the office under the instrument that created the office. Blayney J in *Murphy v The Minster for Social Welfare*[10] referred to the *Glover* case during the course of his judgment and said regarding the contract, that what this contract gave him was simply a right to retain his office for five years; but it did not create the office. Blayney J perused earlier case law regarding the definition of a civil servant and said that the correct test to be applied "would appear to be whether he was a servant of the State in its political capacity". There is an obligation on the State or public body as an employer over and above the contractual obligation to observe the rules of natural and constitutional justice.

Officers of Health Boards

[3.13] Officers employed by Health Boards are governed by separate legislation whereby their appointment, suspension, remuneration and termination are provided for. As their requirements are statutorily provided for this category of worker is excluded from other legislation, most notably the Unfair Dismissal Acts 1977-1993. However, by virtue of s 3 of the Unfair Dismissal (Amendment) Act 1993 a temporary officer of a health board receives the protection of the Unfair Dismissal Acts. Those persons who are employed by Health Boards are also officers as defined in s 14 of the Health Act 1970:

14 (1) In addition to the chief executive officer, there shall be appointed to a health board such and so many other officers and such and so many servants as the board from time to time determines in accordance with the directions of the Minister.

(2) The appointment of an officer referred to in *subsection (1)* or of a servant of a health board shall be a function of the chief executive officer.

(3) An officer or servant of a health board appointed under this section shall hold his office or employment on such terms and conditions and shall perform such duties as the chief executive officer from time to time determines.

The Chief Executive Officer, under the direction of the Minister, appoints officers and determines the terms and conditions of the office having regard to the arrangements that are in operation for either arbitration or conciliation for those who may be affected by the outcome.

Independent Contractor

[3.14] An independent contractor or self employed person is one who is engaged

---

[10] (1988) ILTR 50.

to provide a specific service and is regarded as having a contract for services. He/she does not enjoy the statutory protection given to employees. The courts when examining cases of this kind have given consideration to what the parties themselves intend. *Lamb Bros., Dublin Ltd v Davidson*[11] concerned a painter who changed his status with the company by entering into a new agreement but retained his previous position (self employed). The court was of the view that the parties even if they did not "set down in legal phraseology the exact relationship between them, nevertheless I think it was perfectly clear what they both considered what they were about".

Agency Nursing

[3.15] When a nurse is employed via an agency she does not necessarily have a contract of employment with a hospital, e.g., if employed by a patient for her care exclusively then the only relationship with the hospital is to comply with its general standards of care. In the event of a breach of the standard of care resulting in a claim for negligence, the nurse is the party who is primarily responsible. This situation is similar to that of an independent contractor.

[3.16] In a situation where a nurse is requested to work as a "floor nurse" or the hospital require the services for a specific patient via an agency, then she has a relationship with a hospital authority for short-term employment. There is a grey area as to where the primary liability falls in the event of a claim for negligence. A lot depends on the hospital policy and the terms of the agreement. The same duty and standard of care applies to an agency nurse. Under the Unfair Dismissal (Amendment) Act 1993, agency nurses are now given the protection of the Unfair Dismissal Act 1977.

FAIR PROCEDURES

[3.17] Before an employee can be dismissed, it must be shown that fair procedures have been observed. The basic requirements are those of natural justice, and the opportunity to state one's case. In other words, an employee is entitled to know the case against her and to be given an opportunity to reply prior to a dismissal. In *Garvey v Ireland* [12]Mr Garvey who was Commissioner of the Garda Síochána[13] declined to resign when asked to do so by the Government. It was sought to remove him from the office without any notice being given to him. He brought proceedings for wrongful dismissal. The Supreme Court said that "an employee is entitled to know the case against him and be given an opportunity to reply prior to a dismissal". O'Higgins CJ stated that:

"The Constitution incorporates into our laws and their administration the requirements of natural justice, and by Article 40, s.3, there is guaranteed to every citizen whose

---

[11] Unreported High Court, 4 December 1978.

[12] [1981] IR 95 *per* O'Higgins CJ at 97.

[13] Mr Garvey held this office under the Police Forces (Amalgamation) Act 1925.

rights may be affected by decisions taken by others the right to fair and just procedures. This means that under the Constitution powers cannot be exercised unjustly or unfairly. This applies as well to the Government as to any authority within the State to which is given the power to take action which may infringe the rights of others."

The Chief Justice further stated that the Government was bound to act in a fair manner and must "tell the Commissioner of the reason or reasons for the proposed action" and also give him an opportunity to state his side of the case. In *Glover v BLN*,[14] it was held that:

"That the plaintiff's position as holder of an office, as distinct from being only an employee, required the application of the rules of natural justice to the termination of his employment as a technical director."

[3.18] In *Gearon v Dunnes Stores*[15] it was held that a that an employee has:

"The right to defend herself and have her arguments and submissions listened to and evaluated by the respondent in relation to the threat to her employment is a right of the claimant and not the gift of the respondent or of the Tribunal".

In *Bunyan v United Dominions Trust (Ireland) Ltd*[16] the Tribunal recognised the fact that:

"It may be argued that fair procedures are necessary or of value only to demonstrate that the employer acted fairly in investigating and gathering the information upon which he makes his decision. It is clear that if belief in the culpability of the employee is necessary to justify the dismissal then it is equally necessary that such belief be reasonably held. Fair procedures therefore help to lead an employer to as full possession of information as is reasonably possible and he will then proceed to a decision."

The Tribunal went on to say "As the right is a fundamental one under natural and Constitutional justice it is not open to the tribunal to forgive its breach". In a dismissal situation under the Unfair Dismissals Act the Tribunal will have regard to what a reasonable employer would do in similar circumstances.

DUTIES OF AN EMPLOYER

[3.19] Both parties under a contract of employment are obliged to conform with the mutual obligations which arise under the contract. At the heart of the contract the employer has a duty to remunerate the employee for work performed. The rate may be fixed by contract, collective agreement or statutory authority. The right to

---

[14] [1973] IR 383.
[15] UD 367/1988.
[16] UD 66/1980.

be paid while on sick leave may be incorporated as a term of the contract, if not it may be possible to incorporate this term as being one of custom in that particular job. Under the common law the manner of payment was not regulated, but the methods of payment and compulsory deductions are now governed by the Payment of Wages Act 1991. The employer is obliged to provide a safe place of work, and safe systems and equipment[17]and to select skilled workers in the work place. Both parties owe to each other duties of trust, fidelity and confidence. Both parties under a contract of employment are obliged to conform with their mutual obligations. These duties arise both under the common law and by statute. In *Dalton v Frendo*[18] the Chief Justice, regarding the duty of care which is owed to an employee expressed the view that:

> "The duty of an employer towards a servant is to take reasonable care for the servant's safety in all the circumstances of the case. This duty has also been described as a duty so to carry on operations as not to expose those employed to unnecessary risks. Whatever way the duty is described it must involve an element of foreseeability. What is reasonable care for the safety of a workman must be measured by such risks and hazards as are known or ought to be known and by those which can reasonably be apprehended."

The court went on to say that all the circumstances must be considered in each case such as the age, experience, skill of the worker and the nature of the work and the court concluded with the statement that the employer is not an insurer.

DUTIES OF AN EMPLOYEE

[3.20] A nurse is obliged to serve honestly and faithfully when handling the property of her employer or when protecting confidential information that is acquired as a result of her employment. A nurse is obliged to use reasonable skill in the performance of her duties and be proficient in the qualifications she holds herself out as possessing. Trust and confidence are the essential elements of the contract and a nurse is also obliged to obey all lawful orders. She also has a duty to care for her own safety at work.[19]

[3.21] Section 9 of the Safety, Health and Welfare at Work Act 1989 provides that:

> (1) It shall be the duty of every employee while at work-
>
>   (*a*) to take reasonable care for his own safety, health and welfare and that of any other person who may be affected by his acts or omissions while at work;

---

[17] Safety, Health and Welfare at Work Act 1989.

[18] Unreported, Supreme Court 15 December 1977.

[19] Safety, Health and Welfare at Work Act 1989.

(*b*) to co-operate with his employer and any other person to such extent as will enable his employer or the other person to comply with any of the relevant statutory provisions;

(*c*) to use in such manner so as to provide the protection intended, any suitable appliance, protective clothing, convenience, equipment or other means or thing provided (whether for his use alone or for use by him in common with others) for securing his safety, health or welfare while at work; and

(*d*) to report to his employer or his immediate supervisor, without unreasonable delay, any defects in plant, equipment, place of work or system of work, which might endanger safety, health or welfare, of which he becomes aware.

(2) No person shall intentionally or recklessly interfere with or misuse any appliance, protective clothing, convenience, equipment or other means or thing provided in pursuance of any of the relevant statutory provisions or otherwise, for securing the safety, health or welfare of persons arising out of work activities.

[3.22] An employee is obliged not only to look after her own safety but also the safety of her co-workers. The standard is that of reasonable care for the safety, health and welfare of any other employee or any person to whom it is reasonably foreseeable may be affected by their acts or omissions. Where protective clothing is supplied by an employer a employee is under a duty to utilise it, e.g., lead aprons when in the proximity of x-rays.

SAFETY IN THE WORKPLACE

[3.23] Safety in the workplace is governed by the Safety, Health and Welfare at Work Act 1989. The employer is obliged as far "as reasonably practicable" to ensure an employee's safety. Section 6(1) and (2) provides that:

6 (1) It shall be the duty of every employer to ensure, so far as is reasonably practicable, the safety, health and welfare of all his employees,

(2) Without prejudice to the generality of an employer's duty under *subsection (1)*, the matters to which that duty extends include in particular -

(*a*) as regards any place of work under the employer's control, the design, the provision and the maintenance of it in a condition that is, so far as is reasonably practicable, safe, and without risk to health;

(*b*) so far as is reasonably practicable, as regards any place of work under the employer's control, the design, the provision and the maintenance of safe means of access to and egress from it;

(*c*) the design, the provision and the maintenance of plant and machinery that are, so far as is reasonably practicable, safe and without risk to health;

(*d*) the provision of systems of work that are planned, organised, performed and maintained so as to be, so far as is reasonably practicable, safe and without risk to health;

(*e*) the provision of such information, instruction, training and supervision as is necessary to ensure, so far as is reasonably practicable, the safety and health at work of his employees;

(*f*) in circumstances in which it is not reasonably practicable for an employer to control or eliminate hazards in a place of work under his control, or in such circumstances as may be prescribed, the provision and maintenance of such suitable protective clothing or equipment, as appropriate, that are necessary to ensure the safety and health at work of his employees;

(*g*) the preparation and revision as necessary of adequate plans to be followed in emergencies;

(*h*) to ensure, so far as is reasonably practicable, safety and prevention of risk to health at work in connection with the use of any article or substance;

(*i*) the provision and the maintenance of facilities and arrangements for the welfare of his employees at work; and

(*j*) the obtaining, where necessary, of services of a competent person (whether under a contract of employment or otherwise) for the purpose of ensuring, so far as is reasonably practicable, the safety and health at work of his employees.

[3.24] Section 7 sets out the general duties of employers and the self-employed to persons other than their own employees:

7 (1) It shall be the duty of every employer to conduct his undertaking in such a way as to ensure, as far as is reasonably practicable, that persons not in his employment who may be affected thereby are not exposed to risks to their safety or health.

(2) It shall be the duty of every self-employed person to conduct his undertaking in such a way as to ensure, as far as is reasonably practicable, that he and other persons (not being his employees) who may be affected thereby are not exposes to risks to their safety or health.

(3) In such cases as may be prescribed, it shall be the duty of every employer and self-employed person, in the prescribed circumstances, and in the prescribed manner to give to persons (not being his employees) who may be affected by the way in which he conducts his undertaking the prescribed information about such aspects of the way he conducts his undertaking as might affect their safety or health.

[3.25] The Act makes provision for the selection of a safety representative with specific functions,[20] which include the right to represent fellow employees with

---

[20] Section 13.

regard to their safety and health at work and the right to such information as the employer has regarding same. The Act also provides that the representative is entitled to paid time off to attend to these functions. The Act specifies an obligation on the employer to prepare a safety statement[21] which specifies the manner in which safety and health are secured at work.

VICARIOUS LIABILITY

[3.26] The law sometimes holds one person liable for the wrongs committed by another person, even though the person held liable is not personally at fault. A master is liable for the wrongs of his servants if they are committed within the scope of their employment. When the acts of an employee are outside the scope of her employment, then these acts do not belong to the class of acts which are impliedly authorised by her employer. In this instance the employee is liable for her own acts and the employer may well be entitled to be reimbursed by the employee for any loss or damage. An employer will not be held liable for an act carried out by a nurse within the hospital premises which is outside the scope of her employment. However the employer may be liable if the employee acted negligently or criminally within the scope of their employment. In determining an employer's liability, the test favoured nowadays is whether the act in question was within the scope of the employee's duty, not whether the act was permitted by the employer.[22]

TERMINATION

[3.27] A contract of employment may be brought to an end in a variety of ways depending on the type of contract. The parties may agree to terminate the contract, or an employee may resign or be dismissed or the contract may cease by operation of law. A contract is brought to an end, when it is for a fixed term and purpose and both have ceased.[23] Wrongful dismissal arises when a breach of the contract by the employer occurs. An employer or employee may lawfully terminate the contract when a breach of one of the fundamental terms of the contract occurs. Notice as provided for in the contract or by statute[24] or what is regarded as reasonable notice in that job is normally given of the proposed termination.

[3.28] Either party which is aggrieved by a breach of the terms of the contract can seek a remedy in the courts for a declaration that the termination is valid or bring a claim for damages. The appropriate court will depend on the amount of damages claimed - the Circuit Court for claims up to £30,000 and the High Court for any claims greater than £30,000.

---

21 Section 12.

22 See Chapter 6.

23 See the Unfair Dismissal Acts 1977-1993 s 3(B).

24 Minimum Notice of Terms of Employment Act 1973.

[3.29] The contract may also provide for summary dismissal. This arises where an employee is dismissed without notice, normally for incidents involving serious misconduct such as alcohol or drug abuse, violence or intimidation or failure to obey a lawful and reasonable order that is related to the employment. It will depend upon the circumstances of each case and the nature of the employment.

[3.30] Dismissal occurs when an employer seeks to bring an employee's contract of service to an end. Certain procedures must be complied with in order for the dismissal to be lawful. These procedures are to be found generally at common law and statute including the Health Act 1970 and the Unfair Dismissal Acts 1977 - 1993. There are a variety of ways that a dismissal can occur:

1. Expiry of a fixed term contract.
2. Summary dismissal.
3. Unfair dismissal.
4. Constructive dismissal.
5. Dismissal under the Health Act 1970.
6. Wrongful dismissal (Common Law).
7. Redundancy.
8. Nurses Act 1985.

Expiry of a fixed term contract

[3.31] A fixed term contract is a contract for a specified period of time or can be for a particular purpose. When that purpose or time comes to an end then the contract of employment expires.

Expiry at Common Law

[3.32] Whether a contract is oral or in writing, once the purpose or period of time of the contract comes to its natural end, the employment ceases and the employee has no method of redress.

Summary Dismissal

[3.33] Summary dismissal occurs when an employee is dismissed instantly, i.e. on the spot. Most written contracts set out the grounds where a summary dismissal can occur.[25]

Dismissal under the Health Act 1970

[3.34] Nurses appointed under the 1970 Health Act are governed by s 2 in relation to their appointment to office, suspension and removal. Section 22 provides for the suspension of an officer, where the chief executive officer has reason to believe that an officer has been guilty of misconduct or is unfit to hold office:

> **22** (1) Whenever, in respect of an officer of a health board other than the chief executive officer, there is, in the opinion of the chief executive officer, reason to

---

[25] See para **[3.29]** *supra*.

believe that the officer has misconducted himself in relation to his office or is otherwise unfit to hold office, the chief executive officer may, after consultation with the chairman, or in his absence, the vice-chairman of the board, suspend the officer from the performance of the duties of his office while the alleged misconduct or unfitness is being inquired into and any disciplinary action to be taken in regard thereto is being determined.

The chief executive officer is obliged to notify the Minister, within one month, of the suspension and the reasons for same.

[3.35] Remuneration upon suspension is only paid for the period prior to the suspension:

22 (5) An officer suspended under this section shall not be paid any remuneration (other than remuneration for a period prior to his suspension) in respect of his office during the continuance of his suspension and, on termination of his suspension, the remuneration which he would, had he not been suspended, have been paid during the period of suspension shall be wholly or partly forfeited or paid to him or otherwise disposed of as may be directed by-

(*a*) in the case of a suspension of not more than one month's duration, the chief executive officer, and

(*b*) in any other case, the Minister.

(6) Whenever an officer of a health board is suspended under this section, the chief executive officer may, if he thinks fit, make with the consent of the Minister an *ex gratia* payment to the suspended officer.

(7) Any sum paid under *subsection (6)* shall be repayable by the officer to the health board and may be deducted from any moneys payable by the board to him.

Removal of Officers under the Health Act 1970

[3.36] Section 23 provides that the chief executive officer may remove an officer or servant from the board:

23 (1) Subject to *subsections (2) to (4)*, an officer or servant of a health board appointed under section 14 may be removed from being such officer or servant by the chief executive officer to the board.

(2) A permanent officer shall not be removed under this section because of misconduct or unfitness except-

(*a*) on a direction by the Minister under *subsection (3)*, or

(*b*) on the recommendation of a committee under *section 24* or on a direction by the Minister under *section 24(11)*.

(3) Where a permanent officer has misconducted himself by absenting himself from duty without leave or without reasonable cause, the Minister may direct his removal from office.

(4) A permanent officer shall not be removed under this section for a reason other than misconduct or unfitness except with the approval of the board.

[3.37] Section 23(5) states that the removal of officers and servants must be carried out in such a manner that the officer or servant in question is given notice of the reason for the removal and that any representation which he makes himself or which is made on his behalf must be given consideration. When an officer or servant is in a position where her livelihood is in jeopardy she is entitled, when appearing before a body with power to remove her from office, to be told the reason for the purported dismissal and given an opportunity to defend herself and reply to any allegations. These proceedings must be conducted in a fair manner. Full-time officers are expressly excluded by s 2 (*f*) of the Unfair Dismissal Act 1977 from these provisions. However, by virtue of s 3 of the Unfair Dismissal (Amendment) Act 1993, a temporary officer of a health board is now protected under the Unfair Dismissal Act 1977. They also enjoy the protection of the Redundancy Acts, the Minimum Notice and Terms of Employment 1973 and Industrial Relations Act 1990.

Dismissal under the Unfair Dismissal Acts 1977 - 1993

[3.38] There is an abundance of labour law legislation which now gives employees greater job security. The hallmark piece of legislation was the Unfair Dismissal Act 1977. The rights of the employee received statutory recognition over and above that recognised at common-law. However it is necessary to have one year's continuous service and to be normally expected to work eight hours per week when seeking redress under this Act. Certain categories of employees are excluded from this legislation as their rights and benefits are protected by specific legislation for their area. Excluded employees include those employed by health boards, local authorities and the State.

[3.39] Section 6(1) deems a dismissal to be unfair unless there were "substantial grounds" by which it can be justified. The onus is on the employer to prove the dismissal was fair. Dismissal will be regarded as being automatically unfair if it results from one of the following:

1. Membership of a trade union or trade union activities.

2. For religious or political grounds.

3. By bringing civil or criminal proceedings against an employer or in a situation where an employee is likely to be a witness.

4. Race or colour.

5. Because of pregnancy or matters related to the pregnancy.

6. Sexual orientation.

7. Age of the employee.

8. Being a member of the travelling community.

9. Unfair selection for redundancy.

[3.40] It is not necessary to have one year's service prior to bringing a case for wrongful dismissal under any of the above headings. A finding of unfair dismissal could also arise where there has been a breach of fair procedure or lack of reasonableness on the employer's part or for a serious breach of a code of practice. Dismissal may also occur in a situation where the employee terminates the contract as a result of the conduct of the employer and it was reasonable for her to do so. This is referred to as a constructive dismissal.

[3.41] If an employee seeks particulars of the reasons why she was dismissed the employer is obliged under the Act to furnish them. Other substantial grounds may be taken into account by a tribunal or court at the hearing. A dismissal will be deemed to be fair if the substantial grounds result wholly or mainly from one or more of the following as set out in s 6(4):

6 (4) Without prejudice to the generality of *subsection (1)* of this section, the dismissal of an employee shall be deemed, for the purposes of this Act, not to be an unfair dismissal, if it results wholly or mainly from one or more of the following:

(*a*) the capability, competence or qualifications of the employee for performing the work of the kind which he was employed by the employer to do,

(*b*) the conduct of the employee,

(*c*) the redundancy of the employee, and

(*d*) the employee being unable to work or continue to work in the position which he held without contravention (by him or his employer) of a duty or restriction imposed by or under any statute or instrument made under statute.

An illegal contract is not precluded under the Act. The onus is on the employer to show that the dismissal resulted from the above.

Employer Investigation
[3.42] When an employer finds that it is necessary for him to terminate an employee's contract the obligations of fair procedures and natural justice must be complied with. Where a complaint has been made about an employee with regard to her work performance, the employer is obliged to have the matter investigated

and to inform the employee of the complaint. It is vital that an employer should conduct the investigation in a fair and reasonable manner. An employee should be given the choice of representation at any such meeting and be given an opportunity to give an explanation and due regard should be given to that explanation. A warning should also be given to the employee in either written or oral form.

Redundancy Payments Acts 1967-1979

[3.43] Redundancy is a form of dismissal, whereby employment ceases when the employer is unable to provide work for an employee. The Redundancy Acts provide a statutory basis for compensation in these situations. The redundancy payment is made by the employer who then claims a rebate from a statutory fund which amounts to approximately 60% of the claim. The Employment Appeals Tribunal deals with disputes relating to redundancies. An appeal lies to the High Court on a point of law.

[3.44] Employees entitled to receive redundancy payments are :

(a) Employees who have worked continuously for the same employer for 104 weeks.

(b) Employees who normally work 88 hours per week prior to termination for redundancy.

(c) Regular part-time employees who are normally expected to work 8 hours per week.

(d) Employees between the ages of 16 and 66 years of age.

(e) Employees who are insurable for the purposes of the Social Welfare Acts.

Certain categories of employees are excluded from the Redundancy Acts such as those employed in a household.

[3.45] To qualify for a statutory redundancy payment, an employee must be in insurable employment for a minimum of two years in order to receive all benefits under the Social Welfare Acts. Nurses employed under the Health Act 1970 are excluded since they are not in insurable employment. The amount of the statutory lump sum varies depending on the length of service, the age of the claimant and the claimant's gross ongoing weekly wage. The amount payable is subject to a ceiling figure. Where an employee is laid off or kept on short-time for stated periods then the Redundancy Acts are applicable to them provided they are in insurable employment.

Definition of redundancy under the Redundancy Acts and the Unfair Dismissals Acts 1977-1993

[3.46] Legislation identifies five situations in which a dismissal may give rise to redundancy:

(1) Where the business is closing down or intending to close down.

(2) Where the employer's requirements of an employee with a particular type of skill have ceased or are expected to cease or diminish.

(3) Where fewer employees are required due to re-organisation and the work may be carried out by another employee.

(4) Where an employer decides that the work is to be conducted in a different manner and the employee is not sufficiently trained or qualified.

(5) Where the work being done by the employee may be carried out by a person who is capable of doing other work and the employee is not sufficiently trained.

[3.47] An employer who makes an employee redundant may face a challenge for unfair selection under s 6(3) of the Unfair Dismissal Act 1977, if the circumstances "constituting" the redundancy applied equally to one or more other employees in similar employment with the same employer who have not been dismissed. Therefore, if a "last in first out" policy is in force it should be adhered to unless there are special reasons which would justify departing from it. The redundancy payment is calculated on the length of service and whether the service is continuous.

Remedies

[3.48] Where an employee has been found to be unfairly dismissed the Tribunal may make an award of not more than 104 weeks compensation for any financial loss. Where there has been no financial loss then there is provision for a basic award of up to four weeks pay.[26] In some circumstances an employee may be returned to the position held prior to dismissal with all rights preserved or re-employed in a suitable similar position.

OTHER STATUTES WHICH PROVIDE PROTECTION IN THE WORKPLACE

Minimum Notice and Terms of Employment Act 1993

[3.49] This Act provides that minimum periods of notice, provided an employee has thirteen weeks continuous service, must be given upon termination of a

---

[26] Unfair Dismissal (Amendment) Act 1993.

contract of employment. The period of notice will vary depending upon the length of service. An employee who resigns is obliged under the Act to give one weeks notice regardless of the length of service.

[3.50] While most employees are covered under this Act, there are some who are excluded. These include:-

(a) Members of the immediate family, who also live with [the employer] and are employed in the house or farm.

(b) Civil Servants who are employed pursuant to the Civil Service Commissioners Act 1956.

(c) Members of the Defence Forces (with the exception of temporary staff in the Army Nursing School).

(d) Members of the Garda Síochána.

(e) Seamen who are employed under the Merchant Shipping Act.

It is acceptable for a contract of employment to provide for greater periods of notice but not for less than the statutory entitlement. The rules regarding the calculation of continuity of service are contained in the schedule to the Act.

[3.51] There may be occasions when an employee is entitled to longer periods of notice under the common law. These are determined by the courts, having regard to such matters as the status of the employee, e.g., managerial status, and the degree of responsibility, in deciding what is reasonable in the circumstances. Under the Act it is permissible to accept payment in lieu of notice. However an employer is entitled to effect a dismissal without due notice where there is serious misconduct on the part of the employee.

Terms of Employment (Information) Act 1994

[3.52] There is an obligation on the employer to provide a written statement of the terms of employment to the employee within one month of commencement of employment.[27] There is also an obligation by virtue of the Terms of Employment (Information) Act 1994[28] to provide a statement of the terms of employment to those who commenced employment after 16 May 1994. The nature of the terms to be contained in the written statement are set out in s 3 (1)(*a*)-(*m*):

3 (1) An employer shall, not later than 2 months after the commencement of an employee's employment with the employer, give or cause to give to the employee a

---

[27] Section 9.

[28] This Act implements an EU Directive and the Act came into force on 16 May 1994.

statement in writing containing the following particulars of the terms of employment, that is to say -

(*a*) the full names of the employer and employee,

(*b*) the address of the employer in the State or, where appropriate, the address of the principal place of the relevant business of the employer in the State or the registered office (within the meaning of the Companies Act 1963),

(*c*) the place of work or, where there is no fixed or main place of work, a statement specifying that the employee is required or permitted to work at various places,

(*d*) the title of the job or nature of the work for which the employee is employed,

(*e*) the date of commencement of the employee's contract of employment,

(*f*) in the case of a temporary contract of employment, the expected duration thereof or, if the contract of employment is for a fixed term, the date on which the contract expires,

(*g*) the rate or method of calculation of the employee's remuneration,

(*h*) the length of the intervals between the times at which remuneration is paid, whether a week, a month or any other interval,

(*i*) any terms or conditions relating to hours of work (including overtime),

(*j*) any terms or conditions relating to paid leave (other than paid sick leave),

(*k*) any terms or conditions relating to -

  (i) incapacity for work due to sickness or injury and paid sick leave, and
  (ii) pensions and pension schemes,

(*l*) the period of notice which the employee is required to give and entitled to receive (whether by or under statute or under the terms of the employee's contract of employment) to determine the employee's contract of employment or, where this cannot be indicated when the information is given, the method for determining such periods of notice,

(*m*) a reference of any collective agreements which directly affect the terms and conditions of the employee's employment including, where the employer is not a party to such agreements, particulars of the bodies or institutions by whom they were made.

The statement must be signed and dated by the employer.

[3.53] Upon failure by an employer to provide such information or where the employer has contravened the Act, an employee can bring a claim to a Rights Commissioner, provided she has at least one month of service. A recommendation of a Rights Commissioner may, in accordance within s 7(2):

(*a*) Declare that the complaint was not well founded,

(*b*) confirm all or any of the particulars in the statement provided by the employer,

(*c*) alter or add to the statement,

(*d*) require the employer to provide the employee with a written statement,

(*e*) order the employer to compensate the employee.

The recommendation of the Rights Commissioner can be appealed to the Employment Appeals Tribunal.

Holidays (Employees) Act 1973

[3.54] This Act deals with an employee's entitlement to annual leave and public holidays. The Act provides for three weeks holidays *per annum* provided an employee has twelve qualifying months of service. In order to be classed as a qualifying month of service it is necessary that 120 hours are worked. Where there are less qualifying months of service there are lesser amounts of holidays due. Regular part-time employees who earn more than £25 a week and are fully insurable under the Social Welfare Acts are entitled to annual leave of six hours per one hundred hours worked, and to benefit from public holidays as are applicable to full-time employees.[29]

Holiday Pay

[3.55] Holiday pay is based on an employee's regular salary excluding overtime but including regular bonuses which is not applied to the amount of work carried out. Where an employee is not on a fixed salary then the calculation is made on the average weekly earnings for the preceding thirteen weeks prior to the start of the annual leave. This payment is to be paid in advance of the holiday.

Annual Leave

[3.56] Section 6 provides when annual leave may be taken. As will be seen an employer may decide when this will be taken. Section 3 provides that:

3 (1) An employee shall be entitled to paid leave (in this Act referred to as annual leave) in respect of a leave year in which he has at least one qualifying month of service.

---

[29] There is a requirement that at least 4 of the previous 5 weeks have been worked when employment has ceased when seeking benefit.

(2) Annual leave shall be equivalent to three working weeks where there are twelve qualifying months of service and, subject to the next subsection, to proportionally less where there are eleven or fewer such months.

The Act provides penalties for failure to provide the holiday entitlement provided the prosecution takes place within twelve months of the offence. A fine of £25 is imposed for the first offence and £50 for further offences.

Remedy

[3.57] The Act provides a remedy by means of a liquidated claim (meaning a claim for a guaranteed amount) to the District/Circuit Courts. It is not possible to bring a claim to the Employment Appeals Tribunal.

Public Holidays

[3.58] The Act provides for eight public holidays per year. It is not necessary to have worked any minimum number of months in order to be entitled to paid public holidays, however there are excluded categories of employees such as: day to day workers and regular part time employees unless they are normally expected to work eight hours per week.

[3.59] Where an employee is not given a holiday on the day the public holiday fell due, s 4(1) provides that:

4 (1) (*a*) An employee shall, in respect of a public holiday, be entitled to-

    (i) a paid day off on that day, or
    (ii) a paid day off within a month, or
    (iii) an extra day's annual leave, or
    (iv) an extra day's pay,

as the employer may decide.

(*b*) Notwithstanding that a public holiday falls on a day on which an employee, if it were not a holiday, would normally work for less than a full days pay, "paid" and "pay" in this subsection refer, as respects that day, to a full days pay.

The employer can decide whether to give the holiday on the day it falls due or any of the above or it may be given on a church holiday.

Maternity Protection of Employees Act 1981

[3.60] This Act entitles female employees to unpaid time off before and after the birth of a child. Section 8 provides for a right to maternity leave. An employee must give not less than four weeks notice in writing to her employer. The employee must specify the expected week of confinement and the end of the leave which has to be four weeks after the expected week of confinement. All rights of employment are preserved while on maternity leave, with the exception of an entitlement to be paid. These periods of leave are specified as being:

10 Subject to *sections 11* to *13*, the minimum period of maternity leave shall commence on such day as the employee selects, being not later than four weeks before the end of the expected week of confinement, and shall end on such day as she selects, being not earlier than four weeks after the end of the expected week of confinement.

There are also provisions for both extended and additional maternity leave. The main provision of the Act provides the right to return to work, provided that the conditions as laid down in the Act are complied with.

Return to work

[3.61] Section 20 provides an employee with a general right to return to work on the expiry of her maternity leave to the job she "held immediately before the start of the period":

20 (1) Subject to this Part, on the expiry of a period during which an employee to whom this Part applies was absent from work while on maternity leave or additional maternity leave, she shall be entitled to return to work -

(*a*) with the employer with whom she was working immediately before the start of that period or, where during her absence from work there was a change of ownership of the undertaking in which she was employed immediately before her absence, with the owner (in this Act referred to as "the successor") of the undertaking at the expiry of her period of absence,

(*b*) in the job which she held immediately before the start of that period, and

(*c*) under the contract of employment under which she was employed immediately before the start of that period, or, where a change of ownership such as is referred to in *paragraph (a)* has occurred, under a contract of employment with the successor which is identical to the contract under which she was employed immediately before the start of that period, and (in either case) under terms or conditions not less favourable than those that would have been applicable to her if she had not been so absent from work.

(2) For the purpose of *subsection (1)(b)*, where the job held by an employee before the start of the period of her absence on maternity leave or additional maternity leave was not her normal or usual job, she shall be entitled to return to work, either in her normal or usual job or in that job as soon as practicable without contravention by her or her employer of a provision of a statute or instrument made under that statute.

(3) In this section "job", in relation to an employee, means the nature of the work which she is employed to do in accordance with her contract of employment and the capacity and place in which she is so employed.

[3.62] Where a dismissal occurs as a result of pregnancy or matters connected therewith, because the employee is unable safely or adequately to continue to work, this will not be considered an unfair dismissal. However where there is a suitable alternative vacancy, then this should be offered to her.

Intention to Return

[3.63] It is vital that an employee notifies her employer of her intention to return, in writing, not later than four weeks before the date on which she expects to return. Failure to comply with this will lose the employee her right to return to work. There is no obligation on the employer to notify an employee of the requirement. Section 22(2) states that:

> **22** (2) A notification under *subsection (1)* shall subsequently be confirmed in writing not earlier than four weeks and not later than two weeks before the date on which the employee concerned expects to return to work.

Where an employee is dismissed because of her pregnancy or an employer refuses to allow her to return, she can bring a claim under the Unfair Dismissals Act or this Act, provided that she is not in one of the excluded categories.

[3.64] Legislation is currently being drafted in order to give additional protection and leave to women who suffer illness or health risks connected with their pregnancy. This is in compliance with an EU Directive.[30]

Anti-Discrimination Pay Act 1974 and the Employment Equality Act 1977

[3.65] The main thrust for change in the conditions of work, so as to ensure equality, comes from the European Commission. The Employment Equality Act 1977 and the Anti-Discrimination Pay Act 1974 were enacted in compliance with Ireland's obligations under EU Directives. These Acts comprise a code which gives protection to employees in the area of equal pay when doing "like work".

Anti-Discrimination Pay Act 1974

[3.66] This Act entitles men and women to equal pay, who are working in the same employment or for an associated employer, engaged in like work and working in the same place, i.e. city or locality. Section 2(1) of the Act implies an entitlement to equal pay in the contract of employment:

> **2** (1) Subject to this Act, it shall be a term of the contract under which a woman is employed in any place that she shall be entitled to the same rate of remuneration as a man who is employed in that place by the same employer (or an associated employer if the employees, whether generally or of a particular class, of both employers have the same terms and conditions of employment), if both are employed on like work.

Remuneration

[3.67] Remuneration for the purposes of equal pay includes payment in cash or in kind, whether received directly or indirectly in respect of employment. It has been established in cases before the Labour Court and the European Court of Justice that equal pay includes the following:

---

[30] EU Directive 92/85. See the Appendix.

(1) All benefits enjoyed by an employee which arise out of the employment relationship, including bonus payments for equal levels of output, marriage gratuities and preferential loans;

(2) Pension Benefits, or allowances based on the wage or salary received by an employee; e.g., travel and subsistence rates, preferential insurance cover;

(3) Contributions made to a pension scheme made by the employer in the name of the employee (but not benefits or contributions under compulsory State schemes);

(4) Non-pension benefits made available on retirement, such as free travel, goods or services, where these are granted by the former employer;

(5) Benefits made available to dependents or relatives of the employee, whether in cash or in any other form.

"Like Work"

[3.68] Section 3 defines "like work" as follows:

3 Two persons shall be regarded as employed on like work-

(*a*) where both perform the same work under the same or similar conditions, or where each is in every respect interchangeable with the other in relation to the work, or

(*b*) where the work performed by one is of similar nature to that performed by the other and any differences between the work performed or the conditions under which it is performed by each occur only infrequently or are of small importance in relation to the work as a whole, or

(*c*) where the work performed by one is equal in value to that performed by the other in terms of the demands it makes in relation to such matters as skill, physical or mental effort, responsibility and working conditions.

The work which the parties are engaged in may have some differences, e.g., additional duties or a different range of duties, nevertheless it will be regarded as similar work. All the different aspects of the job have to be weighed up and they may amount to work being of equal value, in order that a claim may be brought under that heading.

Grounds for Different Rates of Pay

[3.69] The Act allows for different rates of pay in an area where workers are doing "like work" provided the different rates of pay are based "on grounds other than sex". Therefore, if there are genuine reasons for differences in pay this will be a defence for an employer. The reason could include experience and grading structures provided they are not discriminatory. These grounds are not an exhaustive list.

Procedure

[3.70] Compliance with the Acts is overseen by an Equality Officer[31] appointed in accordance with the Act. Initially, a complaint is made to the Labour Court, which may refer the complaint to an Equality Officer, who also has the power to enforce the decision of an Equality Officer. The Labour Court issues a recommendation which is binding on the parties.

Employment Equality Act 1977

[3.71] This Act applies to all employees both male and female. Section 2 states that discrimination is said to occur in the following instances:

2 For the purposes of this Act, discrimination shall be taken to occur in any of the following cases-

(*a*) where by reason of his sex a person is treated less favourably than a person of the other sex.

(*b*) where because of his marital status a person is treated less favourably than another person of the same sex,

(*c*) where because of his sex or marital status a person is obliged to comply with a requirement, relating to employment or membership of a body referred to in *section 5*, which is not an essential requirement for such employment or membership and in respect of which the proportion of persons of the other sex or (as the case may be) of a different marital status but of the same sex able to comply is substantially higher.

[3.72] The Act does not apply in the following instances:

- where, in rare instances, the sex of the employee or prospective employee is an occupational qualification for the job, e.g. where an actor or model is required to be of a particular sex;

- where there are statutory restrictions on the employment of women;

- where the nature or location of the employment requires the employee to live in premises which do not have separate sleeping and sanitary facilities for men and women. The employer must show that he could not reasonably be expected to provide these facilities;

- where the job is likely to involve duties outside the State in a country whose laws and customs are such that these duties could not be performed by a man or woman.

---

[31] Section 6 provides that these officers are now officers of the Labour Relations Commission.

[3.73] It is unlawful for an employer to discriminate against a prospective employee on the grounds of sex or marital status in:

- the arrangements made for recruitment, e.g. the criteria for selection interview procedures, the instructions given to an employment agency;

- the terms on which the employer offers the job;

- or by refusing or deliberately omitting to offer the person the job.

An employer must not discriminate in any of the following instances:

- the provision of training, on or off the job,

- the regrading or classification of jobs,

- work counselling,

- the provision of work experience,

- the promotion opportunities offered,

- in dismissal, disciplinary measures or in any other disadvantages to which employee may be subjected to, e.g. redundancies, shorter working hours,

- by having discriminatory rules or instructions.

[3.74] The Labour Court is the body which adjudicates on whether or not discrimination has occurred and details of any complaint must be referred to the Court within six months of the alleged act of discrimination occurring. The Labour Court may refer a complaint to an Equality Officer.[32] If the Labour Court upholds a complaint it may:

- declare the rights of the parties, or

- recommend a specific course of action to comply with the law, or

- award compensation of up to a maximum of 104 week's pay.

In the case of discriminatory dismissal, the Labour Court may also order re-instatement or re-engagement.

[3.75] The Act also deals with the display or publishing of discriminatory advertisements, membership and benefits of various bodies including trade

---

[32] Section 19.

unions, employment agencies and professional organisations. All employees, including those employed by a local authority come within the scope of the Act except those in the Defence Forces. However the Act will not apply where an essential requirement of the job is that the applicant be of a particular sex or where the work performed is of a personal nature. Men by virtue of s 11 became entitled to become midwives.

European Communities (Safeguarding of Employees' Rights on the Transfer of Undertakings) Regulations 1980

[3.76] Under common law, a contract of employment was deemed to come to an end upon the sale of the employer's business, unless the parties agreed otherwise. These Regulations seek to provide protection for employees where there is a change of employer upon the sale of a business. They also seek to preserve and safeguard employees' statutory rights, e.g., rights as to the length of service, collective agreements etc., that were previously in existence with the first employer. The court will have regard as to whether the same business is being carried on by the new employer notwithstanding that the identity of the company has changed. However these do not apply to employees' rights to old age, invalidity or survivor's benefits under supplementary company or inter-company pension schemes outside the Social Welfare Acts 1952-1979. In the event of a contract of employment being terminated because a transfer involves a substantial change in working conditions to the detriment of the employee concerned, the new employer shall be regarded as having been responsible for the termination.

Notification

[3.77] There is an obligation in the Regulations on the party selling and the party acquiring the business to inform the representatives of their respective employees affected by the transfer in good time before the transfer is carried out of:

1. The reason for the transfer.
2. The legal economic and social implication for the employees.
3. The measures envisaged which may affect the employees.

Details of any measure envisaged in relation to employees must be discussed with representatives of the employees with the view to obtaining their agreement. If there are no representatives then the statement is to be given in good time to each employee with particulars and also a notice of the transfer must be displayed at the place of work. An inspector from the Department of Enterprise and Employment may request the parties to make such information available to him as he may reasonably require and to enter the premises at all reasonable times. There are penalties for failure to comply with the above.

Payment of Wages Act 1991

[3.78] This Act sets out the manner in which wages are to be paid and what lawful deductions can be made. The Act applies to all employees including those employed by a local authority or health board. Section 2 of the Act sets out the various methods of payment of wages:

> **2** Wages may be paid by and only by one or more of the following modes:
>
> (*a*) a cheque, draft or other bill of exchange within the meaning of the Bills of Exchange Act 1882,
>
> (*b*) a document issued by a person who maintains an account with the Central Bank or a holder of a licence under section 9 of the Central Bank Act 1971, which, though not such a bill of exchange as aforesaid, is intended to enable a person to obtain payment from that bank or that holder of the amount specified in the document,
>
> (*c*) a draft payable on demand drawn by a holder of such a licence as aforesaid upon himself, whether payable at the head office or some other office of the bank to which the licence relates,
>
> (*d*) a postal, money or paying order, or a warrant, or any other like document, issued by or drawn on An Post or a document issued by an officer of a Minister of the Government that is intended to enable a person to obtain payment from that Minister of the Government of the sum specified in the document,
>
> (*e*) a document issued by a person who maintains an account with a trustee savings bank within the meaning of the Trustee Savings Bank 1989, that is intended to enable a person to obtain payment from the bank of the sum specified in the document,
>
> (*f*) a credit transfer or another mode of payment whereby an amount is credited to an account specified by the employee concerned,
>
> (*g*) cash,
>
> (*h*) any other mode of payment standing specified for the time being by regulations made by the Minister after consultation with the Minister for Finance.

In the event of a strike effecting a financial institution, e.g., a bank strike and cash is to readily available, then with the consent of the employee, employers are obliged to make alternative arrangements by one of the modes set out above. However in the event the employee does not consent, then the wages are to be paid in cash. Failure to comply with the above shall be an offence and may result in a fine.

Wages

[3.79] The Act defines wages as any sum of money paid by the employer to the employee "in connection with his employment". Those payments which are not covered by the Act include expenses incurred in the carrying out of his employment, pension contributions, redundancy payments and any payments made to an employee in any other capacity and benefits in kind.

Statement of Wages

[3.80] Under s 4 of the Act the employee is entitled to a written statement of wages with every payment of wages showing the gross amount of wages and deductions therefrom. Where payment is made by credit transfer then this statement should be given as soon as possible after the credit transfer has taken place. An employer is obliged to treat this information with confidentiality.

Deductions

[3.81] Section 5 sets the valid deductions which may be made by the employer, such as PAYE or PRSI. All other deductions may only be made with the prior consent of the employee. Where an employer seeks to make deductions regarding matters such as breakages, bad workmanship or the provision of goods or services such as the cleaning of uniforms etc. then these deductions must be provided for and agreed to by the employee. The deduction must be "fair and reasonable" having regard to all the circumstances and the employee must be given reasonable notice of the deduction.

Unlawful Deductions

[3.82] A complaint may be made to a Rights Commissioner within six months of the date where there has been an unlawful deduction from an employee's wages. In the event of the Rights Commissioner deciding that the complaint is well founded, he shall order the employer to pay the employee such amount as he considers reasonable but not exceeding:

6 (2)(*a*) the net amount of the wages (after the making of any lawful deduction therefrom) that-

(i) in case the complaint related to a deduction, would have been paid to the employee in respect of the week immediately proceeding the date of the deduction if the deduction had not been made, or

(ii) in case the complaint related to a payment, were paid to the employee in respect of the week immediately preceding the date of payment, or

(*b*) if the amount of the deduction or payment is greater than the amount referred to in *paragraph (a)*, twice the former amount.

[3.83] An employee must elect to go to a Rights Commissioner. Either the employer or the employee may appeal his decision to the Employment Appeals Tribunal. This must be done within six weeks of the date when the decision has been communicated to the parties. There is an appeal from this forum to the High Court on a point of law.

Time Limit

[3.84] Any deduction must be made within six months after the employer knows of the act or omission of his employee. Any deductions made must not exceed the loss or damage suffered by the employer and if a service or goods have been supplied the deduction must not be more than the initial cost to the employer. A receipt should be issued to the employee in respect of deductions for any of the above.

Enforcement

[3.85] A decision of the Rights Commissioner or a determination of the Employment Appeals Tribunal may be enforced as if it were issued by the Circuit Court. A contract of employment which seeks to preclude or limit the provisions of this Act will be of no effect, i.e. void.

[3.86] *Shalvey v Telecom Éireann*[33] a case which came before the High Court, concerned a debt owed by Mr Shalvey to his employer Telecom Éireann, who sought to deduct the amount from his wages. The Court was of the opinion that under s 5(5) of the Act, the employer was unable to do this as the section only applies where an employee has given his consent in writing prior to the deduction and that s 5(5)(g) only caters for payments to a third party pursuant to a court order.

Worker Protection (Regular Part-Time Employees) Act 1991

[3.87] This Act protects those who are in continuous part-time employment and who are normally expected to work not less than eight hours per week or have thirteen weeks service. Regular part-time employees benefit from the following Acts:

Unfair Dismissals Acts 1977-1993.
Minimum Notice and Terms of Employment Act 1993.
Worker Participation (State Enterprises) Acts 1977 and 1988.
Holidays (Employees) Act 1973.
Redundancy Payments Acts 1967 - 1990.
Maternity Protection of Employees Act 1981.
Protection of Employees (Employers' Insolvency) Act 1984.

This Act applies to those employees who earn more than £25 per week and who are fully insurable under the Social Welfare Acts. There is an entitlement to annual leave of six hours per one hundred hours worked and to benefit from public holidays in the same way as full time employees. However the employee needs to have worked at least four of the previous five weeks to benefit from the public holiday entitlement where employment ceases.

---

[33] Unreported High Court, July 28 1992.

[3.88] Section 4 provides that an employee is entitled to three weeks holiday so long as there are twelve qualifying months worked, one hundred and twenty hours worked in a month is a qualifying month. Upon termination there is an entitlement under s 5 to compensation of one quarter of the normal weekly rate for each qualifying month of service.

[3.89] The Act also deals with situations where an employer seeks to get around the Act by dismissing an employee or by reducing her hours. In such situations the Tribunal will deem the employee to be protected.

Remedy

[3.90] A regular part-time employee may bring a claim to the Employment Appeals Tribunal provided they are employed under a contract of service. There is an appeal from the Tribunal to the High Court on a point of law only.

SEXUAL HARASSMENT

[3.91] Sexual harassment is defined by the European Commission as "unwanted conduct of a sexual nature, or other conduct based on sex which affects the dignity of women and men at work, this can include physical, verbal or non-verbal conduct."[34]

[3.92] The European Commission gives examples of conduct which would fall within their definition:

"Physical conduct of a sexual nature is commonly regarded as meaning unwanted physical contact ranging from unnecessary touching, patting or pinching or brushing against another employee's body to assault and coercing sexual intercourse. Much of this conduct, if it took place in the street between two persons, would amount to a criminal offence."[35]

[3.93] The Commission gives guidance on the range and characteristics of such behaviour. Thus, a range of behaviour may be considered to constitute sexual harassment. Conduct is unacceptable if it is unwanted, unreasonable and offensive to the recipient; a person's rejection of or submission to such conduct on the part of employers or workers (including superiors or colleagues) is used explicitly or implicitly as a basis for a decision which affects that person's access to vocational training or to employment, continued employment, promotion, salary or any other employment decisions; and/or such conduct creates an intimidating, hostile or humiliating working environment for the recipient.

---

[34] Council Resolution on the Protection of the Dignity of Women at Work (OJ C157, 27/6/1990).

[35] *How to Combat Sexual Harassment at Work*, Commission of the European Communities, 1993 p. 21.

[3.94] The essential characteristics of sexual harassment are that it is unwanted by the recipient and that it is for each individual to determine what behaviour is acceptable to them and what they regard as offensive. Sexual attention becomes sexual harassment if it is persisted in, once it has been made clear that it is regarded by the recipient as offensive. One incident of harassment may constitute sexual harassment if sufficiently serious. It is the unwanted nature of the conduct which distinguishes sexual harassment from friendly behaviour, which is welcome and mutual.

[3.95] The Employment Equality Agency defines sexual harassment as:

> "behaviour which includes unreciprocated and unwelcome comments, looks, jokes, suggestions or physical contact that might threaten a person's job security or threat, i.e., a stressful or intimidating working environment."

Sexual harassment of a worker may take many forms, e.g., leering, ridicule, unwelcome remarks about their dress or appearance, deliberate abuse, unwanted physical contact. Social relationships mutually entered into by work colleagues do not form the basis of a charge of sexual harassment. It is only in cases where the behaviour is unwanted that a claim for sexual harassment may arise. In general, sexual harassment creates a hostile environment for the person being harassed and in some instances sexual compliance is expected for a job or promotional opportunity. If a person is being sexually harassed at work, that person should:

- Tell the harasser that his behaviour is not welcome and ask him to stop.
- Report the matter as soon as possible to the employer and/or trade union personnel.
- Keep a record of individual incidents as they happen.
- Contact the Employment Equality Agency.

Enforcement

[3.96] A case may be brought to the Labour Court within six months of the alleged act of harassment. In certain circumstances the time limit may be extended. When the matter comes before the Labour Court it may decide to have an investigation by an Equality Officer who will then issue a recommendation or it may seek to reach settlement there and then.

Appeals

[3.97] An appeal against an Equality Officer's recommendation or the non-implementation of a decision, may be lodged in the Labour Court not later than forty-two days from the date of the recommendation.

The Labour Court

[3.98] The Labour Court may issue a declaration which states that the act complained of did or did not occur and make a recommendation. Failure to comply with an order of the Labour Court is an offence. An appeal lies to the High Court on a point of law.

Case-law

[3.99] In a recent case which came before the High Court[36] a female employee of a health board suffered a violent sexual assault by two fellow employees. For six weeks prior to this she was subject to "lewd and coarse" remarks and unwanted touching. She threatened to complain but did not do so. After the attack she complained immediately and the board took action in that one employee was dismissed and the other was suspended without pay for five weeks. The High Court was of the view that even if the assailants were found not guilty of indecent assault at the criminal trial that followed, nevertheless this verdict did not affect the fact that she had suffered a "violent sexual assault at the hands of her attackers". A claim was brought under the Act and the claimant succeeded before the Equality Office and the Labour Court. The matter was then appealed to the High Court on a point of law. The question for determination was whether the act of her fellow employees was "discrimination" and if it was whether the health board was vicariously liable under the Employment Equality Act. The Court was of the view that the conduct complained of prior to the assault was clear sexual harassment and had a detrimental effect on the conditions in the workplace. The Court referred to both the English and Northern Ireland provisions in this area which show that there is a gap in the Irish law as there is no express provision that renders an employer liable for the discriminatory acts of his employees. Under English legislation an employer is automatically liable for any discriminatory act of his employees. In this case the Court said that the health board was not vicariously liable for what occurred as the fellow employees were acting outside the scope of their employment. In the event of a complaint of sexual harassment being made to an employer, the employer then is obliged to take steps to keep the workplace free of sexual harassment and failure to do so may lead to a claim for compensation.

TRADE UNION ACTIVITIES

[3.100] Many nurses opt to become members of a trade union. Membership of a trade union is a right protected by the Constitution but it is not obligatory to join a trade union. One of the functions of a trade union is to negotiate with employers as to the terms and conditions of service and to represent its members in disputes.

---

[36] *The Health Board v BC and the Labour Court*, judgment of Costello J delivered 19 January 1994.

Most trade unions have full time officials but normally day to day matters are dealt with by employees appointed for that purpose. An employee can not be dismissed by an employer for engaging in trade union activities, either outside her normal hours of work or during times permitted by her contract of employment.[37]

Trade Dispute

[3.101] Interference with another person's contract of employment constitutes an actionable tort. However, the Industrial Relations Act 1990 provides protection from civil liability, provided a *bona fide* dispute exists.[38] The Act defines a trade dispute as being any dispute which is between the employer and worker and which is connected to the employment or non-employment or the terms and conditions of same. In the event of a dispute being concerned with only one worker there is a statutory requirement that all agreed grievance procedures be exhausted before any strike action is taken, otherwise the protection of the Act is lost. In the event of a dispute arising which cannot be resolved and provided certain conditions are met, the employee may engage in strike action or the parties may agree to refer the dispute to conciliation. These matters are governed by the Industrial Relations Act 1990.

[3.102] In the event of a strike occurring as a result of a *bona fide* dispute and a nurse wishes to withdraw her labour then she may do. However those nurses who are officers of a local authority employed by health boards, with the exception of psychiatric nurses, do not enjoy protection under the Act.

Picketing

[3.103] The Act allows for peaceful picketing by employees either acting on their own behalf or on behalf of a trade union provided it is in "contemplation or furtherance of a trade dispute." The picket may be at or near a place where their employer works or carries on business, if they so attend merely for the purpose of peacefully obtaining or communicating information or of peacefully persuading any person to work or abstain from working.

[3.104] It may also be possible to place a picket peacefully at the premises of an employer who is not a party to the dispute, only if it is reasonable to believe that this other employer has "directly assisted their employer", who is a party to the dispute and the purpose of the assistance is to frustrate the strike or industrial action. However if an employer in the Health Services does take action to "maintain life-preserving services" this will not be regarded as assistance of the type which might otherwise be a ground for legal secondary picketing.

Secret Ballots

[3.105] It is necessary before any industrial action is taken that a secret ballot be

---

[37] Unfair Dismissal Act 1977 s 2 as amended by Unfair Dismissal (Amendment) Act 1993.

[38] See ss 10-12 of the Industrial Relations Act 1990 regarding the number of licensed Trade Unions.

conducted of all members and one week's notice be given by the union to the employer.[39] The ballot must be conducted in accordance with the Act. Failure to observe this will result in loss of protection under the Act which could result in an employer obtaining an injunction for preventing the placing of a picket and/or damages.

[3.106] Under the provisions of s 42 of the Industrial Relations Act 1990, a code of practice relating to the procedure to be adopted in the case of a dispute regarding essential services has been drawn up.[40] Section III provides that:

> **20** While the primary responsibility for the provision of minimum levels of services rests with managements, this Code recognises that there is a joint obligation on employers and trade unions to have in place contingency plans and other arrangements to deal with any emergency which may arise during an industrial dispute. Employers and trade unions should co-operate with the introduction of such plans and contingency arrangements. In particular, employers and trade unions in each employment providing an essential service should co-operate with each other in making arrangements concerning:
>
> (a) the maintenance of plant and equipment,
>
> (b) all matters concerning health, safety and security;
>
> (c) special operational problems which exist in continuous process industries;
>
> (d) the provision of urgent medical services and supplies,
>
> (e) the provision of emergency services required on humanitarian grounds.
>
> **21** In the event of the parties encountering problems in making such arrangements they should seek the assistance of the Labour Relations Commission.

The Code recognises that there is a joint obligation on employers and trade unions to draw up contingency plans to deal with any emergency arising during a dispute. The dispute procedures set out in the Code are aimed at bolstering the methods of negotiation, with strike action being a last resort.

[3.107] It is important to note that all the immunities granted under this Act may not extend to nurses where they know or have reasonable cause to know that their actions would result in human life being endangered or cause serious bodily injury. This could result in a criminal charge. When the conditions as outlined above have been complied with, a nurse may withdraw her labour.

---

[39] See s 19 of the Industrial Relations Act 1990.

[40] SI 1/92. Code of Practice: *Dispute Procedures including Procedures in Essential Services*, issued by the Department of Labour.

STATUTORY INSTITUTIONS

[3.108] Over the years a number of institutions have been established to ensure that both employers and employees comply with statute law with regard to contracts of employment and to assist in the resolution of any disputes. These include the Labour Court, the Equality Employment Agency, Equality Officers and the Employment Appeals Tribunal.

The Labour Court

[3.109] The Labour Court was established under the Industrial Relations Act 1946. The Court also has certain functions under the Anti-Discrimination (Pay) Act 1974 and the Employment Equality Act 1977. The Industrial Relations Act 1990 transferred the Court's conciliation functions and the Equality Officer service to the Labour Relations Commission, which was established under that Act. The Labour Court's functions are as follows:

- To investigate trade disputes and issue recommendations for their settlement.

- To make determinations on appeals against the recommendations of Equality Officers.

- To make orders on cases of alleged dismissal under the Anti-Discrimination (Pay) Act 1974, the Employment Equality Act 1977 and the Pensions Act 1990.

- To decide on appeals against recommendations of the Rights Commissioner under the Industrial Relations Act.

- To establish and service Joint Labour Committees.

- To register and vary certain employment agreements.

- To provide conciliation and advisory service or industrial relation and the preparation of codes of practice.

[3.110] The Labour Court may on its own initiative offer its services in the event of a trade dispute or give assistance on request. The Labour Court at present consists of a chairman, two deputy chairmen and six ordinary members, all of whom are appointed by the Minister for Labour. Not all Labour Court recommendations are binding on the parties concerned, but the following decisions are binding and may be enforced through a court of law:

(1) Determinations and Orders under equal pay, employment equality.

(2) Decisions and Orders under ss 32, 33, 57 of the 1946 Act and s 10 of the 1969 Act, concerning registered employment Agreements.

A decision by the Labour Court on an appeal against a Rights Commissioner's recommendation is binding on the parties.

Equality Officers

[3.111] Equality officers were established by s 6 of the Anti-Discrimination (Pay) Act 1974. They are officers of the Labour Relations Commission but are independent in the performance of their functions. Claims for breach of equal pay provisions of the Anti-Discrimination (Pay) Act 1974 and the Employment Equality Act 1977 are investigated by the equality officers and recommendations are made. These may be referred to the Labour Court whose decision is final except on a point of law where an appeal lies to the High Court.

Employment Equality Agency

[3.112] The Employment Equality Agency was established by the Employment Equality Act 1977. This Agency provides information and advice about employment opportunities, placements in a job, and other employment related services. It also oversees that employees are not discriminated against either on grounds of sex or marital status. The Agency has the power to hold formal investigations and if it is satisfied that practices or conduct contravene the Employment Equality Act or the Equal Pay legislation can issue non-discrimination notices requiring that they cease. For certain formal investigations the Agency has the power to require any person to furnish information and attend hearings to give evidence. There are penalties for failure to comply with such requirements. The Agency is empowered to seek a High Court injunction in respect of persistent discrimination. Only the Agency can bring proceedings in matters to do with:

- Discriminatory advertisements.

- Pressure on persons to discriminate.

- General policy of discriminatory practices.

Employment Appeals Tribunal

[3.113] The Employment Appeals Tribunal (E.A.T.) was established by s 39 of the Redundancy Payments Act 1967. Its function was to administer redundancy compensation introduced by that Act. Its jurisdiction has been extended by a number of Acts, most significantly by the Unfair Dismissal Act 1977 and the Unfair Dismissal (Amendment) Act 1993. The present day workload of the E.A.T. concerns the resolution of disputes which arise under the following Acts:

The Redundancy Payments Acts.
The Minimum Notice and Terms of Employment Act 1973.
The Unfair Dismissals Acts 1977-1993.
The Maternity Protection of Employees Act 1981.
The Protection of Employees (Employers' Insolvency) Act 1984.
The Payment of Wages Act 1991.
Holidays Employees Act 1973.

Worker Protection (Regular Part-Time Employees) Act 1991.
Acquired Rights of Employees Directive 77/187.
Terms of Employment (Information) Act 1994.

[3.114] The E.A.T. has the power to administer oaths, take evidence on oath, seek the attendance of witnesses and the production of documents. Witnesses have the same privileges and immunities as if they were witnesses in the High Court. The rules and procedures of the E.A.T. are regulated by statutory regulation under the relevant Acts and it is subject to the principles of fair procedures and natural justice. The members of the E.A.T. are appointed by the Minister for Labour and when sitting it consists of a practising barrister, solicitor, a member of the Irish Congress of Trade Unions and a member of an employers organisation. The decisions of the E.A.T. relating to unfair dismissal and maternity protection may be appealed to the Circuit Court by way of a full rehearing and a further full rehearing to the High Court.

SUMMARY

[3.115] The above chapter outlines the types of contracts which usually apply to persons in the nursing profession. It outlines the various duties of both the employer and employee and also the relevant statutes that apply to employment law. However, it must be remembered that an employee also has recourse to the civil courts in the event of a dispute and does not necessarily have to pursue her grievance through the statutory tribunals.

CHAPTER 4

THE FITNESS TO PRACTISE COMMITTEE

DISCIPLINARY PROCEDURES

[4.01] Nursing legislation has always provided for procedures whereby the Nursing Board may discipline a nurse when she is in breach of professional standards or the code of conduct. Disciplinary proceedings for some health professions are regulated by statute, e.g., the Medical Practitioners Act 1978, the Dentists Act 1985 and the Nurses Act 1985. The disciplinary committees will have regard to judicial decisions on the application of each other's guidelines in reaching a decision to discipline one of their members. Each of these committees when disciplining their members, applies the standards generally accepted by their profession and contained in their code of conduct. The Acts empower the various professions to develop their own professional code. These codes have persuasive value and the Boards have a duty to publish a code which members of the professions must observe or have regard to in exercising their professional duties. Under the Nurses Act 1985, the Code of Professional Conduct for Nurses and Midwives[1] was drawn up. This is updated as the need arises.

FORMATION OF THE FITNESS TO PRACTISE COMMITTEE

[4.02] The provisions of the Nurses Act 1985 require the Nursing Board to form a Fitness to Practise Committee. This committee for all intents and purposes is a body of people who, when a complaint is made about the professional conduct of a nurse, sit and look into all the circumstances and validity of the complaint. Its main function is to apply the generally accepted standards of the nursing profession to the complaint made.

[4.03] Under s 13(2) it is mandatory that the Board establish the Fitness to Practise Committee whose function it is to investigate complaints made by any "person". Section 13(3) requires that this committee must comprise of members from the Board only, whereas other committees established by the Board may include non-members of the Board:

> **13** (1) The Board may, subject to the subsequent provisions of this section, from time to time establish committees to perform such, if any, functions of the Board as, in the opinion of the Board, may be better or more conveniently performed by a committee, and are assigned to a committee by the Board.

---

[1] An Bord Altranais (The Nursing Board) January 1988. See the Appendix.

(2) In particular and without prejudice to the generality of *subsection (1)* of this section, the Board shall establish a committee in relation to its function under *Part V* of this Act.

COMPOSITION OF THE COMMITTEE

[4.04] This Committee is composed of members of the Board, a majority of whom are nurses. A third of the Committee of the Board is appointed by the Minister for Health. Section 13 provides as follows:

13(5) Every member of the Committee established under *subsection (2)* of this section shall be a member of the Board.

(6) A majority of the members of the Committee referred to in *subsection (2)* of this section shall be persons who have been appointed by election to the Board and at least one-third of the members of that Committee shall be persons other than persons who have been appointed by election to the Board.

(7) The acts of a Committee established under this section shall be subject to confirmation by the Board unless the Board, at any time, dispenses with the necessity for such confirmation.

POWERS OF THE COMMITTEE

[4.05] Section 38(6) of the Nurses Act 1985 gives the Committee, when holding an inquiry, the powers, rights and privileges of the High Court. These would include a power to obtain documents for examination, compel witnesses to attend for examination under oath. The Committee is also vested with the power to issue summonses for the purposes of obtaining necessary evidence to hold an inquiry. In the event of non-compliance with the Committee's request for either attendance, documents or for refusal to take the oath, a criminal conviction or a fine of £1000 may be imposed.

[4.06] The 1985 Act clearly sets out that it is the Board and not the Committee which decides whether a nurse's name should be erased or suspended from the register.

[4.07] In the event of a nurse not being satisfied with the result of the inquiry, she is entitled to a full rehearing. In *K v An Bord Altranais*[2] Finlay CJ said that under the provisions of the Nurses Act 1985, the High Court alone retained the power to suspend or erase a nurse from the Register. He explained that:

"The necessity for that procedure to vest that power unequivocally in the courts, in my view arises from the constitutional frailty that would attach to the delegation of any such power to a body which was not a court established under the Constitution having regard to the decision of the former Supreme Court in *In Re Solicitors Act...*"

---

[2] [1992] IR 369.

[4.08] The constitutionality of ss 45-48 of the Medical Practitioner's Act were challenged in *M v The Medical Council* [3] (there are similar provisions in the Nurses Act 1985) on the grounds that the powers of the Committee of the Medical Council were judicial powers (which are vested in the courts under Article 37 of the Constitution) and were not limited powers in relation to disciplinary matters. Finlay P applied the test laid down by the Supreme Court in *Re The Solicitors Act 1954*[4] and said:

"Neither the Committee nor the [Medical] Council has any power to erase the name of a practitioner from the register, to suspend him from his practice, to attach conditions to the continuation of his practice, to make him pay compensation or to award costs against him. The only power vested in them in regard to any of these matters (other than payment of compensation) which is not provided for in the Act at all is to initiate proceedings in the High Court which may lead to an order being made by the High Court in respect of any of these matters."

Finlay P concluded that the powers vested in the Committee were not judicial in nature and that even if they were, they were very clearly "limited" in nature:

"The only powers of the Committee of the Council which could be said to be final and, in a sense, binding are the publication of a finding by the Committee of misconduct or unfitness to practice and the Council's power to advise, admonish or censure a practitioner. Even if it could be said that the publication to the public of a finding by a committee of inquiry of misconduct or unfitness was something affecting the rights of a practitioner...or if the same could be said of advising, admonishing or censuring...these would be functions so clearly limited in their effect and consequence that they would be within the exception provided by Article 37...even if they constituted the administration of justice."

CONFIDENTIALITY OF PROCEDURES

[4.09] The findings of the Fitness to Practise Committee shall not be made public without the consent of the nurse, unless a finding of professional misconduct has been made or the nurse has been declared unfit to engage in the practice of nursing. Section 38(5) of the Nurses Act 1985 provides that:

38(5) The findings of the Fitness to Practise Committee on any matter referred to it and the decision of the Board on any report made to it by the Fitness to Practise Committee shall not be made public without the consent of the person who has been the subject of the inquiry before the Fitness to Practise Committee unless such person has been found, as a result of such inquiry to be:

(*a*) guilty of professional misconduct, or

(*b*) unfit to engage in the practice of nursing because of physical or mental disability, as the case may be.

---

[3] [1984] 1 IR 485.

[4] [1960] IR 239.

PRIVILEGE

[4.10] Under s 45 of the Nurses Act 1985 the proceedings of the Fitness to Practise Committee are protected by absolute privilege:

> **45** Proceedings under *section 38* of this Act, proceedings of or communications to or by the Board pursuant to *sections 39, 40, 41* and *42* of this Act, reports made by the Fitness to Practise Committee to the Board under this Part of this Act and any other communications between the Committee and the Board made in the exercise or performance of the powers, duties or functions of the Committee or the Board, as the case may be, shall in any action for defamation, be absolutely privileged.

CONSTITUTIONALITY

[4.11] The constitutionality of a Fitness to Practise Committee and its powers to hold an inquiry were challenged in the High Court. In *In re M, a Doctor*[5] Finlay P was of the view that since the powers vested in the Medical Council were not final and binding, the sections were not unconstitutional. It was held *per* Finlay P in dismissing the plaintiff's claims:

> "1. That at the hearing by the High Court of the plaintiff's application for the cancellation of the decision of the defendant Council made pursuant to s 46 of the Act of 1978, the true construction of that Act would require, (a) that an onus of proof should lie upon the defendant Council to establish (i) the correctness of the finding that the plaintiff had been guilty of an act or acts of professional misconduct and (ii) the correctness of the defendant Council's decision that the plaintiff's name should be erased from the said register and (b) that, in the event of the court affirming the finding of professional misconduct, the plaintiff be given an opportunity to address the court upon the appropriate penalty to be imposed on him.

> 2. That, apart from the power to publish the finding of the Committee or the decision of the Council and the power of the Council under s 48 to advise, admonish or censure a medical practitioner, neither the Committee nor the Council was invested by the impugned enactments with any powers that were final and binding on the medical practitioner whose conduct had been investigated under s 45 of the Act and that, accordingly, the exercise of those powers (apart from the two exceptions) did not constitute the administration of justice within the meaning of Article 34, s 1, of the Constitution."

Finlay P referred to the powers exercised by the Medical Council as follows:

> "3. That the powers mentioned in those two exceptions, even if they involved the administration of justice, were limited functions and powers of a judicial nature and, as such, were permitted by the exemption provided by Article 37 of the Constitution.

> 4. That, in view of the onus of proof to be discharged by the defendant Council at the hearing of the plaintiff's application for cancellation of that defendant's decision, the

---

[5] [1984] IR 479.

fact that the plaintiff would make that application as a person already condemned by the Committee and the Council did not constitute a lack of fair procedures, nor did the fact that the plaintiff had no opportunity to make submissions to the defendant Council before it made its decision."

In relation to the question of the publication of an adverse finding, which is permitted by s 46 of the Act of 1978, the court was of the view that this would not "constitute an unjust attack on the good name" of the practitioner.

[4.12] Dr. M further challenged the Council's power to erase him from the register upon a finding of professional misconduct and also sought a full re-hearing of his case. When the case came before Finlay P it was held as follows:

"1. That the hearing by the High Court of an application under s 46 of the Act of 1978 constitutes an entire trial of the issues involved and is not a mere appeal from the combined decisions of the committee and the council."

The Court was of the opinion that the onus fell on the Council to establish the alleged misconduct and said:

"2. That, at such hearing, the onus is on the council to establish the alleged misconduct and the aptness of the penalty chosen by the Council.

3. That, in view of the first two findings and the ultimate role of the High Court, the lack of any right of the petitioner to be heard by the Council before it reached its decision on the report of the Committee did not constitute unfair procedure or want of natural justice."[6]

SUMMARY

[4.13] An Bord Altranais possesses statutory powers to discipline and question members of the nursing profession regarding matters of conduct and discipline in order to uphold the professional standards of its profession. The nurse has statutory protection in Part V of the Nurses Act 1985 with regard to the powers of the Fitness to Practise Committee. Before a suspension or erasure can occur, it is necessary for the Board to obtain an order of the High Court.

---

[6] This was followed in *K v An Bord Altranais* [1990] 2 IR 396.

CHAPTER 5

THE FITNESS TO PRACTISE INQUIRY

INTRODUCTION

[5.01] A number of professions have statutory powers which enable them to deal with the discipline of their members within the parameters of their own profession and to maintain the standards pursuant to their code of conduct. In the nursing profession disciplinary matters are dealt with by a Fitness to Practise Committee, which consists of members elected by the profession and statutory appointments by the appropriate Minister. Part V of the Nurses Act 1985[1] contains provisions whereby a Fitness to Practise Committee can examine the conduct and professional practices of members of the nursing profession.

[5.02] Section 38(1) of the Nurses Act 1985 lays down the procedure to be followed when a complaint is made in relation to a nurse's general conduct and fitness to practise:

38 (1) The Board or any person may apply to the Fitness to Practise Committee for an inquiry into the fitness of a nurse to practise nursing on the grounds of-

(*a*) alleged professional misconduct, or

(*b*) alleged unfitness to engage in such practice by reason of physical or mental disability,

and the application shall, subject to the provisions of this Act, be considered by the Fitness to Practise Committee.

The complaint can be made by "any person" and this may be another nurse, a relative, a patient, a visitor or any member of the public in general, or any member of the hospital staff.

PROCESSING THE COMPLAINT

[5.03] A complaint may refer either to the professional conduct or any mental or physical disability effecting a nurse's competence. The Fitness to Practise Committee (hereinafter referred to as the Committee) have to consider the *bona fides* of the complaint, i.e. is there a case to answer? In reaching a conclusion the

---

[1] See the Appendix.

Committee may make the necessary inquiries as to the veracity of the complaint and complainant. A report is then submitted to the Board. Having considered the report the Board then directs whether an inquiry will be held or not regardless of the Committee's recommendations. Section 38(2) of the Nurses Act 1985 provides that:

> **38** (2) Where an application is made under this section and the Fitness to Practise Committee, after consideration of the application, is of opinion that there is not sufficient cause to warrant the holding of an inquiry, it shall so inform the Board and the Board, having considered the matter, may decide that no further action shall be taken in relation to the matter and shall so inform the Committee and the applicant, or it may direct the Committee to hold an inquiry into the matter in accordance with the provisions of this section.

THE INQUIRY

[5.04] When it has been proposed to hold an inquiry the chief executive officer of the Board must notify the subject of the complaint (the respondent) at her address as recorded on the live register by pre-paid registered post. This notice must contain the nature of the evidence to be adduced at the inquiry. Section 38(4) also provides that the respondent may be present and be represented by "any person" at the hearing. This section must be strictly complied with. While there is no mention of a required length of notice, reasonable notice of the inquiry should be given:

> **38** (4) When it is proposed to hold an inquiry under *subsection (3)* of this section the person who is the subject of the inquiry shall be given notice in writing by the Chief Executive Officer sent by pre-paid post to the address of that person as stated in the register of the nature of the evidence proposed to be considered at the inquiry and that person and any person representing him shall be given the opportunity of being present at the hearing.

[5.05] When the Committee notifies a nurse who is the subject of a complaint, the notice must contain all the evidence and charges to which she has to respond. In *K v An Bord Altranais*[2] Blayney J stated that:

> "The applicant contends that the notice sent to her in purported compliance with the provisions of section 38 sub-section 4 was not a notice in compliance (with the section). Her submission in this regard is correct. I am not given a definition of what is required. The term is not very clear. The notice must contain evidence. The notice served in this case did not convey any of the evidence which will be given at the Inquiry. The notice was of particulars of the charge. The charge is of professional misconduct. The notice should have contained the nature of the evidence which will be given to the Inquiry to support that charge."

---

[2] [1990] IR 396.

[5.06] When the preliminary matters and all of the statements from people required to give evidence at the inquiry and the charges of the misconduct have been furnished to the nurse, then arrangements such as the date and venue for the hearing are made by the Committee. The Committee is merely obliged to consider the respondent's representations regarding such arrangements.

[5.07] The nurse is entitled to be represented by any person which can include a lawyer or by her trade union representative or a colleague. The Committee is legally advised throughout the hearing. The chief executive officer is the person who presents the case on behalf of the Board and is also independently represented. The Committee itself acts as the judge and jury and examines any witness including the nurse on any matter which is laid before it.

[5.08] If an inquiry lasts more than a day, then as future dates for the hearing have to be agreed between a considerable number of people, this means that the inquiry may span over a number of weeks before all evidence is adduced.

[5.09] Section 13(8) provides for the making of rules and regulations governing any of the committees established under the Nurses Act 1985, there are as yet none in existence. Section 13(8) provides that:

> **13** (8) The Board may, subject to the provisions of this Act, regulate the procedure of committees established under this section, but, subject to any such regulation, committees established under this section may regulate their own procedure.

In the absence of such regulations the requirements of fair procedures and natural justice have to be complied with.

THE HEARING

[5.10] All the evidence before the Committee is presented on oath and recorded. On completion of the hearing of evidence, both sides make submissions. The Committee then retires and submits its findings in a report to the Board. Section 38(3)(*c*) of the Nurses Act 1985 provides that:

> **38** (3)(*c*) ...therein the nature of the application and the evidence laid before it and any other matters in relation to the nurse which it may think fit to report including its opinion, having regard to the contents of the report, as to-
>
> (i) the alleged professional misconduct of the nurse, or
> (ii) the fitness or otherwise of that nurse to engage in the practice of nursing by reason of alleged physical or mental disability,
>
> as the case may be.

THE REPORT

[5.11] On completion of the inquiry, the Committee shall embody its findings in a report to the Board specifying its recommendations. The nurse is then requested to attend and make submissions regarding the report. If the complaint is upheld the Board then makes a decision as to how to censure the nurse. This decision is communicated to the nurse by registered post.

[5.12] Section 39(1)(*a*) gives the Board the power to initiate proceedings in the High Court to erase, suspend or admonish the nurse:

39 (1) Where a nurse-

(*a*) has been found, by the Fitness to Practise Committee, on the basis of an inquiry and report pursuant to *section 38* of this Act, to be guilty of professional misconduct or to be unfit to engage in the practice of nursing because of physical or mental disability,

the Board may decide that the name of such person should be erased from the register or that, during a period of specified duration, registration of the person's name in the register should not have effect.

(2) On making a decision under this section, the Board shall forthwith send by pre-paid post to the person to whom the decision relates, at his address as stated in the register, a notice in writing stating the decision, the date thereof and the reasons therefor.

EX PARTE APPLICATION TO THE HIGH COURT

[5.13] When a nurse is notified of the decision of the Board, and if after a lapse of 21 days she decides not to appeal the decision, the Board then proceeds by way of an *ex parte*[3] application to the High Court in order to affirm its decision. The Board must exhibit on affidavit the following:

(1) The evidence of the Committee,

(2) The findings.

(3) The report of the Committee.

(4) The decision of the Board.

[5.14] The onus is on the Board to establish that the nurse had an opportunity to be heard, that the finding was correct in all the circumstances and that the Board is seeking to enforce the appropriate sanction. The High Court in *M v Medical Council*[4] affirmed this procedure and Finlay P said as follows:

---

[3] An application to the court by one party in the absence of the other party.
[4] [1984] IR 485.

"Upon the true construction of the Act, in the event of an application by a practitioner under either s 46 or s 47 to cancel a decision of the Council, the onus was on the Council to establish the correctness of any finding of misconduct or unfitness and the correctness of the decision on the penalty that should be imposed. Furthermore, I held that the Council, in discharging that onus, was obliged to prove by oral evidence any fact on which it relied and which was contested by the plaintiff and, lastly, that the court, in hearing such an application, should first make a decision as to whether any finding asserted by the council of misconduct or unfitness to practise was established and, in the event of so finding, should give a further and separate opportunity to the plaintiff to be heard on the appropriate penalty that should be imposed."

POWERS OF THE HIGH COURT

[5.15] The High Court upon hearing the *ex parte* application by the Board, may direct the Board to erase the applicant's name from the register or suspend her for a specific period or some other remedy as the Court thinks proper in the circumstances.

NOTICE OF ERASURE OR SUSPENSION

[5.16] If it has been decided by the Court that a nurse's name is to be erased or suspended from the nurses register, the nurse must be notified in writing by pre-paid post. Notification must take place within a period of seven days prior to the date of erasure.

NOTIFICATION TO THE MINISTER

[5.17] When any of the above occur the Board must comply with s 46 of the Nurses Act as follows:

46 The Board shall notify the Minister, and, in the case of a person the name of whose employer is known to the Board, such employer, on the occasion of-

(a) the erasure of the name of a person from the register,

(b) the restoration of the name of a person to the register,

(c) the suspension of the name of a person from the register,

(d) the termination of a period of suspension from the register, or

(e) the attachment of conditions to the retention of the name of a person on the register,

of the erasure, restoration, suspension, termination of suspension or attachment of conditions, as the case may be.

RESTORATION TO THE REGISTER

[5.18] Where a nurse has been erased from the register she may apply at any time for restoration. The Board may direct that this be done. In doing so the Board may attach conditions which could include the payment of a fee. Where a nurse has been suspended for a specific duration she may apply to the Board to terminate the suspension. Section 39(8) of the Nurses Act 1985 provides that:

> **39** (8) Where the registration of a person in the register has ceased to have effect under this section for a period of specified duration, the Board may, if it so thinks fit, on application made to it by such person, by direction terminate the suspension.

POWER OF THE BOARD TO ADVISE, ADMONISH OR CENSURE

[5.19] Section 41(1) empowers the Board to advise, admonish or censure a nurse where it thinks fit following an inquiry and on receipt of a report by the Fitness to Practise Committee. This may be done by the Board without reference to the High Court. This power can also "be exercised in addition to or in substitution for any of the powers" of erasure[5] and suspension.[6]

SUSPENSION PENDING AN INQUIRY

[5.20] While suspension from the register is provided for in s 39 which has the same procedures as erasure, s 44 provides that these procedures may be dispensed with in limited circumstances. Where the Board is satisfied that the public interest requires protection, in that they require a nurse to be removed from the register, it may apply to the High Court *in camera* for an immediate suspension pending the outcome of the inquiry. In the normal course of events a nurse remains on the register until the High Court directs otherwise:

> **44** (1) Whenever the Board is satisfied that it is in the public interest so to do, the Board may apply to the High Court for an order in relation to any person registered in the register that, during the period specified in the order, registration of that person's name in the register shall not have effect.
>
> (2) An application under this section may be made in a summary manner and shall be heard otherwise than in public.
>
> (3) The High Court may make, in any application under this section, such interim or interlocutory order (if any) as it considers appropriate.

OTHER REASONS FOR ERASURE

[5.21] Where a nurse has failed to pay a retention fee (i.e., a fee to be paid in order to be retained on the register) and the Board has notified her of her default of payment and has requested payment of the fee on more than one occasion after a

---

[5] Section 41(2) of the Nurses Act 1985.

[6] Sections 39, 42.

lapse of not less than two months, the nurse's name may then be erased or suspended from the register by the High Court. At a hearing on 12 July 1993, the High Court heard an application on behalf of the Board for the removal of nurses for non-payment of their registration fees. These nurses were erased from the register by order of Costello J.

WHERE A PERSON IS CONVICTED OF A CRIMINAL OFFENCE

[5.22] Where a nurse is convicted of an indictable offence, e.g., a serious criminal offence, either in the State or outside the State, the Board may decide that such person's name be erased from the register without the necessity of holding an inquiry. Section 42 of the Nurses Act provides that:

42 (1) Where a nurse is convicted in the State of an offence triable on indictment or is convicted outside the State of an offence consisting of acts or omissions which would constitute an offence triable on indictment if done or made in the State, the Board may decide that the name of such person should be erased from the register.

(2) On making a decision under this section, the Board shall forthwith send by pre-paid post to the person to whom the decision relates, at his address as stated in the register, a notice in writing stating the decision, the date thereof and the reasons therefor.

(3) A person to whom a decision under this section relates may, within the period of twenty-one days, beginning on the date of the decision, apply to the High Court for cancellation of the decision.

When the matter is before the High Court, it may do any one of the following:

(*a*) the High Court, on the hearing of the application, may-

(i) cancel the decision, or
(ii) confirm the decision and direct the Board to erase the name of such person from the register, or
(iii) give such other directions to the Board as the Court thinks proper,

(*b*) if at any time the Board satisfies the High Court that such person has delayed unduly in proceeding with the application, the High Court shall, unless it sees good reason to the contrary, confirm the decision and direct the Board to erase the name of such person from the register,

(*c*) the High Court may direct how the costs of the application are to be borne.

[5.23] A nurse has twenty-one days from the date of the decision within which to apply to the High Court for a cancellation of the decision:

42 (4) Where a person to whom a decision of the Board under this section relates does not within the period of twenty-one days, beginning on the date of the decision, apply to the High Court for cancellation of the decision, the Board may apply *ex parte* to the High Court for confirmation of the decision and, if the Board so applies, the High Court, on the hearing of the application, shall, unless it sees good reason to the contrary, confirm the decision and direct the Board to erase the name of such person from the register.

The Board may attach whatever conditions as it thinks fit to the its findings, subject to the approval of the High Court. The nurse must be notified of these conditions.

APPLICATION FOR AN APPEAL

[5.24] A nurse proceeds with her application for an appeal to the High Court by way of special summons and an affidavit. An affidavit is a sworn document which sets out the reasons why she is contesting the decision of the board, e.g. unfair procedure, breach of constitutional or natural justice or where the facts of the evidence before the Board are in dispute. Where it is sought to have a full hearing on oral evidence, special leave of the court is required. In *K v An Bord Altranais*[7] a full hearing was given by the Supreme Court as there was dispute as to the truth or falsity of the evidence of the witnesses. Section 39(3)(*a*) provides:

> **39** (3)(*a*) A person to whom a decision under this section relates may, within the period of 21 days beginning on the date of the decision, apply to the High Court for cancellation of the decision and if he so applies-
>
> > (*a*) the High Court, on the hearing of the application, may-
> >
> > > (i) cancel the decision, or
> > > (ii) declare that it was proper for the Board to make a decision under this section in relation to such person and either (as the Court may consider proper) direct the Board to attach such conditions as the Court thinks fit to the retention of the name of such person in the register, or
> > > (iii) give such other directions to the Board as the Court thinks proper.

PROFESSIONAL CONDUCT OF A NURSE

[5.25] A nurse can be disciplined for misdemeanours by her superiors in the hospital. But where a serious breach of the Code of Practice occurs, which brings the nursing profession into disrepute, a complaint is made to the Board. The Board is empowered under Part V of the Nurses Act 1985 to make the necessary investigations and, if it considers it appropriate, to hold a Fitness to Practise inquiry.

---

[7] [1990] IR 396.

CASE LAW

[5.26] The majority of complaints made to the Board relate to the misconduct of the nurse within her profession. Misconduct is a concept measured by the set of standards applicable to each profession, e.g., there may be situations where misconduct in the nursing profession would not necessarily be regarded as misconduct in the medical profession. The concept of misconduct has been developed by the courts and committees since the last century. The following are a number of important decisions of both the Irish and English courts and committees.[8]

[5.27] One of the earliest cases was *Allinson v General Council of Medical Education*[9] where a doctor published advertisements regarding his fellow doctors in the following manner:

"In this our nineteenth century of boasted civilisation the drug doctors are not so successful in the cure of disease as were the ancients nearly 2000 years ago. Then the healers relied mostly on diet and baths, not having found out the poisonous drugs now employed. A patient is now fed up with useless and disease-producing animal broths, meat-extracts, or so-called beef tea, which contains most of the refuse which the kidneys would have thrown out if the animal had lived. The patient is usually dosed with poisonous drugs which upset his stomach, derange the other organs, greatly lessen his chance of recovery, and lengthen the duration of his illness."

[5.28] The doctor was found guilty of infamous conduct. The test as set out by the Court of Appeal regarding "infamous conduct" in a professional respect is as follows:

"If it be shown that a medical man, in the pursuit of his profession, has done something with respect to it which could be reasonably regarded as disgraceful or dishonourable by his professional brethren of good repute and competency, then it is open to the General Medical Council to say that he has been guilty of "infamous conduct in a professional respect." The question is not merely whether what a medical man has done would be an infamous thing for anybody else to do, but whether it is infamous for a medical man to do it" [10]

[5.29] These principles of misconduct was further developed in *Felix v the General Dental Council*.[11] This case concerned a N.H.S. Dentist who was required to keep records and who was accused of overcharging and wrongful certification of patients treatment. While Mr Felix admitted the fact of

---

8   The most recent Irish cases include *P v Medical Council Fitness to Practise Committee & Beaumont Hospital* [1992] ILRM 469 and *Georgopolous v The Medical Council* unreported High Court, 3 March 1992.

9   [1894] 1 QB 750.

10 *Medical Law: Text and Materials* Kennedy and Grubb (2nd edition) at p 573.

11 [1960] 2 All ER 391.

overcharging he denied doing so with fraudulent or dishonest intent and claimed this arose because of his own carelessness and that of an inadequately supervised secretary. The Court was of the view that the allegation of overcharging fell short. The Court also adopted the definition from the *Allison* case and were of the view that the conduct there was different than in this case. Lord Jenkins said that:

"Granted that in accordance with Lord Esher's definition of "infamous" conduct in a professional respect the full derogatory force of the adjectives "infamous" and "disgraceful" in section 25 of the Act of 1957 must be qualified by the consideration that what is being judged is the conduct of a dentist in a professional respect, which falls to be judged in relation to the accepted ethical standards of his profession, it appears to their Lordships that these two adjectives nevertheless remain as terms denoting conduct deserving of the strongest reprobation, and indeed so heinous as to merit, when proved, the extreme professional penalty of striking-off. To make good a charge of "infamous or disgraceful conduct in a professional respect" in relation to such a matter as the keeping of the prescribed dental records it is not, in their Lordships' view, enough to show that some mistake has been made through carelessness or inadvertence in two or even three cases out of (to quote the figures in the present case) 424 patients treated during the period in which the mistakes occurred, whether the carelessness or inadvertence consisted in some act or omission by the dentist himself or in his ill-advised delegation of the making of the relevant entries to a nurse or receptionist and omitting to check the forms to see that she had done as she was told. To make such a charge good there must, in their Lordships' opinion, (generally speaking) be some element of moral turpitude or fraud or dishonesty in the conduct complained of, or such persistent and reckless disregard of the dentist's duty in regard to records as can be said to amount to dishonesty for this purpose. The question is to some extent one of degree, but in their Lordships' view the cases of overcharging with which this appeal is concerned clearly fall short of the degree of culpability required."

That case turned on the question of what constituted an honestly held opinion and it must be seen in relation to a case where honesty is in issue.

[5.30] In *Doughty v General Dental Council*[12] Lord McKay of Clasfern stated:

"This is an appeal from a decision of the Professional Conduct Committee of the General Dental Council on 12 March 1987 that the appellant had been guilty of serious professional misconduct in relation to three charges and that his name should be erased from the Dentists Register. The three charges in question were:
That being a registered dentist: (1) Between 10th January and 26th October 1984 you accepted 19 patients, whose names and addresses are shown on List 'A' [which is attached to the charge] for dental treatment as National Health Service patients, and thereafter provided them with dental treatment in the course of which, having obtained radiographs of these patients, you: (a) Failed to retain those radiographs for a reasonable period of time after completion of the treatment; (b) Failed to submit those

---

[12] [1988] AC 164.

radiographs to the Dental Estimates Board when required to do so by a letter from the Board dated 27th November, 1984. (2) Between 5th June and 16th November, 1984, you accepted 6 patients, whose names and addresses are shown on List 'B' [which is attached to the charge] for dental treatment as National Health Service patients and thereafter provided them with dental treatment in the course of which you failed to exercise a proper degree of skill and attention. (3) Between 21st August and 5th October, 1984, you accepted 4 patients, whose names and addresses are shown on List 'C' [which is attached to the charge] for dental treatment as National Health Service patients, and thereafter provided them with dental treatment in the course of which you failed satisfactorily to complete the treatment required by the patients... And that in relation to the facts alleged in each of the above charges you have been guilty of serious professional misconduct."

[5.31] The Committee announced their decision in the following terms:

"In relation to the facts alleged in head 1 of the charge which have been admitted, the Committee finds that you have been guilty of serious professional misconduct. In relation to the facts alleged against you in charge 2 in respect of the five remaining patients and in charge 3 in respect of the three remaining patients, the Committee finds that you have been guilty of serious professional misconduct."

The Committee directed that the appellant's name be erased from the Dentists Register. The Court of Appeal was of the view that infamous or disgraceful conduct would be regarded as professional misconduct:

"Their Lordships readily accept that what was infamous or disgraceful conduct in a professional respect would also constitute serious professional misconduct but they consider that it would not be right to require the council to establish now that the conduct complained of was infamous or disgraceful and therefore not right to apply the criteria which Lord Jenkins derived from the dictionary definitions of these words which he quoted in *Felix v General Dental Council*. Their Lordships consider it relevant, in reaching a conclusion on whether Parliament intended by the change of wording to make a change of substance, to notice that in addition to this change and in close conjunction with it the additional and much less severe penalty of suspension for a period not exceeding 12 months was provided. Further, in terms of s 1(2) of the Dentists Act 1984, which is the statute presently applicable, 'It shall be the general concern of the Council to promote high standards of dental education at all its stages and high standards of professional conduct among dentists...'"

[5.32] In *Dr Gregory v General Medical Council*[13] Lord Denning delivered the judgment of the court as follows:

"A doctor gains entry to the home in the trust that he will take care of the physical and mental health of the family. He must not abuse his professional position so as, by act or word, to impair in the least the confidence and security which should subsist

---

[13] [1961] AC 957.

between husband and wife. His association with the wife becomes improper when by look, touch or gesture he shows undue affection for her, when he seeks opportunities of meeting her alone, or does anything else to show that he thinks more of her than he should. even if she sets her cap at him, he must in no way respond or encourage her. If she seeks opportunities of meeting him, which are not necessary for professional reasons, he must be on his guard. He must shun any association with her altogether rather than let it become improper. He must be above suspicion."

[5.33] In *McCoan v General Medical Council*[14] a medical practitioner was found guilty of infamous conduct as he had maintained an improper sexual relationship with his patient (the complainant). The complainant was at the time divorced and the medical practitioner was a widower. The matter was appealed to the Privy Council and during the course of his judgment Lord Upjohn said that:

"One of the most fundamental duties of a medical adviser, recognised for as long as the profession has been in existence, is that a doctor must never permit his professional relationship with a patient to deteriorate into an association which would be described by responsible medical opinion as improper. It is for this reason that the Medical Acts have always entrusted the supervision of the medical advisers' conduct to a committee of the profession, for they know and appreciate better than anyone else the standards which responsible medical opinion demands of its own profession. Sexual intercourse with a patient has always been regarded as a most serious breach of the proper relationship between doctor and patient and their lordships do not see how the finding of the committee, on the facts of this case, that the appellant was guilty of infamous conduct in a professional respect can be successfully challenged before their lordships."

[5.34] *Marten v The Royal College of Veterinary Surgeons Disciplinary Committee*[15] concerned the case of a veterinary surgeon who owned a farm. During the winter months a number of cattle died on his farm from husk. He was charged before the Disciplinary Committee of the Royal College of Surgeons with, *inter alia*, conduct disgraceful to a man in a professional respect, in that he failed to provide adequate nursing care for sick animals in his care and he allowed conditions to exist on his farm which were likely to bring disgrace on the veterinary profession. He was found guilty and he appealed the decision. Lord Parker CJ was of the view that professional misconduct was:

"...not limited either to conduct involving moral turpitude or to a veterinary surgeon's conduct in pursuit of his profession, but might extend to conduct which, though reprehensible in any one, was, in the case of a professional man, so much more reprehensible as to merit the description disgraceful, in the sense that it intended to bring disgrace on the profession which he practised; in the present case there was abundant evidence on which the Disciplinary Committee could have come to the

---

[14] [1964] 3 All ER 143.
[15] [1965] 1 All ER 949.

conclusion that the conduct was disgraceful to the appellant in a professional respect and the court would not interfere with the finding of the committee."

[5.35] In 1993 complaints against a neurosurgeon, Mr O'L, were made to the Medical Council. The complaints generally related to:

(a) His failure to operate or make provisions for the appropriate operation and to ensure prompt and necessary treatment.

(b) That he made recommendations that were not in the best interests and welfare or health of a patient,

(c) That he failed without just cause to operate on a patient.

(d) That he failed to refer a patient to a colleague to carry out the necessary operation.

(e) That he made allegations concerning colleagues in that they operated and managed the National Centre of Neurosurgery in a manner that caused unnecessary and human misery and conducted surgery in such a manner as to give rise to justifiable dissatisfaction so as to make Beaumont Hospital liable for compensation when he knew or ought to have known that there was no foundation or basis to such an allegation.

(f) That he made allegations concerning the professional competence and capacity of a colleague.

The Committee found that Mr O'L was guilty of professional misconduct and recommended that he be suspended. These matters are presently on appeal before the High Court where the case has not yet been concluded.

SUMMARY

[5.36] The above chapter outlines the statutory procedures of the Fitness to Practise Committee when it holds an inquiry and its statutory limits. It also sets out the requirements which a nurse must comply with in the event of her being the subject matter of an inquiry and the protection given to her by statute. The end of this chapter gives some examples as to what the courts and committees have regarded as misconduct and what they take into consideration when deciding that misconduct has occurred. The parameters of misconduct are constantly being scrutinised by the courts and must not be regarded as being settled since each case is determined on its own set of facts.

CHAPTER 6

NEGLIGENCE

TORT

[6.01] The word "tort" comes from the old French meaning "a wrong" and is part of our civil law as distinct from the criminal law. The one set of events may well give rise to both a crime and a civil wrong. For example, a person who causes a road accident by driving dangerously can be guilty of the criminal offence of dangerous driving and can also be liable in the civil courts to the victim of the accident. The purpose of the criminal law is primarily to punish the guilty person whereas the function of the civil courts is to compensate the victim, though in some cases the criminal courts can make an order for an award of compensation to the victim. The other important distinction is how the civil and criminal courts decide the outcome of a case. There are differences in procedure, rules of evidence and the burden of proof. In the example of dangerous driving, if it is to be established that the driver is guilty of a crime, the case against him must be proved "beyond all reasonable doubt" whereas in a civil action against the driver the case has to be proved "on the balance of probabilities". Therefore in a civil action for the plaintiff to succeed, all that is necessary is that he establish that his account of the occurrence is more likely to be right than that of the defendant. As mentioned above a tort is a civil wrong, however there are many types of civil wrong. Examples include slander, defamation, trespass and nuisance. Although a tort is a civil injury not all civil injuries are torts, for no civil injury is to be classed as a tort unless the appropriate remedy for it is an action for damages. Such an action is an essential characteristic of every true tort.

[6.02] From the nineteenth century onwards there has been an emerging body of law defining the nature of duties owed by one person or class of persons to another in certain situations. In a book published in 1889[1] 156 separate duties of care were listed by the author. Underhill defined a tort as follows:

> "An act or omission which, independent of contract, is unauthorised by law and results either-
>
> (a) in the infringement of some absolute right to which another is entitled; or
>
> (b) in the infringement of some qualified right of another causing damage; or

---

[1] *Bevin on Negligence.*

(c) in the infringement of some public right resulting in some substantial and particular damage to some person beyond that which is suffered by the public generally."

Salmond[2] describes the developments of the law in this area as having "been built up in disconnected slabs" and he attempts to formulate a general principle as to why a duty of care should exist in any situation and why the relationship between the different duties of care was rejected by a majority of judges until 1932.

[6.03] The four elements in the tort of negligence are as follows:

1 - A duty of care.
2 - A failure to conform to the required standard.
3 - Actual loss or damage to the interests of the plaintiff.
4 - A sufficiently close casual connection between the conduct and resulting injury to the plaintiff.[3]

When it is alleged that a negligent act has occurred then the injured party may commence proceedings in the civil courts seeking the appropriate remedy. To sustain a negligence action the person doing so must establish that there was some act of omission and that the act of omission inflicted injury.

[6.04] The concept of duty in negligence is relatively modern, but it is now so firmly rooted that there can be no doubt that actions in negligence must fail where a duty is not established. One of the earliest cases was *Heaven v Pender* where Brett MR produced this formula:

"...whenever one person is by circumstances placed in such a position with regard to another that everyone of ordinary sense who did think would at once recognise that if he did not use ordinary care and skill in his own conduct with regard to those circumstances he would cause danger or injury to the person or property of the other, a duty arises to use ordinary care and skill to avoid such danger."[4]

[6.05] The duty of care was widened considerably by Lord Atkin in *Donoghue v Stevenson*.[5] That historic case which has been cited and endorsed by the Irish courts created a new category of duty. In that case Mrs D drank some ginger beer from an opaque glass bottle which had been purchased for her by a friend in a cafe in Paisley, Scotland. When the remainder of the beer was poured she alleged that a decomposed snail emerged from the bottle. Mrs D claimed that she suffered from shock and severe gastro-enteritis and brought proceedings against the

---

[2] *Salmond on Torts*, (20th ed.), para 9(3).

[3] See McMahon and Binchy, *The Irish Law of Torts*, ch 5.

[4] (1883) 11 QBD 503 at 509.

[5] [1932] AC 562 (HL).

manufacturer of the beer. During the course of his judgment Lord Atkin in the House of Lords posed the question "Who is my neighbour?" and went on to say:

> "You must take reasonable care to avoid acts or omissions which you could reasonably foresee would be liable to injure your neighbour. Who, then, in law, is my neighbour? The answer seems to be - persons who are so closely and directly affected by my act that I ought reasonably to have them in contemplation as being so affected when I am directing my mind to the acts or omissions which are called in question"[6]

The House of Lords held that Mrs D was entitled to recover damages arising from the breach by the defendant manufacturer of the duty of care it owed to her. The effect of this case was to expand the class of persons to whom a duty of care could be owed and has since been referred to as the "neighbour principle".

DUTY OF CARE

[6.06] In establishing a negligence action the first principle to be established is that a duty of care exists, which a judge decides as a matter of fact. A factor which must be taken into consideration is reasonable foresight, that is to say that the person who carried out the act and subsequently caused the damage complained of could have reasonably foreseen that the act would cause the damage. The test of reasonable foreseeability was applied in *Condon v CIE*.[7] That case concerned the tragic railway accident in Buttevant in Cork, where a train was derailed causing the deaths of eighteen people and injuries to seventy-five more. The plaintiff was a railway employee who was suspected of being responsible for the accident. Barrington J said:

> "I accept that in determining liability for the consequences of a tortious act of negligence the test to be applied is whether the damage is of such a kind as a reasonable man should have foreseen. I also accept that if the damage is of such a kind as a reasonable man should have foreseen it is quite irrelevant that no one foresaw the actual extent of the damage."

STANDARD OF CARE

[6.07] The general principle of the standard of care that has been adopted is that of the "reasonable man". In 1856 in *Blyth v The Company of Proprietors of the Birmingham Waterworks* [8] it was stated that:

> "Negligence is the omission to do something which a reasonable man, guided upon those considerations which ordinarily regulate the conduct of human affairs, would do, or doing something which a prudent and reasonable man would not do."

---

[6] [1932] AC 580.

[7] Unreported, High Court, 16 November 1984.

[8] [1856] 11 Exch 781.

In *Kirby v Burke* Gavan Duffy J stated that:

> "..the foundation of liability at common law for tort is blameworthiness as determined by the average standards of the community; a man fails at his peril to conform to these standards. Therefore, while loss from an accident generally lies where it falls, a defendant cannot plead an accident if, treated as a man of ordinary intelligence and foresight, he ought to have foreseen the danger which caused injury to his plaintiff"[9]

[6.08] The reasonable man is a hypothetical person and has been described as "the man on the Clapham omnibus." This reasonable man test can arise in a number of ways, e.g., negligence in a motor car accident, in a professional negligence action, in an action against a solicitor or a dentist or an accountant. As the standard of care required will be that measured if that person fails to exercise the skill and knowledge reasonably expected in all of the circumstances.

[6.09] However the standard of the reasonable professional must be elaborated a little. The defendant must exhibit the degree of skill which a member of the public would expect from a person in his or her position. Negligence should not be equated with moral culpability or general incompetence. In *Wilsher v Essex Area Health Authority*,[10] a premature baby was admitted to a specialist neo-natal unit. An error was made in that the medical staff failed to notice that the baby was receiving too much oxygen and as a result went blind. The doctors were held to be negligent and the Court of Appeal held that they must be judged by reference to their "posts" in the unit. In determining the standard required in a particular post, be it a surgeon, nurse or solicitor, expert evidence of proper practice in that profession must be called upon. Where a certain practice is disputed, then conformity with a responsible body of opinion within the profession will suffice. Care must be taken in assessing the standard expected of a professional and must take into account the skills he claims to hold and not demand unrealistic standards of skill and knowledge. A general practitioner consulted by a patient complaining of stomach trouble is not expected to have the same level of knowledge as the consultant gastro-enterologist, but as a reasonable general practitioner he should know when he ought to refer the patient on to a gastro-enterologist.

DAMAGES

[6.10] Damages for negligence are regarded as compensation for an injury sustained and not as punishment for a wrong inflicted. The rule *restitutio in integrum* is applied, i.e. the injured party being placed back into the position they previously held by the award of a sum of money. However in some cases this principle may not be totally effective, a man who has lost his leg in an accident caused by the defendant's negligence will never be capable of being placed in the position he was in prior to the accident. An award of money is however, regarded

---

[9] [1944] IR 207 at 214.
[10] [1987] QB 730.

by the law as better than nothing. The plaintiff's claim for damages is assessed under the following headings:

1 - Medical expenses. These include the cost of the hospital bills, doctors' fees, medications, the cost of rehabilitation training and any miscellaneous medical costs.
2 - Loss of wages both in the past and in the future, if the plaintiff is unable to resume his previous occupation. The wages are actuarially assessed.
3 - The plaintiff is paid damages for pain and suffering to the date of his court hearing and for any future pain and suffering or for any loss of amenity which he suffers.

[6.11] In *Reddy v Bates*,[11] the plaintiff, a twenty-four year old clerk, suffered brain damage due to a car crash caused by the defendant's negligence. The brain damage caused severe physical loss of capacity and impairment of memory and concentration. The plaintiff spent over a year in hospital and rehabilitation and had a number of major operations. The brain damage resulted in a rare form of disabling bone growth which made walking difficult even after the operations and rehabilitation. The plaintiff needed someone to help her in her home. Expert evidence was given to the effect that she would never work again. The jury awarded general damages to date of £100,000 and general damages to the future of £150,000. This was in addition to a sum awarded for special damages making a total award in excess of half a million pounds. This matter was appealed to the Supreme Court on the question of damages only. The Supreme Court reduced the total amount of damages to £400,354.00. Griffin J in the Supreme Court stated:

"In a case of this nature where damages are to be assessed under several headings, the jury having added the various sums awarded and having arrived at a total figure for damages, should consider the total sum (as should this Court on any appeal) for the purposes of ascertaining whether the total sum is, in the circumstances of the case, fair compensation for the plaintiff for the injury suffered, or whether it is out of all proportion to such circumstances. In my view, the income which that capital sum would generate with reasonably careful and prudent investment is a factor which the jury, (and this Court on appeal) should take into consideration in arriving at a conclusion in this behalf. Notwithstanding the ravages of inflation a very substantial income can be obtained, whilst preserving the capital intact. This is a factor which has in fact been taken into consideration by this Court in very many cases within the past ten years."

Griffin J also held that in assessing the amount to award for future loss of earnings actuarial figures are only a guideline. In making such assessments the jury should have to consider evidence relating to the risk of unemployment, redundancy, illness, accident or marriage prospects.

---

[11] [1983] IR 141.

[6.12] In *Cooke v Walsh*,[12] the plaintiff suffered severe brain damage in a road traffic accident, as a result of which it was stated that his mental age would at no time be more than two years of age. In assessing general damages, the Court followed the principles of *Reddy v Bates* above. However the Court went on to consider the plaintiff's awareness of his condition when assessing damages:

> "The general damages did not take into account the plaintiff's lack of awareness or appreciation of his condition, and since a jury, or a trial judge, should also consider whether the total or the global sum awarded is a fair and reasonable compensation to the injured person..."

[6.13] In *Sinnott v Quinnsworth*,[13] the plaintiff suffered severe personal injuries in a road traffic accident. As a result the plaintiff became "quadriplegic, with paralysis, sensory loss, loss of control of bladder and bowel and became totally dependent on others". The plaintiff was awarded damages in excess of one million pounds. Among the issues appealed to the Supreme Court was the question of damages. The Court followed their previous reasoning in that general damages "should represent fair and reasonable compensation for the loss and injury sustained by the plaintiff." The concept of a ceiling figure for general damages unless there are special circumstances was firmed up by the court to be a figure of £150,000. O'Higgins CJ stated that:

> "In a case of this nature unless particular circumstances suggest otherwise damages should not exceed a sum of the region of £150,000...In this case the injury which the plaintiff suffered has changed him from being an active, healthy young man on the threshold of adult life, in to a helpless, dependent, paralysed being, conscious of what he has lost and facing a bleak uncertain and limited future. To talk of compensating for such a terrible transformation is to talk of assaying the impossible. Never the less, it is this impossible task which the court must attempt in endeavouring to determine, in terms of money, compensation for such injury. the danger is that in so doing all sense of reality may be lost."

MEDICAL NEGLIGENCE

[6.14] Medical negligence arises when it is established that a duty of care is owed to a patient and this has been breached with the result that pain and injury have occurred. This involves examining whether the standard of the treatment given by the defendant fell below the standard expected of a nurse by the law. A nurse is deemed to possess certain nursing skills and is obliged accordingly to measure up to the standard of those skills. Also if a nurse can show that she has complied with the accepted standards of her profession, and that there are no foreseeable defects in the procedure carried out, this would not be regarded as negligence.

---

[12] [1983] ILRM 429 (HC); [1984] ILRM 208 (SC).
[13] [1984] ILRM 523.

[6.15] A duty of care arises when a person comes under the care of either a hospital or a doctor or both. When this occurs there is an obligation in law to provide the required standard of care, both in the nursing and medical field. *Halsbury* discussed the duty of care as follows:[14]

"The practice of a profession, art or calling which, from its nature, demands some special skill, ability and experience carries with it a representation that the person practising or exercising it possesses, to a reasonable extent, the amount of skill, ability, and experience which it demands. Such a person is liable for injury caused to another to whom he owes a duty to take care, if he fails to possess that amount of skill and experience which is usual in his profession or calling, or if he neglects to use the skill and experience which he possesses or the necessary degree of care demanded or professed. His duty is honestly and diligently to use that care which would be used by others in the same profession or calling. He will not, however, generally, be held liable for loss resulting either from a mere error of judgment on a difficult point or from want of skill in performance of some act which is not appropriate to be performed by the members of his particular profession. A man should not, however, undertake to do a work of skill unless he is fitted for it, and it is his duty to know whether he is so fitted or not."

[6.16] This standard has been analysed in a number of decisions by the courts. In *R v Bateman*[15] Lord Hewart CJ said:

"In order to establish civil liability, the plaintiff must prove (in addition to pecuniary loss caused by the death) that A owed a duty to B to take care, that duty was not discharged, and that such default caused the death of B. [He further went on to say that] If a person holds himself out as possessing special skill and knowledge, and he is consulted, as possessing such skill and knowledge, by or on behalf of a patient, he owes a duty to the patient to use due caution in undertaking the treatment. If he accepts the responsibility and undertakes the treatment and the patient submits to his direction and treatment accordingly, he owes a duty to the patient to use diligence, care, knowledge, skill and caution in administering the treatment. No contractual relation is necessary, nor is it necessary that the services be rendered for reward."

[6.17] In the Irish case of *Daniels v Heskin*[16] Kingsmill Moore J said that :

"A doctor owes certain well recognised duties to his patient. He must possess such knowledge and skill as conforms to the recognised contemporary standards of his profession and, if he is a specialist, such further and particularised skill and knowledge as he holds himself out to possess. He must use such skill and knowledge to form an honest and considered judgment as to what course, what action, what treatment, is in the best interests of his patient. He must display proper care and attention in treating, or in arranging suitable treatment for, his patient. Any attempt to substitute a rule of

---

[14] First edition, volume 21 para 634.

[15] (1925) 94 KB 791.

[16] [1954] IR 86.

law, or even a rule of thumb practice, for the individual judgment of a qualified doctor, doing what he considers best for the particular patient, would be disastrous. There may be cases where the judgment of the physician is proved by subsequent events to have been wrong, but if it is honest and considered and if, in the circumstances known to him at the time, it can fairly be justified, he is not guilty of negligence. There may indeed be cases where the nature of the judgment formed or the advice given is such as to afford positive evidence that the physician has fallen short of the required standard of knowledge and skill, or that his judgment could not have been honest and considered, but it lies on the plaintiff to adduce evidence from which such a failure of duty can reasonably be inferred."

[6.18] This was further developed in the case of *O'Donovan v Cork County Council*[17] where Walsh J said that:

"A medical practitioner who holds himself out as being a specialist in a particular field is required to attain to the ordinary level of skill amongst those who specialise in the same field. He is not required to attain to the highest degree of skill and competence in that particular field."

[6.19] What has become known as the *Bolam Test* in *Bolam v Friern Hospital Management Committee*[18] which is a statement of the general principles of medical negligence was stated by Lord Nair as follows:

". . . I must explain what in law we mean by "negligence". In the ordinary case which does not involve any special skill, negligence in law means this: some failure to do some act which a reasonable man in the circumstances would do, or doing some act which a reasonable man in the circumstances would not do; and if that failure or doing of that act results in injury, then there is a cause of action. How do you test whether this act or failure is negligent? In the ordinary case it is generally said, that you judge that by the action of the man in the street. He is the ordinary man. In one case it has been said that you judge it by the conduct of the man on the top of a Clapham Omnibus. He is the ordinary man. But where you get a situation which involves the use of some special skill or competence, then the test whether there has been negligence or not is not the test of the man on the top of the Clapham omnibus, because he has not got this special skill. The test is the standard of the ordinary skilled man exercising and professing to have that special skill. A man need not possess the highest expert skill at the risk of being found negligent. It is well established law that it is sufficient if he exercises the ordinary skill of an ordinary competent man exercising that particular art."

[6.20] Finlay CJ in *William Dunne v The National Maternity Hospital and Dr J* [19] took the opportunity to analyse the principles of medical negligence from the existing caselaw. In that case, Mrs Dunne sued The National Maternity Hospital

---

[17] [1967] IR 173.
[18] [1957] 2 All ER .
[19] [1989] IR 92.

on behalf of her infant son for the alleged negligence in the care, management and control of his mother's labour and his own birth as a result of which he was born with severe brain damage. In the High Court the jury found that the defendants were negligent and awarded the plaintiff a sum in excess of one million pounds. Both the Hospital Authority and Dr J were held to be liable. The defendants appealed to the Supreme Court on a number of grounds. The Supreme Court directed a retrial on the issues of liability and damages. The case was begun again in the High Court and after a few days the case was settled. In the course of his judgment the Chief Justice laid down the principles of medical negligence by drawing together and defining earlier cases on both negligence and medical negligence. These principles are listed below. When he had completed setting out the list of principles, he went on to state that in order to understand the "principles and their application to any particular set of facts" it is "helpful to set out parameters which would appear to underline their establishment".

[6.21] Finlay CJ in *Dunne v The National Maternity Hospital and Dr J* set out the following principles applicable to medical negligence:

1 (*a*) A practitioner was negligent in diagnosis or treatment only if guilty of such failure as no other practitioner of equal specialist or general status and skill would be guilty of if acting with ordinary care.

(b) A plaintiff establishes negligence against a medical practitioner by proving his deviation from a general and approved practice only upon proving also that the course taken was one which no other medical practitioner of like specialisation and skill would have followed when taking the ordinary care required from a person of his qualifications.

(c) A medical practitioner who establishes that he followed a practice which was general and approved by his colleagues of similar specialisation and skill is nevertheless negligent if the plaintiff thereupon establishes that such practice has inherent defects which ought to be obvious to any person giving the matter due consideration.

(d) An honest difference of opinion between doctors as to which is the better of two ways of treating a patient does not provide any ground for leaving a question to the jury as to whether the defendant who has followed one course rather than the other has been negligent.

(e) It is not for a jury (or a judge) to decide which of two alternative courses of treatment is in their (or his) opinion preferable, but their (or his) function is merely to decide whether the course of treatment followed, on the evidence, complied with the careful conduct of a medical practitioner of like specialisation and skill to that professed by the defendant.

2 That for a practice to be "general and approved" it need not be universal but must be approved of and adhered to by a substantial number of reputable practitioners holding

the relevant specialist or general qualifications. Where certain statements of principle have referred to "treatment" only, those principles must apply in identical fashion to questions of diagnosis.

[6.22] When dealing with the question of an allegation of negligence against the hospital the Chief Justice said:

"...where allegations are made of negligence against the medical administrators on the basis of a claim that practices and procedures laid down by them for the carrying out of treatment or diagnosis by medical or nursing staff were defective, their conduct is to be tested in accordance with the legal principles which would apply if they had personally carried out such treatment or diagnosis in accordance with such practice or procedure."

The Chief Justice then went on to state the extent of the benefit of the common good that results from medical science and that this has to balance with the standard of medical care that a patient may expect:

"The development of medical science and the supreme importance of that development to humanity makes it particularly undesirable and inconsistent with the common good that doctors should be obliged to carry out their professional duties under frequent threat of unsustainable legal claims. The complete dependence of patients on the skill and care of their medical attendants and the gravity from their point of view of a failure in such care, makes it undesirable and unjustifiable to accept as a matter of law a lax or permissive standard of care for the purpose of assessing what is and is not medical negligence. In developing the legal principles outlined and in applying them to the facts of each individual case, the courts must constantly seek to give equal regard to both of these considerations."

CASE LAW

[6.23] There are few reported cases involving allegations of negligence against nurses in this jurisdiction. However, cases have been reported in other countries with common law jurisdictions and where similar principles apply. In a Canadian case *Cavan v Wilcox*,[20] a nurse administered an injection of bicillin into the deltoid muscle of the upper arm of a patient who had been injured in the buttock. The patient took an action in negligence when part of his hand was amputated. When the matter reached the Supreme Court in Canada, they reviewed the evidence of the lower court and in particular that of the nursing and medical experts. The Supreme Court found the nurse negligent for having improperly injected the patient. The Court referred to the trial judge's findings who noted that the nurse was unable to recall the particular injection in question but relied on what her usual practice was. The Court further said that the nurse was not convincing as she had no recollection of the procedure adopted by her in that particular case:

---

[20] [1974] 44 DLR 42.

"She has also failed to establish that the gangrenous condition suffered by the plaintiff developed, or probably developed, from an unknown cause for which she cannot be held responsible. The evidence is sufficient to support the conclusion that the gangrene would not have developed in the absence of fault in the administering of the injection."

Evidence was given that at that time (1975) nurses were not given training on the dangers attaching to the giving of an injection in the muscle having regard to the pressure of the circumflex artery. The Court was of the view that nursing standards had not been breached even though the amputation was a result of the injection as it had been injected "without fault" on the nurse's part.

[6.24] Traditionally, hospitals were institutions which cared for the sick, wounded and the aged and which were financed by voluntary institutions and charitable trusts. However, in order to function, these institutions had to pay staff and purchase food and equipment. Patients did not contribute to their accommodation. By the mid-nineteenth century those who could afford it made a contribution towards their upkeep, which brought into being a contractual relationship between the hospital and the patient. While the hospital was not liable to the patient for the treatment and professional care carried out by the surgeon, physician or nurse, certain duties were found to exist between the hospital and the patient. In *Hillyer v Governors of St Bartholomew's Hospital*[21] the Court held that:

"The governors of a public hospital, by their admission of a patient to enjoy in the hospital the gratuitous benefit of its care, do, I think, undertake that the patient whilst there shall be treated only by experts, whether surgeons, physicians or nurses, of whose professional competence the governors have taken reasonable care to assure themselves; and further, that those experts shall have at their disposal, of the care and treatment of the patient, fit and proper apparatus and appliances."

Prior to the *Hillyer* case in 1909, hospitals received protection from the courts as they were charitable institutions which were funded by benevolent donations and voluntary subscriptions. That case signalled the end of protection against negligence claims being given to hospitals by virtue of their charitable status.

[6.25] A hospital has a duty to provide a reasonable standard of medical and nursing care. Further duties to the patient include the provision of competent and professionally qualified staff, provision of proper equipment and ensuring that it is properly maintained. The hospital also has a duty to have a safe and proper system in the operation and running of the hospital which would include hospital policies, proper instruction and supervision of the staff. The common law duty of care and the professional standard of care have been developed by the courts over

---

[21] [1909] 2 KB 820.

the years and the following are a number of cases which illustrate how these duties have developed.

[6.26] The facts of *Barnett v Chelsea and Kensington Hospital Management Committee* are as follows:[22]

"At about 5 am on 1 January 1966, three night watchmen drank some tea. Soon afterwards all three men started vomiting. At about 8 am the men walked to the casualty department of the defendants' hospital, which was open. One of them, the deceased, when he was in the room in the hospital, lay on some armless chairs. He appeared ill. Another of the men told the nurse that they had been vomiting after drinking tea. The nurse telephoned the casualty officer, a doctor, to tell him of the men's complaint. The casualty officer, who was himself unwell, did not see them, but said they should go home and call in their own doctors. The men went away, and the deceased died some hours later from what was found to arsenical poisoning."

In his judgment, Nair J considered the duty which the law imposes on persons in the position of the defendants and their servants and agents:

"The authorities deal in the main with the duties of doctors, surgeons, consultants, nurses and staff when a person is treated either by a doctor at his surgery or the patient's home or when the patient is treated in or at a hospital. In *Cassidy v Ministry of Health* Denning LJ dealt with the duties of hospital authorities and said: 'In my opinion, authorities who run hospitals, be they local authorities, government boards, or any other corporation, are in law under the self-same duties as the humblest doctor. Whenever they accept a patient for treatment they must use reasonable care and skill to cure him of his aliment. The hospital authorities cannot, of course, do it by themselves. They have no ears to listen through a stethoscope, and no hands to hold the knife. They must do it by the staff which they employ, and, if their staff are negligent in giving the treatment, they are just as liable for that negligence as is anyone else who employs other to do his duties for him. Is there any possible difference in law, I ask, can there be, between hospital authorities who accept a patient for treatment and railway or shipping authorities who accept a passenger for carriage? None whatever. Once they undertake the task, they come under a duty to use care in the doing of it and that is so whether they do it for reward or not.' "

[6.27] The Court considered the extent of the duty that is owed when a person presents themselves at a casualty department complaining of an illness and prior to treatment. When the night watchmen made their way into the hospital they complained to the nurse who in turn communicated with the casualty officer who then responded through the nurse to the men and this created the relationship which gave rise to the duty of care owed to the patient by the hospital. Nair J went on to say:

"Thus I have no doubt that Nurse C and Doctor B were under a duty to the deceased to

---

[22] [1968] 1 All ER 1068.

exercise that skill and care which is to be expected of persons in such positions acting reasonably, or, as it is, I think very helpfully put by the learned author of *Winfield on Torts* (7th Ed.)p.183.... 'where anyone is engaged in a transaction in which he holds himself out as having professional skill, the law expects him to show the average amount of competence associated with the proper discharge of the duties of that profession or trade or calling, and if he falls short of that and injures someone in consequence, he is not behaving reasonably.'

Moreover, the author proceeds to give a warning that the rule must be applied with some care to see that too high a degree of skill is not demanded, and he gives as an example 'a passer-by who renders emergency first-aid after an accident is not required to show the skill of a qualified surgeon'."

[6.28] The judge continued to say that there was no complaint against Nurse C and that she had not failed in her duty. The question to be considered was whether Doctor B was negligent and if so whether that negligence caused the deceased's death :

"Let me say at this stage that there is no complaint against Nurse C that she failed in her duty. There are two main questions here; has the plaintiff established, on the balance of probabilities, (i) that Doctor B was negligent, and, if so, (ii) that such negligence caused the death of the deceased?"

The judge then subdivided question 1 into four further questions:

"(i) Should Doctor B have seen the deceased?
(ii) Should he have examined the deceased?
(iii) Should he have admitted the deceased to the wards?
(iv) Should he have treated or caused to be treated the deceased?

The first of these four questions can be answered together. It is not, in my judgment, the case that a casualty officer must always see the caller at his department. Casualty departments are misused from time to time. If the receptionist, for example, discovers that the visitor is already attending his own doctor and merely wants a second opinion, or if the caller has a small cut which the nurse can perfectly well dress herself, then the casualty officer need not be called."

The Court then considered the views of a witness, Doctor L, who stated that:

" In my view, the duty of a casualty officer is in general to see and examine all patients who come to the casualty department of the hospital." He then cited some exceptions such as I have given. " When a nurse is told that three men have been vomiting, having drunk tea, and have abdominal pains her duty is to report it, and she should report accurately to the doctor. The first step she should take to deal with the matter is to take a history" and the doctor put it most emphatically in this way: " I cannot conceive that after a history of vomiting for three hours a doctor would leave the matter to a nurse, however experienced the nurse." Without doubt Doctor B should have seen and examined the deceased. His failure to do either cannot be described as an excusable error as has been submitted, it was negligence. It is unfortunate that Doctor B was himself at the time a tired and unwell doctor, but there was no-one else to do that which was his duty to do. Having examined the deceased I think the provisional diagnosis would have been of food poisoning."

When dealing with the final question the judge was of the view that the patient should have been admitted for observation and diagnosis.

"Having reviewed the questions the judge was of the view 'thus it is that I find under all four headings the defendants were negligent and in breach of their duty in that they or their servants or agents did not see and did not examine and did not admit and did not treat the deceased'."

[6.29] In *Gold v Essex County Council,*[23] a young child was administered Grenz Rays by a radiographer who was an employee of the hospital. Due to negligence on the radiographer's part the child was severely disfigured. The Court went on to hold the local authority liable for this negligence:

" A local authority carrying on a public hospital owes to a patient the duty to nurse and treat him properly, and is liable for the negligence of its servants even though the negligence arises while a servant is engaged on work which involves the exercise of professional skill on his part. Where, therefore, a patient being treated in such a hospital was injured by the negligence of a competent radiographer, who was a whole-time employee of the hospital, the local authority was liable for his negligence. The same duty and liability is owed by and attaches to the governors of a voluntary hospital, whether the services be rendered gratuitously or for reward."

[6.30] In *Cassidy v Ministry of Health,*[24] the patient was suffering from a contraction of the finger of his left hand and underwent an operation at the defendant's hospital. After the operation the patient's hand and forearm were bandaged in a splint for some fourteen days during which he complained of pain. No action other than the administration of sedatives was taken. When the bandages were removed the fingers were stiff and the hand practically useless. The case taken by the patient concerned the post-operative treatment and he sued both the hospital and the doctors involved. Denning LJ in the Court of Appeal said as follows:

"Even if he is so poor that he can pay nothing, and the hospital treats him out of charity, still the hospital authorities are under a duty to take reasonable care of him just as the doctor is who treats him without asking a fee. In my opinion, authorities who run a hospital, be they local authorities, government boards, or any other corporation, are in law under the self-same duty as the humblest doctor; whenever they accept a patient for treatment, they must use reasonable care and skill to cure him of his ailment. The hospital authorities cannot, of course, do it by themselves. They have no

[23] [1942] KB 293.
[24] [1954] 2 KB 66.

ears to listen through the stethoscope, and no hands to hold the knife. They must do it by the staff they employ, and if their staff are negligent in giving the treatment, they are just as liable for that negligence as is anyone else who employs others to do his duties for him. What possible difference in law, I ask, can there be between hospital authorities who accept a patient for treatment and railway or shipping authorities who accept a passenger for carriage? None whatever. Once they undertake the task, they come under a duty to use care in the doing of it, and that is whether they do it for reward or not."

[6.31] Denning LJ then looked at the facts of the case:

"... the hospital authorities accepted the plaintiff as a patient for treatment, and it was their duty to treat him with reasonable care. They selected, employed, and paid all the surgeons and nurses who looked after him. He had no say in their selection at all. If those surgeons and nurses did not treat him with proper care and skill, then the hospital authorities must answer for it, for it means that they themselves did not perform their duty to him."

[6.32] In *Roe v Minister of Health*,[25] two patients in a hospital were operated on the same day. Both operations were of a minor character and in each case Nupercaine, a spinal anaesthetic, was injected by means of a lumbar puncture by a specialist anaesthetist. The ampoules of Nupercaine were stored in a solution of phenol. After the operations both patients developed spastic paraplegia caused by phenol which had percolated into the ampoules through invisible undetectable cracks. The English Court of Appeal was of the view that:

"...applying the test of what was the standard of medical knowledge in 1947 in respect to the detection of the presence of the phenol in the ampoules, at the time of the operations, neither the anaesthetist nor any member of the hospital staff had been guilty of negligence and the appeals failed."

[6.33] In *Kelly v St Laurences Hospital*,[26] the facts were that in 1974 Mr. Kelly was diagnosed as showing symptoms of epilepsy and was referred to the defendants' hospital by his general practitioner. He was diagnosed as suffering from right temporal lobe epilepsy. In 1981 his epilepsy attacks appeared to be out of control and accompanied on occasion by some evidence of automatism and by further psychotic abnormal behaviour. He was referred back to the defendants' hospital. His was a routine admission for observation and tests on 12 July 1981. During his stay in the hospital he was taken off all medication as a necessary part of his treatment. In the early hours of 16 July, Mr. Kelly left the ward and entered the toilet cubicles and was observed by a staff nurse. He removed bottles from the window sill and placed a mobile commode underneath. He then climbed through

---

[25] [1954] 2 All ER 131.
[26] [1988] IR 402.

the window and fell about twenty feet to the yard below, landed on a car and sustained severe personal injuries. O'Higgins CJ regarded this case as:

> "more precisely a case where the issue is one of nursing care and attention than it is of one where the allegation of negligence is to be categorised as negligence in medical treatment. Undoubtedly, the extent and nature of the care and attention which a reasonable careful hospital would have afforded to the plaintiff whilst he was an in-patient there on the 15th of July 1981 and in particular, of course, the question as to whether a reasonable careful hospital staff would have arranged for a person to attend him when he left the ward in the middle of the night to go the toilet, depends to a very large extent on the foreseeability from a medical point of view of the risk that the plaintiff would, if allowed to go unattended to the toilet in the middle of the night, injure himself in some way."

[6.34] The Chief Justice did not see this case as one that should be tested solely by the standard of professional medical people when he said:

> "That does not, however, seem to me to make this a case solely to be tested by the standards which have been accepted by the courts with regard to allegation of negligence in treatment afforded to their patients by professional medical people."

The required standard of care that is owed to a patient when under the care of a hospital and staff was stated as follows:

> "In law the duty that the defendants owed to the plaintiff as a patient in their hospital was in general to take reasonable care of him to avoid his being exposed to risk of injury which a reasonable person ought to foresee."

RES IPSA LOQUITUR

[6.35] When a person brings a negligence action the burden of proof under the common law lies with the person alleging the wrongdoing, i.e. it is necessary to prove that the care and treatment given to him fell below the accepted standard of care required by law. *Res ipsa loquitur* is a legal maxim which means that something speaks for itself. It applies whenever it is so improbable that without negligence on the part of the defendants that such an accident could have happened. In such a situation the defendant is called upon by the plaintiff for an explanation as to how the accident occurred. The doctrine has arisen in a number of cases one of which was *Kelliher v The Board of Health and Public Assistance for County Tipperary and Leahy* [27] where FitzGibbon J stated:

> "In actions founded upon negligence the principle embodied in the maxim *res ipsa loquitur* is called in aid to shift the onus of proof, and to relieve the party who relies upon the maxim from the necessity for producing any evidence other than the bare occurrence of an accident. Where the maxim is applied, the mere occurrence of an

---

[27] [1938] IR 43.

accident of a peculiar kind is treated as casting upon the defendant without any further evidence on behalf of the plaintiff, the onus of showing the accident was not caused by his negligence."

[6.36] In *Lindsay v Midwestern Health Board*[28] a seventeen year old girl in March 1982 attended the casualty department of the regional hospital in Limerick complaining of abdominal pain and vomiting after eating a meal. She was diagnosed in casualty by the senior house officer as suffering from acute appendicitis. She was admitted to a ward and then taken to theatre where she was operated upon and returned to the recovery room. She regained consciousness but shortly afterwards slipped into unconsciousness which deepened. She never regained consciousness and remains in a deep coma to date. The essence of the case made on behalf of the plaintiff was that she went into hospital with a common complaint of acute appendicitis, that she was a normal and healthy girl. She was put through a routine anaesthetic reducing her to a state of unconsciousness and her situation is that she was never brought back to a state of consciousness. The plaintiff succeeded in her case in the High Court where Morris J said that the defendant had failed to discharge the burden of proof cast upon it. The Supreme Court overturned the decision of the High Court and O'Flaherty J said regarding the findings of Morris J:

"The learned trial judge, having held that the effect of the application of the maxim *res ipsa loquitur* was to throw the burden of proof onto the defendant to prove, on the balance of probabilities, what caused the plaintiff's brain damage, and it having failed to do so - having propounded possibilities only of what caused her condition - that that would amount to a court adopting a theory based on pure speculation; that was not sufficient for the defendant to meet the case and, therefore, he held that negligence was to be inferred. On that basis, he found for the plaintiff."

O'Flaherty J continued:

"I believe that the trial judge was, however, correct in regarding this as a *res ipsa loquitur* case. Disparity between the situation of the respective parties is crucial in this regard. As Ó Dálaigh CJ said in *Dowd v Kerry County Council* [1970] IR at 41: 'It should also be said that in an action with regard to a surgical operation the patient rarely knows anything; what has happened is known only to the defendants..' ."

O'Flaherty concluded that, *inter alia*, that one of the courses open to the defendant was to establish was that there was no negligence on its part:

"...This it did decisively and, in those circumstances, it appears to me that it rebutted the burden of proof that rested on it to displace the maxim *res ipsa loquitur* and so the case returned to the plaintiff's bailiwick to prove negligence..."

---

[28] [1993] 2 IR 177.

SUMMARY

[6.38] The above chapter gives an overview of the general principles of the law of negligence, in particular the law relating to medical negligence. The extracts from the various cases will help the reader to understand the practicalities of a medical negligence action and all it entails. Medical negligence is itself a vast topic and there are many different circumstances in which a medical negligence claim can arise. It is outside the scope of this book to conduct a detailed study of this area of the law. However, the general principles outlined above apply to all cases of medical negligence but each individual case will depend on its own particular facts.

CHAPTER 7

THE HOSPITAL

INTRODUCTION

[7.01] A hospital is a complex entity. In the previous chapters we dealt with the liability which can arise as a result of negligence by nurses in the performance of their medical duties and the liability that may fall on the hospital authorities as an employer of a negligent employee. However the duties of a hospital authority do not stop there. A hospital owes duties to both patients and other people visiting the hospital. A visitor, whether a patient or not, does not expect to suffer any injury as a result of the visit and so there is a considerable complexity of relationships between a hospital authority and others. In this chapter we intend to deal with the liability of a hospital in relation to others in so far as any such liability might affect a nurse or the manner in which she carries out her duties. Hospital premises include all parts of the hospital under the control and management of the hospital authority including out-patient and x-ray departments and all places within the hospital environs.

THE HOSPITAL AS AN EMPLOYER

[7.02] The duties which are owed to a nurse by a hospital as her employer, including her health and safety, are outlined in chapter 3. The hospital is responsible for the actions of its staff during the course of their employment, provided they act within the scope of their employment. This is known as vicarious liability. In the event of harm befalling a patient while under the care of the hospital, or a visitor, as a result of any action or inaction on the part of a nurse during the course of carrying out her duties, there may be cause for an action by the patient or visitor. Therefore the hospital is reliant on its medical staff to provide the appropriate standard of care in everything they do. Thus if a nurse knocked over a cleaner's bucket causing the floor to become slippery, the hospital could be held liable if someone suffered an injury as a result.

THE HOSPITAL PATIENT

[7.03] Upon entry to any part of a hospital's premises a patient is entitled to expect a reasonable standard of care. This duty was outlined in *Kelly v St Laurences Hospital* [1] by Finlay CJ:

---

[1] [1988] IR 402.

"In law the duty that the defendants owed to the plaintiff as a patient in their hospital was in general to take reasonable care of him to avoid his being exposed to risk of injury which a reasonable person ought to foresee."

ACCIDENTS IN THE HOSPITAL

[7.04] In the event of an accident occurring when a patient is under the care of the hospital, for example falling out of bed or falling on a wet floor, the nurse in charge or the person who accepts responsibility should take the following steps:

(1) Call a medical doctor for the injured person.

(2) Ascertain who saw the accident.

(3) Ascertain how the accident happened.

(4) Obtain a report from the person who witnessed the accident.

(5) If there was no witness to the accident, then a report should be compiled by the person who found the injured party.

(6) This report is then sent to the Matron's office.

PATIENTS' PROPERTY

[7.05] When a patient hands over property to a servant or agent of the hospital for safekeeping, the hospital becomes the bailee of the property and owes a duty to take reasonable care of that property. A nurse or any other person who misappropriates or takes without consent the property of another may be guilty of the offence of stealing. This is defined in the Larceny Act 1916 as:

1 (1) A person steals who, without the consent of the owner, fraudulently and without a claim of right made in good faith, takes and carries away anything capable of being stolen with intent, at the time of such taking, permanently to deprive the owner thereof.

[7.06] Thus it can be seen that the elements of the offence of stealing are: (1) no consent of the owner, (2) acting without honest excuse, (3) taking the property away, and (4) the intention to permanently deprive the owner. If all four elements are not present the a prosecution will not succeed. There is a further proviso to s 1 which is as follows:

Provided that a person may be guilty of stealing any such thing notwithstanding that he has lawful possession thereof, if, being a bailee or part owner thereof, he fraudulently converts the same to his own use of the use of any person other that the owner.

If a patient voluntarily hands over goods into the possession of a nurse who subsequently takes the goods with the intention of permanently depriving the patient, the original consent to the handing over is not a defence. Goods may also be stolen if they are removed by a trick or intimidation.

[7.07] Generally patients are advised by a hospital not to bring valuables with them when attending a hospital and most hospitals have a policy regarding the arrangements to be carried out when patients do bring valuables with them. This policy should be adhered to by the nurse as the hospital may be held liable in the event of goods or valuables being lost or stolen.

DISCLAIMER CLAUSES

[7.08] Notices are often found in hospitals stating that the hospital's liability is limited with regard to patients' property. This notice must be clear and unambiguous and be displayed in a prominent position and must also be brought to the attention of the patient.

OCCUPIERS LIABILITY

[7.09] The hospital as an occupier in control of the premises owes a general duty of care to all those who enter the premises. The extent of this duty will vary depending upon the category of the entrant. This duty of care to entrants on the premises arises both from common law and statute. The relevant statutes are the Civil Liability Act 1961 and the Safety Health and Welfare at Work Act 1989.

[7.10] The common law recognises four categories of entrant to whom a duty of care is owed while the entrant is on the hospital premises. This aspect of the law has been the subject of much litigation and it would appear that the position at present is as follows:[2]

> (a) Contractual entrants.
> (b) Invitees.
> (c) Licensees.
> (d) Trespassers.

Contractual entrants

[7.11] A person who enters a premises under this heading will normally have a contract with the occupier of the building, e.g. a cinema patron. The duty that is owed here is to take reasonable care in all the circumstances for the safety of the entrant. The duty of reasonable care imposes an obligation on the occupier with regard to his own acts, his omissions and those of his employees.

Invitees

[7.12] Invitees are those persons who bring a benefit to the occupier, these would include a delivery man, or a messenger. What has to be looked at is the nature of the purpose for which the visitor comes, and whether the occupier would

---

[2] For further information on this area see McMahon & Binchy, *The Irish Law of Torts*, ch 12.

normally have a material interest in visits made for that purpose.[3] The duty that is owed here is to use reasonable care "to prevent damage from unusual danger which he knows or he ought to know."[4] happening to the invitee. An employee is also regarded as an invitee, though in the event of an injury arising during the normal course of her work, she would sue on foot of her contract of employment.

Licensees

[7.13] These are persons who have permission to enter the premises, but who bring no benefit to the occupier, e.g., visitors to a church or public park and visitors to a patient in a hospital. The duty of a hospital here is to warn of any concealed or unusual danger that the occupier actually knows exists. Historically the duty owed by an occupier to licensees coming onto his premises was said to be analogous to the duty owed to a donee of a gift; the licensee must take it as he found it. The licensee was not entitled to a higher standard of care for the very reason that he was getting something for nothing. He must not look a gift horse in the mouth.[5] The only duty on the occupier is not to set a trap. However if the dangers are obvious then they do not require a warning, e.g., a lighted candle in a church, may well be a concealed danger for a nine year old child,[6] but may not be so for an adult. Different and higher standards apply when dealing with children.

Trespassers

[7.14] A trespasser is a person who enters an occupier's premises "without an invitation of any sort and whose presence is either unknown to the proprietor or, if he knows, has practically objected to".[7] It was commonly said that an occupier owed no duty to a person entering his premises as a trespasser. The trespasser was regarded as a wrongdoer and entitled to little or no consideration and was certainly not entitled to the same degree of care reserved for contractual entrants, invitees and licensees. However, a qualification must be added: the occupier must do no act so as to intentionally or recklessly to injure the trespasser, whose presence was known or ought to have been known. The only duty that is owed here is not to set a trap. Different and stricter standards apply to children if the premises or the danger itself is such that it amounted to an "allurement" to a child to trespass. Thus for example an unfenced building site adjacent to a housing estate could be so classed and the contractor or owner held liable for any injury as a result of children playing on the site or with machinery.

[7.15] A nurse's duty to her employer as his servant or agent extends to seeing that the part of the premises in which she works is reasonably safe and free from

---

[3] *Boylan v Dublin Corporation* [1949] IR 60.

[4] *Indermaur v Dames* LR 1 CP (1867).

[5] See McMahon & Binchy, *The Irish Law of Torts*, p. 217.

[6] See *Rooney v Connolly* [1987] ILRM 768.

[7] See *Addie and Sons v Dunbreck* [1929] AC 358.

concealed dangers which ought to have been known to her. A danger that she is aware of should be brought to a visitor's notice, e.g., a broken tile.

WILLS IN HOSPITALS

[7.16] If a patient informs a nurse that she wishes to make a will, the nurse is obliged to inform a relative or the patient's solicitor, whichever is requested. Where a nurse has witnessed a patient's signature it should be borne in mind that she may be called at some future date as a witness in a court action to attest the validity of the signature or the capacity of the patient to understand the nature of the document. However, where hospital policy dictates that a nurse should never become involved in the signing or witnessing of legal documents she should comply with this policy.

SUMMARY

[7.17] This chapter outlines the general duties which a hospital owes to various categories of visitors, and in particular to its patients. The duties of a hospital both as an employer and as an occupier of premises have been defined by common law and statute. As well as providing a safe building, safe equipment and systems, a hospital must ensure that there are clear rules and regulations to be followed by its employees in relation to all matters of safety and conversely a hospital relies on its employees to comply with these.

CHAPTER 8

CONSENT

INTRODUCTION

[8.01] The acts of assault and battery constitute the tort of trespass to the person and are actionable *per se*, i.e., no proof of damage to the person is necessary. In the strict sense, to touch a person without their consent is battery. When members of the medical profession carry out treatment on patients, they must have the patient's consent to do so, otherwise the treatment could be regarded as trespass to the person.

[8.02] Early legal authorities have defined the torts of assault and battery as follows:[1]

> "An assault is an offer or attempt to apply force or violence to the person of another in an angry or hostile manner; and if force be actually applied, either illegally or without the consent of the person assaulted, and in an angry, rude, revengeful, or violent manner, the assault becomes a battery, however slight the force may be. Every battery includes an assault.

> Mere words can never amount to an assault. There must be some act indicating an intention of assaulting, or which an ordinary person might reasonably construe as indicating such an intention, or some act amounting to an attempt.

> If no actual violence is used, there must, to constitute an assault, be some threatening act sufficient to raise in the mind of the person threatened a fear of immediate violence; therefore, if an offer is made to strike a person with the fist, at such a distance as to make it impossible for a blow to reach, there is no assault; so, too, where a pistol is presented at a range to which the ball cannot by any possibility carry."

[8.03] The tort of battery therefore involves the application of physical contact upon a person without their consent, either express or implied. For example, a slap on the face constitutes a battery. However, there does not have to be physical contact involved; pulling a chair from under a person so that they fall on the ground will be a battery. In order to come within the definition of assault, a threatening gesture indicating an intention to inflict a battery will be sufficient provided the person concerned is put in fear. However when consent is given, this

---

[1] *Halsbury's Laws of England*, 1st ed. Vol. 9 p. 606.

then negatives the tort of assault. In the normal course of events this is unlikely to arise where nursing is carried out in good faith.

> "Generally speaking, in order to constitute an assault it is necessary that the act should be done against the will of the person assaulted, and, in consequence, consent is usually a good defence to a charge of assault. If, however, the act amounts to a breach of the peace or has a direct tendency to cause a breach of the peace, and is therefore injurious to the public, or if the act be a dangerous one, consent will afford no defence. For these reasons all persons taking part in or aiding and abetting a prize fight are guilty of assault."[2]

[8.04] When a person is receiving medical treatment, consent is necessary otherwise an interference with their person would regarded as a battery. An early definition in 1914 in USA by Cordozo J described bodily integrity in the following way:

> "... every human being of adult years and sound mind has a right to determine what shall be done with his own body; and a surgeon who performs an operation without his patient's consent commits an assault, for which he is liable in damages. However this cannot be taken beyond the compass of its words to support an action of battery where there has been consent to the very surgical procedure carried out upon a patient but there has been a breach of the duty of disclosure of attendant risks. In my opinion, actions of battery in respect of surgical or other medical treatment should be confined to cases where surgery or treatment has been performed or given to which there has been no consent at all or where, emergency situations aside, surgery or treatment has been performed or given beyond that to which there was consent."[3]

CONSENT

[8.05] Consent has been defined as follows:

> "The consent must be that of a rational person who knows the nature of the act consented to; and fraud as to the nature of the act done, or as to the identity of the person doing it, vitiates consent. Therefore if a medical man strips a female patient naked on the pretence that he is thereby diagnosing her case, or has connection with a female child of fourteen on pretence that he is treating her medically, he is guilty of an assault."[4]

[8.06] Consent may be obtained in various ways. There is no requirement in law that a valid consent should be in writing. It may be verbal: specifically expressed or implied. It is only necessary to record whatever has been agreed between the parties. A prudent practitioner would ensure that the consent is reduced to writing, explaining the nature and consequence of the treatment and signed by the

---

[2] *Ibid.* at p. 607.

[3] *Schlonloendorff v Society of the New York Hospital* (1914) 501 NE 92.

[4] Halsbury's Laws of England, p.607.

parties.[5] If a dispute were to arise at a later date the written consent is evidence of what was agreed between the parties.

The Requirement for a Valid Consent

[8.07] A patient must have the capacity to give consent. The nature and consequences of the treatment must be fully disclosed to the patient. Finally the consent must be voluntarily given by the patient.

Capacity

[8.08] A person is deemed to have the capacity to give his consent when that person is of adult years and of sound mind; in other words there is a requirement that the person understands the nature and consequence of the treatment. To constitute a valid consent, the capacity of the person to decide and express their will must be taken into account. Notwithstanding the fact that the person concerned is a minor without the capacity to make a medical decision, or a person with an impaired mental disorder, they may, in appropriate circumstances be considered to have the necessary capacity.

Full Disclosure

[8.09] In order to constitute full disclosure the nature and consequences of the proposed treatment must be fully disclosed to the patient. In *Walsh v Family Planning Services Ltd and others*,[6] the plaintiff, Mr Walsh attended Family Planning Services Ltd for an interview regarding a vasectomy at the clinic. At the initial meeting documents and literature regarding the operation were read to Mr Walsh. He was told that it would be a safe, secure, painless operation and was also irreversible. He then decided to have the operation. After the operation he developed the rare condition known as "orchialgia" which is a condition of pain in the testicles. Mr Walsh sued the doctor who carried out the operation and Family Planning Services Ltd. Finlay CJ described the action in the following terms:

> "He sued the defendants for negligence in the performance of the operation and for negligence, assault, and battery in failing to advise him as to the consequences of the operation and because he had not consented to the third defendant's surgery against which shortcomings were alleged. In a seven day trial in the High Court the plaintiff testified that no warning had been given to him about the possibility of indefinite ongoing pain; Dr S testified she had given the warning and had mentioned "but this occurrence was very rare". Expert evidence pinpointed the plaintiff as suffering from orchialgia, a known but exceptionally rare and not properly accounted for consequence of vasectomy operations and that there was no general and approved practice of warning prospective patients as to its incidence."

---

[5] See Appendix for a sample of a consent form.

[6] [1992] 1 IR 496 .

[8.10] Mr Walsh succeeded in his action in the High Court on the grounds of assault and battery, though the judge made a finding that the vasectomy operation was properly performed and without negligence. Family Planning Services Ltd successfully appealed to the Supreme Court. The Court was of the view that a warning should be given even if the consequences are rare:

"On the evidence and in the circumstances of the case there was an obligation on the defendants to warn the plaintiff of the possible consequences of any condition such as orchialgia notwithstanding the rarity of its incidence, particularly since the operation was elective, rather than under any compulsion and the Court would not disturb on appeal the trial judge's determination that a warning had been given and that it had been sufficient."[7]

When dealing with the question of assault the Chief Justice went on to say:

"Assault should be confined to cases where there is no consent to the particular procedure or where an apparent consent has been vitiated by fraud or deception."

Finlay CJ continued:

"I am satisfied that there is, of course, where it is possible to do so, a clear obligation on a medical practitioner carrying out or arranging for the carrying out of an operation, to inform the patient of any possible harmful consequence arising from the operation, so as to permit the patient to give an informed consent to subjecting himself to the operation concerned. I am also satisfied that the extent of this obligation must, as a matter of common sense, vary with what might be described as the elective nature of the surgery."

Similar sentiments were expressed by O'Flaherty J:

"A claim of assault should be confined to cases where there is no consent to the particular procedure and where it is feasible to look for consent."

Voluntary Consent

[8.11] For consent to be voluntarily given, both capacity to give the necessary consent and full disclosure of the possible consequences are required. A person must make a free choice and be aware of the consequences that follow. The consent would not be regarded as voluntary where there was any element of fraud or misrepresentation.

Medical Treatment

[8.12] A nurse is obliged to obtain consent for nursing treatment. Very often this consent is implied by a gesture, e.g., the holding out of an arm for an injection. It is the doctor's duty to explain and be satisfied that the patient understands the

---

[7] [1992] 1 IR 497.

nature and consequences of the medical treatment proposed to be carried out before a valid consent form is signed. Where a patient seeks an explanation or clarification from a nurse regarding the contemplated procedure the nurse is obliged to refer this matter back to the doctor, otherwise the consent obtained does not comply with the requirements for a valid consent.

EXCEPTIONS

[8.13] In certain areas the law steps in and overrides the necessity for consent. This often arises in the case of notifiable diseases, e.g., tuberculosis, measles and other infectious diseases. In many countries at the point of entry there are requirements which must be complied with, for example, such as when returning from a farm (in case of contact with Foot and Mouth disease). Section 66 of the Health Act 1970 provides for medical inspection in schools and the written consent of the parent is required. The following categories deal with situations where consent cannot be obtained from a patient due to a mental incapacity, an emergency situation, an unconscious patient, age or where the treatment is compelled by law.

Adults with a Mental Incapacity

[8.14] If adults with a mental incapacity or those who have an impaired mental capacity fail to understand the nature of treatment in order to give consent, e.g., Alzheimer's disease, Hemiplegia (strokes) and the mentally retarded, consent in these instances is obtained from their next-of-kin. If dealing with a ward of court the President of the High Court is the appropriate person from whom to seek the consent. Notwithstanding the person's incapacity to give his consent, all procedures are to be explained fully and if the person objects to a procedure this must be taken into consideration.

Emergency

[8.15] If a situation occurs where it is necessary to commence immediate treatment or perform an operation to save the life or the health of a person, then a doctor can proceed without consent. Such situations occur in road traffic accidents, in the case of comatose patients or any other emergency situation that requires immediate attention. In such a situation the doctor could rely on the "necessity principle" where the benefit to the patient outweighs the lack of adherence to the law. Finlay CJ went on to say in the *Walsh*[8] case that:

> "I am satisfied, however, that the standard of care to be exercised by a medical practitioner in the giving of the warning of the consequences of proposed medical surgical procedures is not in principle any different from the standard of care to be exercised by medical practitioners in the giving of treatment or advice, and that there are not good grounds for suggesting that the issue of negligence arising under this heading is outside the general principles which have been enunciated by this Court in

---

[8] [1992] IR 497.

previous cases concerning the standards of care and the methods of ascertaining them arising in medical negligence cases... It is, I am satisfied, true, however, that if a medical practitioner charged with negligence consisting of a failure to give sufficient warning of the possible consequences of an operation, defends his conduct by establishing that he followed a practice which was general, that it may be, certainly in relation to very clearly elective surgery, that the Court might more readily reach a conclusion that the extent of the warning given or omitted contained inherent defects which ought to have been obvious to any person giving the matter due consideration than it could do in a case of complicated medical or surgical procedures, and an allegation that, although generally adopted they were inherently unsafe."

When dealing with a situation where the person's health is at risk the Chief Justice said:

"Quite obviously, and apart even from cases of emergency surgery which has to be carried out to persons who are unconscious or incapable of giving or refusing consent, or to young children, there may be instances where as a matter of medical knowledge. notwithstanding substantial risks of harmful consequence, the carrying out of a particular surgical procedure is so necessary to maintain the life or health of the patient and the consequences of failing to carry it out are so clearly disadvantageous that limited discussion or warning concerning possible harmful side-effects may be appropriate and proper. On the other hand, the obligation to give warning of the possible harmful consequences of a surgical procedure which could be said to be at the other end of the scale of the extent to which it is elective, such, undoubtedly, as would be the operation of the vasectomy, may be more stringent and more onerous."

Age

[8.16] Parents are the guardians of children unless a guardian is appointed by the court, i.e. orphans and wards. When treatment of a child is anticipated consent may be obtained from either parent. When dealing with separated parents the wiser course would be to enquire if the absent spouse has been informed of the proposed treatment. However any proposed treatment must be explained to a child who is capable of understanding. While this position has not been explored in the Irish courts it was fully examined in *Gillick v West Norfolk and Wisbech Area Health Authority and the DHSS.*[9] (It should be remembered also that in England the Family Law Reform Act 1969 allows a minor to give consent to surgical treatment when the age of sixteen has been attained. There is no similar provision in Irish law.) In that case guidelines were issued by the DHSS concerning family planning services for young people which stated or implied that in "exceptional" circumstances a doctor, without the consent of the parent, could prescribe contraception and give advice on family planning. Mrs Gillick who had five daughters sought to prevent this by alleging that the guidelines had no authority in law, and were unlawful and adversely affected her parental rights.

---

[9] [1986]AC 112; [1985] 3 All ER 402.

[8.17] The case went to the House of Lords which was of the view that the guidelines were not unlawful, and that a parent's interest in a child did not amount to a "right", it was more correct to regard this interest as a "responsibility or duty". Their Lordships considered that parental rights existed so long as they were needed for the protection of the child and such rights yielded to the child's own right to make his own decision when a sufficient level of intelligence and understanding was reached by that child. Just because a child was at a particular age did not mean he lacked the legal capacity to consent.

[8.18] The following are extracts from the above case, where the majority of the Law Lords were of the view that in order for a minor to give consent, "understanding" is the key principle:

Per Lord Fraser: "Provided the patient, whether a boy or a girl, is capable of understanding what is proposed, and of expressing his or her own wishes, I see no good reason for holding that he or she lacks the capacity to express them validly and effectively and to authorise the medical man to make the examination or give the treatment which he advises. After all, a minor under the age of 16 can, within certain limits, enter into a contract. He or she can also sue and be sued, and can give evidence on oath. Moreover, a girl under 16 can give sufficiently effective consent to sexual intercourse to lead to the legal result that the man involved does not commit the crime of rape."

Per Lord Templeman: "I accept also that a doctor may lawfully carry out some forms of treatment with the consent of an infant patient and against the opposition of a parent based on religious or any other grounds. The effect of the consent of the infant depends on the nature of the treatment and the age and understanding of the infant. For example, a doctor with the consent of an intelligent boy or girl of 15 could in my opinion safely remove tonsils or a troublesome appendix."

Per Lord Scarman: "In the light of the foregoing I would hold that as a matter of law the parental right to determine whether or not their minor child below the age of 16 will have medical treatment terminates if and when the child achieves a sufficient understanding and intelligence to enable him or her to understand fully what is proposed. It will be a question of fact whether a child seeking advice has sufficient understanding of what is involved to give a consent valid in law. Until the child achieves the capacity to consent, the parental right to make the decision continues save only in exceptional circumstances. Emergency, parental neglect, abandonment of the child or inability to find the parent are examples of exceptional situations justifying the doctor proceeding to treat the child without parental knowledge and consent; but there will arise, no doubt, other exceptional situations in which it will be reasonable for the doctor to proceed without the parent's consent."

The Age of Majority Act 1985

[8.19] In 1985 the age of majority was reduced by law from twenty-one to eighteen years of age:

2 (1) Where a person has not attained the age of twenty-one years prior to the commencement of this Act, he shall, subject to section 4, attain full age-

(*a*) on such commencement if he has attained the age of eighteen years or is or has been married, or

(*b*) after such commencement when he attains the age of eighteen years or, in case he marries before attaining that age, upon his marriage.

(2) *Subsection (1)* applies for the purposes of any rule of law and, in the absence of a definition or of any indication of a contrary intention, for the construction of "age of majority", "full age", "infancy", "infant", "minor", "minority" and of other cognate words and expressions in-

(*a*) any statutory provision passed or made before, on or after the commencement of this Act, and

(*b*) any deed, will, court order or other instrument (not being a statutory provision) made on or after such commencement.

(3) Where there is, in any statutory provision passed or made before the commencement of this Act, a reference to the age of twenty-one years, such provision shall, subject to *subsection (4)*, be construed and have effect as if the reference therein were a reference to full age.

Prisons

[8.20] Persons are obliged to submit to routine physical examination on entry to prison, though any blood samples that are taken may not be subject to testing for HIV without the consent of the prisoner.

SUMMARY

[8.21] In this chapter we have discussed the way in which medical treatment can be lawfully carried out without committing the torts of assault or battery or trespass to the patient. It is the nurse's duty to ensure that consent to treatment by a doctor has been obtained, it is not her duty to obtain consent for the doctor's treatment.

CHAPTER 9

DRUGS

INTRODUCTION

[9.01] The control and administration of drugs is an essential part of a nurse's training and work since if drugs are administered in a careless and improper way, serious injury or death could result. The administration of drugs is governed by the Misuse of Drugs Acts 1977 and 1984. These Acts set out in detail in the circumstances in which controlled drugs are to be stored, dispensed and administered. Controlled drugs comprise both scheduled drugs and dangerous drugs.

CATEGORIES OF CONTROLLED DRUGS

[9.02] Drugs are divided into four different categories. These are set out in schedule form at the back of the 1977 Act.[1] These schedules are updated on a regular basis by the Minister for Health by means of regulations. Schedule 1 consists of a list of raw drugs some of which have no medical use but from which useful drugs derive from, e.g., cannabis, opium and LSD. These are used by manufacturers for research and are only permitted by licence. While possession is permitted under licence, this does not authorise "use". Schedule 2 contains a list of dangerous drugs and includes morphine, pethidine and ononopon. Schedule 3 contains a list of drugs in a more diluted form than those in the above mentioned categories and would include such drugs as valium, phenobarbitone, ponston and antibiotics. Schedule 4 contains a list of drugs that usually can be bought over the counter in a pharmacy, e.g., panadol and aspirin.

PRESCRIBING AND ADMINISTRATION

[9.03] Those drugs contained in Schedule 2 and 3 may only be obtained and administered in the prescribed form as set out in the 1977 Act and the regulations made thereunder. The Misuse of Drugs Regulations 1979 defines a "prescription" as follows:

> **3** "prescription" means a prescription issued by a registered medical practitioner for the medical treatment of an individual, by a registered dentist for the dental treatment of an individual or by a registered veterinary surgeon for the purposes of animal treatment.

---

[1] The Principal Act is the 1977 Act which with the Misuse of Drugs Act 1984 may be cited together as one Act.

[9.04] The 1977 Act sets out the prescribed form for a prescription of a controlled drug:

(1) It must be signed by a practitioner in ink.
(2) It must be completed in the practitioners handwriting.
(3) It must contain the following information:
  (a) the name and address of patient, and
  (b) the quantity in both numbers and figures of the prescribed drug.

[9.05] Section 18 prohibits the forging or alteration of a prescription:

18 (1) A person shall not forge a document purporting to be a prescription issued by a practitioner (which document is in this Act referred to as a forged prescription).

(2) A person shall not with intent to deceive either alter or use a prescription which has been duly issued by a practitioner (which document is in this Act referred to as a duly issued prescription).

(3) A person shall not have in his possession either a forged prescription or a duly issued prescription which has been altered with intent to deceive.

[9.06] When dealing with a hospital patient it is sufficient for the information relating to prescribed drugs to be on the patient's drug sheet:

13 (2) In the case of a prescription issued for the treatment of a patient in a hospital or nursing home, it shall be a sufficient compliance with *sub-article (1)(e)* if the prescription is written on the patient's bed card or case sheet.

[9.07] The Misuse of Drugs Regulations 1979 control the supply of a controlled drug as follows:

14 (1) A person shall not supply a controlled drug other than a drug specified in *Schedule 4* on a prescription-

(*a*) unless the prescription complies with the provisions of *article 13*,

(*b*) unless the address specified in the prescription as the address of the person issuing it is an address within the State,

(*c*) unless he either is acquainted with the signature of the person by whom it purports to be issued and has no reason to believe that the signature is not genuine, or has taken reasonably sufficient steps to satisfy himself that it is genuine,

(*d*) before the date specified in the prescription,

(*e*) subject to *sub-article (3)* later than one month after the date specified in the prescription.

(2) Subject to *sub-article (3)*, a person dispensing a prescription for a controlled drug, other than a drug specified in *Schedule 4*, shall -

(*a*) at the time of dispensing it, mark thereon the date on which it is dispensed, and

(*b*) except in the case of a health prescription, retain it on the premises at which it was dispensed.

(3) In the case of a prescription for a controlled drug other than a drug specified in *Schedule 4*, which contains a direction that specified instalments of the total amount may be dispensed at stated intervals, the person dispensing it shall not supply the drug otherwise than in accordance with that direction and -

(*a*) *sub-article (1)* shall have effect as if for the requirement contained in *paragraph (e)* thereof there were substituted a requirement that the occasion on which the first instalment is dispensed shall not be later than one month after the date specified in the prescription,

(*b*) *sub-article (2)* shall have effect as if for the words "at the time of dispensing it" there were substituted the words "on each occasion on which an instalment",

provided that no instalment shall be dispensed later than three months after the date specified in the prescription.

The above must be strictly complied with and this means that drugs may not be prescribed over the telephone or verbally.

RECORDING OF DRUGS

[9.08] When administering dangerous drugs (listed in Schedule 2 of the 1977 Act) the following must be complied with:

1. The prescribed drug is checked by two people.

2. The prescribed drug is entered in the Dangerous Drug Book with the following details:

(*a*) Name and dose of drug.

(*b*) Name of patient.

(*c*) Time and method of administering.

(*d*) Signature of both persons who checked the drug.

(*e*) Prescription on patient's chart checked.

(*f*) When administered this is recorded on patient's drug chart according to hospital policy.

Drugs listed in Schedules 3 and 4 are recorded on the patient's drug chart. It is part of a nurse's duty, as outlined in her training, to ensure that all prescribed medication has been consumed in her presence and also recorded.

[9.09] The following persons are entitled to supply controlled drugs provided they comply with the Regulations:

12 (4) The persons referred to in *sub-article (2)* are-

(a) a registered medical practitioner,

(b) the matron or acting matron of a hospital or nursing home,

(c) a person referred to in *article 8(1)(c)*,[2]

(d) the owner of a ship, or the master of a ship which does not carry a registered medical practitioner on board as part of her complement,

(e) the master of a foreign ship in a port in the State,

(f) the installation manager of an offshore installation.

[9.10] In a hospital or a nursing home the matron or acting matron may hold the keys of the pharmacy but may not dispense the drugs except under the following stringent conditions. This deals with requisitions in different institutions and not just in hospitals:

12 (5) A requisition furnished for the purposes of *sub-article (2)* shall-

(a) where it is furnished by the matron or acting matron of a hospital or nursing home, be signed by a registered medical practitioner or a registered dentist employed or engaged in that hospital or nursing home,

(b) where it is furnished by the master of a foreign ship, contain a statement, signed by a medical officer of health of the health board within whose functional area the ship is, that the quantity of the drug to be supplied is the quantity necessary for the equipment of the ship,

(c) where it is furnished by the installation manager of an offshore installation, contain a statement signed by the Industrial Medical Adviser of the Department of Labour that the quantity of the drug to be supplied is the quantity necessary for the equipment of that installation.

(6) Where the person responsible for the dispensing and supply of medicines at any hospital or nursing home supplies a controlled drug to a sister or acting sister for the

---

[2] See para **[9.12]**.

time being in charge of a ward, theatre or other department in that hospital or nursing home he shall-

(*a*) obtain a requisition in writing, signed by the sister or acting sister, which specifies the total quantity of the drug to be supplied, and

(*b*) mark the requisition in such manner as to show that it has been complied with,

and any requisition obtained for the purposes of this sub-article shall be retained in the dispensary at which the drug was supplied and a copy of the requisition or a note of it shall be retained or kept by the sister or acting sister for the time being in charge of that ward, theatre or other department.

STORAGE

[9.11] Drugs are prescribed by a registered medical practitioner and dispensed by a pharmacist to a person in charge of the ward. There are strict instructions as to the proper method of storage. Those drugs as set out in Schedule 3 and 4 are stored in a locked press on the ward (including those in either liquid and tablet form). Those drugs as contained in Schedule 1 and 2 must be kept in a locked press within a locked press on the ward with the keys in the possession of the person-in-charge.[3]

CATEGORIES OF LAWFUL USE

[9.12] The Misuse of Drugs Regulations 1979 sets out a list of persons who can lawfully supply drugs or have in their possession these drugs as set out in Schedules 2, 3 and 4. Article 8(1) provides that:

8 (1) A person may supply or offer to supply any drug specified in *Schedule 2, 3, or 4* to any person who may lawfully have that drug in his possession where the person so supplying or offering to supply the drug is a person acting in his capacity as -

(*a*) the matron or acting matron of a hospital or nursing home which is wholly or mainly maintained by a public authority out of public funds or by a charity or by voluntary subscriptions,

(*b*) the sister or acting sister for the time being in charge of a ward, theatre or other department in such a hospital or nursing home where the drug is supplied to her by a person responsible for the dispensing and supply of medicines at such hospital or nursing home,

(*c*) a person in charge of a laboratory the recognised activities of which consists in, or include, the conduct of scientific education or research and which is attached to a university or a hospital referred to in *paragraph (a)* of this sub-article, or a person in charge of any other laboratory engaged in the conduct of scientific education, research or analysis approved for the purpose by the Minister.

---

[3] SI 321/ 1982, Safe Custody Regulations 1982.

MIDWIFE

[9.13] Once a midwife is on the "live" registrar and has notified the relevant Health Board of her intention to practice pursuant to the Nurses Act she is then permitted to possess and administer pethidine. A midwife is obliged to return to the medical practitioner any pethidine "she no longer requires". The method by which she can obtain pethidine is set out in article 10(2) of the Regulations. The prescription must be signed by the midwife, and the medical practitioner[4] and must contain the name and address of the midwife and the quantity to be administered. A midwife is empowered under article 10(1) to administer and prescribe pethidine in limited amounts to a woman in labour:

10 (1) A midwife who has in accordance with the provisions of section 45 of the Midwives Act, 1944, notified to a health board her intention to practice may, subject to the provisions of this article -

(*a*) so far as is necessary for her practice as a midwife, have in her possession or administer pethidine, and

(*b*) surrender to an appropriate medical practitioner any pethidine in her possession which is no longer required by her.

(2) Nothing in *sub-article (1)* shall be construed as authorising a midwife to have pethidine in her possession unless it has been obtained on foot of a written order signed by the midwife and an appropriate medical practitioner setting out the name and address of the midwife, the purpose for which the pethidine is required and the quantity to be obtained.

ADMINISTRATION OF DRUGS

[9.14] As part of her training a nurse is educated in the methods of recording and administering drugs. Drugs may be administered in any of the following ways: (a) sub-lingually, (b) subcutaneously, (c) *per* rectum, (d) orally, (e) inter-muscularly, and (f) intravenously. When administering drugs, a nurse is obliged to comply with her syllabus and the Drugs Act. An Bord Altranais have issued guidelines[5] for the administration of drugs.

[9.15] Directors of nursing homes, matrons, chief nursing officers, superintendent public health nurses, and other persons in authority are responsible for ensuring that the guidelines are brought to the attention of nurses. Nurses who administer medical preparations are responsible for their safe administration. Employers should have written policies and procedures for nurses with regard to the administration of medical preparations. These should have regard to the different

---

[4] The doctor must be practising in the area in which the midwife practises.

[5] *Guidelines for the Administration of Medical Preparations*, An Bord Altranais, March 1990.

competencies of nurses and the various settings in which they practice. Nursing management must be involved in the formulation of such policies and procedures.

[9.16] A nurse may administer an intravenous drug, cytotoxic drug or an epidural analgesic after she has had specific training consisting of theoretical instruction and clinical practice in the appropriate procedures which has been approved by An Bord Altranais.

[9.17] A nurse may administer an intravenous medical preparation by the following methods:

(*a*) by the addition to an intravenous infusion (bag, buretol or infusion pump), or

(*b*) through the appropriate section of an intravenous giving set.

Individual nurses in specialist areas as identified by directors of nursing, matrons, chief nursing officers and superintendent public health nurses may administer specified medical preparations directly into a vein by venepuncture. These nurses must receive appropriate specialist training. Registered midwives in accordance with currently accepted midwifery practice, may administer specified medical preparations directly into a vein by venepuncture.

SUMMARY

[9.18] As can be seen from the above chapter, the administration and recording of drugs is governed by statute and guidelines from An Bord Altranais. It is an integral part of a nurse's training and it cannot be emphasised enough that a nurse must be proficient and informed about drugs and their administration. It is a criminal offence to be in breach of the Misuse of Drugs Acts and Regulations and such a breach could result in payment of a fine and/or a term of imprisonment. A failure to follow approved guidelines could also result in a disciplinary procedure by an employer. All training institutions are now advised to have their own written policy on safety for the administration of drugs.

CHAPTER 10

RECORDS AND CONFIDENTIALITY

INTRODUCTION

[10.01] Each hospital has its own policy as regards how it is to function and hospital records are an integral part of this. Records are required so that the persons treating and caring for the patient have a complete picture as to the patient's condition, treatment and care on an ongoing basis. In the event of a complaint being made to a hospital by or on behalf of any person treated there, with regard to the treatment or lack of, the malpractice or the negligence of any employees or agents of the hospital, the hospital relies on the records in order to deal with any such complaint.

KEEPING OF RECORDS

[10.02] Records must be kept accurately, legible, clear and correct. Records should not contain criticism of medical personnel or patients, expressions of opinion, personal abbreviations, or allegations against medical staff. It is vital that on no account should a record be altered or interfered with in any way other than by the person who recorded it. Any changes to a record should be done at the time and not at a later time or date, and must be for the purpose of correcting mistakes. A correct legible signature should be used and initials should not be used. The importance of keeping correct records cannot be over-emphasised.

[10.03] Since a patient's medical history is contained within the records and this will be relied on by different medical personnel over a period of time not only for ongoing treatment, it is of great importance that this record is factually legible and correct so that the hospital provides the appropriate standard of care, e.g., a patient's allergies are correctly recorded and past medical history.

[10.04] In the course of a negligence action those records (which are made at the time) are subject to the scrutiny of the court. Records should contain the following (which is not an exhaustive list):

(1) The patient's name, age, address, next of kin, religion.

(2) Date and time of admission and discharge.

(3) Medical history, doctors' instructions, treatment.

(4) Drug records including prescription and administration pursuant to the Drugs Act.

(5) Record facts only.

(6) Should not be altered retrospectively.

(7) Correct signature (not initials).

(8) Name of the consultant.

(9) International abbreviations only, e.g., S.T.A.T., B.I.D., T.I.D., Q.I.D., NOCTE, P.R.N.

(10) A record of nursing care, medical instructions, condition of the patient, accurately, factually and correct.

In the event of a mistake being made, a single line should be drawn through the incorrect entry and initialled. It is important that the previously incorrect entry be legible. The correct entry can then be written in.

[10.05] There are no statutory provisions or guidelines for the keeping of records other than those provided for in the hospital policy which varies from hospital to hospital. However the Nursing Homes (Care and Welfare) Regulations 1993 set out the method by which records are to be kept in a nursing home. Article 18 provides as follows:

18.1 In every nursing home there shall be kept in a safe place a bound register of all independent persons resident in the home, which shall include the following particulars in respect of each person:

(a) the first name, surname, address, date of birth, marital status and religious denomination of the person;

(b) the name, address and telephone number, if any, of the person's relative or the other person nominated to act on the person's behalf as a person to be notified in the event of a change in the person's health or circumstances,

(c) the name, address and telephone number of the person's medical practitioner,

(d) the date on which the person was last admitted to the nursing home,

(e) when the person has left the nursing home, the date on which he or she left and a forwarding address,

(f) when the person is admitted to the hospital, the date of and the reasons for the admission and the name of the hospital, (*g*) when the person dies in the nursing home, the date, time and the certified cause of death.

18.2 Each part of the register kept under *article 18.1* shall be retained for a period of not less than five years, beginning with the date on which the last entry was made.

However any material which is stored on computer is covered by the Data Protection Act 1988. The standard of care required in the keeping of records is one of reasonable care.

RIGHT OF ACCESS TO RECORDS

[10.06] Whenever information is stored on computer a person (the subject) is entitled to access provided the following conditions are fulfilled. Upon payment of a fee and after satisfying the Data Controller that they are the subject of the information on file, then they are entitled to the personal data that is stored on the computer within forty days subject to the exceptions contained in s 4(1) of the Data Protection Act 1988. If the information is coded then they are entitled to an explanation of the terms used. The Minister for Justice in consultation with the Minister for Health is empowered to modify this right of access regarding data on physical or mental health by the making of regulations.[1]

DATA PROTECTION ACT 1988

[10.07] When a person requires information about themselves, stored on computer, regarding hospital records, they are entitled to same within forty days under s 4 of the Data Protection Act 1988:

4 (1)(*a*) Subject to the provisions of this Act, an individual shall, if he so requests a data controller in writing-

(i) be informed by the data controller whether the data kept by him includes personal data relating to the individual, and

(ii) be supplied by the data controller with a copy of the information constituting any such data.

[10.08] The Health Regulations 1989 made pursuant to s 4 contain the following definitions:

3 In these Regulations-

"care" includes examination, investigation and diagnosis;
"health data" means personal data relating to physical or mental health;
"health professional" means-

---

[1] The Health Regulations 1989.

(*a*) a person who is a medical practitioner, dentist, optician, pharmaceutical chemist, nurse or midwife and who is registered under the enactments governing his profession, and

(*b*) a chiropodist, dietician, occupational therapist, orthoptist, physiotherapist, psychologist, child psychotherapist or speech therapist.

[10.09] There are situations where information is not to be supplied and the Act specifies such a situation where the data is likely to cause serious harm to the physical and mental health of the person seeking the information:

(1) Information constituting health data shall not be supplied by or on behalf of a data controller to the data subject concerned in response to a request under *section 4(1)(a)* of the Act if it would be likely to cause serious harm to the physical or mental health of the data subject.

(2) Nothing in *paragraph (1)* of this Regulation excuses a data controller from supplying so much of the information sought by the request as can be supplied without causing the harm referred to in that paragraph.

OWNERSHIP OF RECORDS

[10.10] There are conflicting opinions in this area as to where ownership lies. Records may, if required by a patient, be obtained in one of two ways:

(1) They are given on a voluntary basis by the hospital and consultant doctor.

(2) By order of the High Court by way of discovery, but this may only be done after legal proceedings have commenced.

CONFIDENTIALITY

[10.11] Confidentiality is recognised by Article 40.3.1 of the Constitution as it is regarded as an unenumerated personal right of a citizen.

40. 3. 1° The State guarantees in its laws to respect, and, as far as practicable, by its laws to defend and vindicate the personal rights of the citizen.

By virtue of the nature of the relationship between the nurse and the patient, information is imparted under the veil of confidentiality and in good faith. Breach of confidence would arise if the nurse were to divulge such information otherwise than for the purpose for which it is imparted.

CONFIDENTIALITY IN THE WORKPLACE

[10.12] Confidentiality arises in a hospital between matron, sister, sister tutor, staff nurse and student, patient and doctor and any para-medical staff or members of the medical team. Reports concerning a nurse's progress, performance or conduct that arise during the course of training/employment are private and confidential. Confidentiality may also be incorporated as a term in a contract of employment.

[10.13] Breach of confidentiality is regarded as a serious breach of the nurse's code of conduct and will result in an inquiry being held by An Bord Altranais into the fitness to practise of the nurse (see chapters 4 and 5).

[10.14] When a breach of confidentiality occurs, a patient may have a right to compensation by the courts for any damage caused to him and members of his family. It will depend on the circumstances surrounding the breach as to whether the nurse would be held personally liable, though this depends on hospital policy, but it is most likely that she would be held personally liable. The hospital employer could argue that the nurse was acting outside the scope of her employment.

PRIVILEGE

[10.15] There are certain circumstances when information is communicated to a third party when privilege can be claimed. This means that there has been no breach of confidentiality as it was in the proper interests of all concerned that the information was communicated to a third party. Such a situation would arise when reporting on a patient or where the sister or staff nurse or any other person is reporting to the nurse on duty. Information can only be communicated within the medical team caring for that patient and where it is necessary for the patient's care and treatment.

INFORMATION TO RELATIVES

[10.16] The doctor is the primary source of disclosing information to a patient's relatives whereas a request for information regarding the well-being and needs of the patient lies within the compass of the nurse. Information should not be divulged over the telephone as it is not possible to verify the identity of the caller.

TO WHOM IS INFORMATION IS GIVEN?

[10.17] The information recorded on a patient's chart is normally supplied to the next-of-kin. In the event of a patient's request for non-disclosure it then becomes the doctor's decision whether or not it is in the best interests of the patient. Where the patient is a child the information should be disclosed to both parents, particularly if they are living apart.

SUMMARY

[10.18] Records and confidentiality are an integral part of a patient's care. Hospital authorities are totally reliant on their staff being proficient and vigilant in both the keeping of records and the proper disclosure of the information received during the course of their employment.

CHAPTER 11

NURSING HOMES

INTRODUCTION

[11.01] The development of geriatric nursing as a specialist area of expertise has been notable over recent years and specialist nursing courses in the care of the elderly have been developed by An Bord Altranais.[1] Nursing homes are regulated by statute. The Health (Nursing Homes) Act 1990 (hereafter referred to as "the Act") repealed the Health (Homes for Incapacitated Persons) Act 1964. Under the Act the following Regulations were brought into force:

1. Nursing Homes (Subvention) Regulations 1993.[2]
2. Nursing Homes (Fees) Regulations 1993.[3]
3. Health (In-Patient Services) Regulations 1993.[4]
4. Nursing Homes (Care and Welfare) Regulations 1993.[5]

These Regulations provide for the implementation of the Act which was brought into force with effect from 1 September 1993.

THE HEALTH (NURSING HOMES) ACT 1990

[11.02] A nursing home is defined in the Act as an institution that cares for more than one dependent person. Section 2 provides that:

> **2** In this Act, except where the context otherwise requires, "nursing home", subject to *subsection (2)*, means an institution for the care and maintenance of more than two dependent persons excluding-
>
> (*a*) an institution managed by or on behalf of a Minister of the Government or a health board,
>
> (*b*) an institution in which a majority of the persons being maintained are being treated for acute illnesses,

---

[1] See *The Future of Nurse Education and Training in Ireland*, An Bord Altranais, 1994.

[2] SI No 277 of 1993.

[3] SI No 223 of 1993.

[4] SI No 224 of 1993.

[5] SI No 226 of 1993.

(*c*) a maternity home carried on by a person who is registered under the Registration of Maternity Homes Act 1934,

(*d*) a mental institution within the meaning of the Mental Treatment Acts 1945 to 1966,

(*e*) an institution for the care and maintenance of mentally handicapped persons operated otherwise than for profit and to which grants are paid by the Minister or a health board,

(*f*) premises in which children are maintained in pursuance of an arrangement with a health board,

(*g*) an institution operated otherwise than for profit-

    (i) that is for the care and maintenance of physically handicapped persons a majority of whom do not receive whole time nursing care in the institution,

    (ii) in the management of which representatives of the Minister or a health board and representatives of the persons being maintained in the institution participate with other persons,

    (iii) to which grants are paid by the Minister or a health board, and
    (iv) to which paragraphs (a) and (b) of section 333(1) of the Income Tax Act 1967 apply, and

(*h*) premises in which a majority of the persons being maintained are members of a religious order or priests of any religion (other than premises in relation to which a payment has been made under *section 7*),

but maintenance by a person of his spouse or of a parent, step-parent, child, step-child, grandchild, brother, step-brother, sister, step-sister, uncle, aunt, niece or nephew of the person or of his spouse shall, for the purposes of this definition, be disregarded.

(2) If the Minister becomes of the opinion that this Act ought to apply to a class of institution for the care and maintenance of persons that it does not apply to, he may by regulations amend the definitions of "nursing home" accordingly and that definition shall have effect in accordance with any regulation for the time being in force under this subsection.

[11.03] The Act contains a prohibition on the "registered proprietor" or the person "in charge" to carry on a nursing home without registration.[6]However there is a period of grace of one year from 1 September 1993 to enable a registered proprietor to register a nursing home where he was carrying on or in charge of the nursing home prior to the commencement of the Act.

---

[6] Section 3.

REGISTRATION

[11.04] Registration is dealt with in s 4 of the Act. Each health board is obliged to maintain a register of nursing homes in its functional area. The public are allowed to inspect the register free of charge. Registration is for a period of three years and once the proprietor is registered he is furnished with a certificate of registration.

WHO CAN APPLY FOR REGISTRATION?

[11.05] Prior to registration a person who wishes to carry on a nursing home must apply for a declaration that he is a "suitable person to carry on a nursing home" and applies to the health board in his functional area. Section 4(8) empowers the health board to attach conditions to the certificate of registration and these are either stated on the certificate or notified in writing to the registered proprietor of the nursing home. The appropriate fee has to be paid.[7] In the event of the registered proprietor not being the person "in charge" then both names are required to be on the certificate.[8] In a situation where a nursing home "continues to be carried on by a person other than the registered proprietor, then the home is no longer registered.[9] Pending registration a nursing home is deemed to be registered.[10]

APPEAL PROCEDURE

[11.06] Where a health board refuses to either (1) give a certificate, or (2) register, a representation may be made to the health board within 21 days. The board is obliged to state its reasons for the refusal in writing. An appeal against the decision is made to the District Court and must be made within 21 days. Section 5 provides that:

> **5** (1) A person, being the registered proprietor or, as the case may be, the person intending to be the registered proprietor, of a nursing home, may appeal to the District Court against a decision of a health board to refuse to register the home, to refuse to give, or to revoke, a declaration under *section 4 (4)*, to remove a home from the register or to attach a condition, or to amend or revoke a condition attached, to the registration of the home and such an appeal shall be brought within 21 days of the receipt by the person of the notification of the decision under section 4 and that court may, as it thinks proper, confirm the decision or direct the health board, as may be appropriate, to register, or to restore the registration of, the home, to give, or to withdraw the revocation of, a declaration under *section 4 (4)*, to withdraw the condition or the amendment to or revocation of a condition, to attach a specified condition to the registration or to make a specified amendment to a condition of the registration.

---

[7] Section 59.
[8] Section 4(11).
[9] Section 4(12)(ii).
[10] Section 4(12).

(2) The jurisdiction conferred on the District Court by this section shall be exercised by the justice of the District Court for the time being assigned to the District Court district in which the nursing home concerned is situated.

(3) A decision of the District Court under this section on a question of fact shall be final.

Note that a further appeal lies only on a point of law.

REGULATIONS FOR THE MAINTENANCE OF PROPER STANDARDS

[11.07] Section 6 of the Act empowers the Minister to make regulations concerning "adequate and suitable accommodation", food and care and the conduct of nursing homes:

6 (1) The Minister shall, for the purpose of ensuring proper standards in relation to nursing homes, including adequate and suitable accommodation, food and care for dependent persons while being maintained in nursing homes, and the proper conduct of nursing homes, make such regulations as he thinks appropriate in relation to nursing homes.

(2) Without prejudice to the generality of *subsection (1)*, regulations under this section may-

(*a*) prescribe requirements as to the maintenance, care, welfare and well-being of dependent persons while being maintained in nursing homes,

(*b*) prescribe requirements as to the numbers, qualifications and availability of members of the staffs (including the medical staffs) of nursing homes,

(*c*) prescribe requirements as to the design, maintenance, repair, cleaning and cleanliness, ventilation, heating and lighting of nursing homes,

(*d*) prescribe requirements as to the accommodation (including the amount of space in bedrooms and wards, the washing facilities and the sanitary conveniences) provided in nursing homes,

(*e*) prescribe requirements as to the food provided for dependent persons while being maintained in nursing homes,

(*f*) prescribe requirements as to the description of nursing homes in written communications by or on behalf of the registered proprietors or the persons in charge of the homes and the display in nursing homes of specified notices,

(*g*) prescribe requirements as to the records to be kept in nursing homes and for the examination and copying of any such records or of extracts therefrom by officers of health boards, (*h*) provide for the effecting by the registered proprietors of nursing homes of contracts of insurance against injury to dependent persons being maintained in the homes while in the homes,

If a health board has reasonable cause to believe that proper care is not being provided for the dependent person, then the Board may provide for the holding and conduct of-

> (i) interviews (including interviews in private) and examinations of dependent persons while being maintained in nursing homes, and
> (ii) interviews (including interviews in private) of persons employed in nursing homes...

The Board may also provide for the inspection of premises in which nursing homes are being carried on or are proposed to be carried on or that are reasonably believed by a health board to be premises in which a nursing home is being carried on and otherwise for the enforcement and execution of the regulations by the appropriate health boards and their officers.

[11.08] Regarding training for staff members the health board may also:

6 (2)(*k*) authorise the provision by the appropriate health boards of training for members of the staffs of nursing homes upon such terms and conditions and to such extent as the health boards may determine,

(*l*) require the provision by the registered owners of nursing homes or, at the option of such owners, by the health boards concerned of specified health services for dependent persons while being maintained in nursing homes..

(*m*) (i) for the consideration and investigation by the health board concerned of a complaint made to it in writing by or on behalf of a dependent person being maintained in a nursing home in relation to any matter concerning the home or the maintenance, care, welfare or well-being of the person while being so maintained or any specified related matter, and

(ii) in case a complaint under *subparagraph (i)* is upheld by a health board, for the issue by the board to the registered proprietor of the nursing home concerned, if the board considers it appropriate to do so, of a direction requiring the taking by such proprietor of specified action in relation to the matter complained of,

(*n*) authorise the provision by or on behalf of the appropriate health boards to nursing homes of such services (being services of a kind provided by or on behalf of health boards for the purposes of their functions), upon such terms and conditions and to such extent as the health boards may determine, and

(*o*) require the provision of specified information to interested persons by the registered owners or the persons in charge of nursing homes in relation to the homes and the accommodation, services and facilities provided for registered persons while being maintained therein.

[11.09] Where a person fails to comply with the Regulations the following applies:

6(3)(*a*) Where, in relation to a nursing home, there is a contravention of a provision of the regulations the registered proprietor and the person in charge of the home shall be guilty of an offence.

(*b*) A person who fails or refuses to comply with a requirement of a direction under the regulations shall be guilty of an offence.

(4)(*a*) Where a person is convicted of an offence under this section, the Circuit Court may, on the application of the health board concerned, brought not more than six months after the conviction or, in the case of an appeal against the conviction, the final determination of it or of any further appeal (if it is a determination affirming the conviction) or the withdrawal of any such appeal therefrom, by order declare that the person shall be disqualified during such period as may be specified in the order for carrying on, being in charge, or concerned with the management, of the nursing home to which the conviction related or, at the discretion of that Court, any nursing home.

(*b*) A person in respect of whom an order is made under this subsection shall not during the period specified in the order carry on, be in charge, or concerned with the management, of the nursing home specified in the order, or if the order so specifies, of any nursing home.

(*c*) A person who contravenes *paragraph (b)* shall be guilty of an offence.

(*d*) Notice of an application under this subsection shall be given to the person convicted of the offence concerned and he shall be entitled to appear, be heard and adduce evidence on the hearing of the application.

(*e*) The jurisdiction conferred on the Circuit Court by this subsection shall be exercised by the judge of the Circuit Court for the time being assigned to the circuit in which the premises concerned are situated.

(5) A person who wilfully obstructs or interferes with a health board or an officer of a health board in the performance of functions under the regulations or who fails or refuses to comply with a requirement of a health board or an officer of a health board under such regulations shall be guilty of an offence.

(6) Regulations under section 2 of the Health (Homes for Incapacitated Persons) Act, 1964. in force immediately before the commencement of this section shall continue in force after such commencement, and may be amended or revoked, as if made under this section.

Nursing Homes (Care and Welfare) Regulations 1993

[11.10] The Nursing Homes (Care and Welfare) Regulations 1993 were brought into force by the Minister for Health to ensure that adequate and suitable care and accommodation are provided for dependent persons in nursing homes. Both the "registered proprietor" and "the person in charge" shall ensure these are complied with. These include such matters as:

1. Contract of care.
2. Nursing care.
3. Personal possessions.
4. Accommodation.
5. Hygiene and sanitation.
6. The keeping of a register and records including staffing records.
7. Inspection.
8. Fire precautions.
9. Extra training facilities for nursing staff.
10. Discharging a dependent person.

These Regulations are legally binding and breach of such may give rise to prosecution.

Contract of Care

[11.11] This contract deals with the care, welfare and services provided in the nursing home and the fees to be charged. Article 7(3) provides that:

> **7.3** Such contract shall deal with the care and welfare of that person in the nursing home and shall include details of the services to be provided for that person and the fees to be charged.

This is to be signed by the dependent person or a person on their behalf. The normal rules of contract apply to the contract.

Nursing Care

[11.12] A high standard of nursing care is required and a minimum of one nurse is required to be on duty at all times. A medical practitioner is to be available for emergencies.

Personal Possessions

[11.13] Provision must be made for the "safe keeping" of personal possessions.

Accommodation

[11.14] Adequate accommodation must be provided in order to ensure the comfort and privacy of persons staying in the nursing home. A minimum level of heating in the bedroom must be maintained at a temperature of 65°F. Emergency call facilities should be provided at each bed.

Hygiene and Sanitation

[11.15] Proper ventilation, prevention of infection, laundry including linen and clothing and sluicing are dealt with under articles 14 and 15. Adequately piped hot and cold water for the provision of baths and showers, properly designed toilets and adequate supply of incontinence sheets and pads must be provided.

Inspection

[11.16] Inspection shall be made by a "designated officer" once every six months. Article 23 provides that:

23.1 The registered proprietor and any member of staff of the nursing home shall:-

(*a*) permit designated officers to enter and inspect the nursing home and shall afford the said officers such facilities and information as they require for that purpose;

(*b*) subject to *article 23.2*,[11] permit designated officers to examine records kept by the nursing home and to obtain copies of any such records or of extracts therefrom;

(*c*) subject to *article 23.3*, permit designated officers to conduct interviews (including interviews in private) with persons (including staff) in the home and to examine any dependent person in the home, where the officer has reasonable cause to believe that a person in the nursing home is not or has not been receiving proper care, maintenance or medical or other treatment;

(*d*) provide facilities for the conducting of interviews and the carrying out of examinations by designated officers.

Only a designated officer is permitted to inspect the medical records or to examine a person in a nursing home.

23.2 Nothing in *article 23.1* authorises any person other than a designated officer who is a medical practitioner to inspect any medical record relating to a person in a nursing home.

23.3 Nothing in *article 23.1* authorises any person other than a designated officer who is a medical practitioner or a registered nurse to carry out an examination of a person in a nursing home.

Fire Precautions

[11.17] Adequate precautions and means of escape and fire drill (dependent persons, as far as is practicable should know the procedure) must be provided for. Article 28 (1) provides that:

---

[11] See SI 379/93.

28.1 In every nursing home there shall be kept in a safe place a record of:-

(*a*) all fire practices which take place at the home;

(*b*) all fire alarm tests carried out at the home together with the result of any such test and the action taken to remedy defects;

(*c*) the number, type and maintenance record of fire-fighting equipment.

28.2 In every nursing home the procedure to be followed in the event of a fire shall be displayed in a prominent place in the nursing home.

DISCHARGE

[11.18] It is necessary to inform the dependent person or a person acting on their behalf fourteen days prior to their discharge. Article 9 provides that:

9 Where the registered proprietor or the person in charge intends discharging a dependent person, they shall inform the person and the person nominated to act on the person's behalf of the date of the proposed discharge, the reasons for the discharge and give fourteen days notice to make alternative arrangements.

For those involved in the operation of a nursing home it is advisable to have a working knowledge of the Regulations.

TEMPORARY MANAGEMENT OF A NURSING HOME

[11.19] Where the person to whom the certificate was issued fails to comply with the regulations as provided in the Act then the Health Board has a statutory power to take charge and manage the home under s 9 of the Act:

9(1) (*a*) Where a health board is of the opinion that, in relation to a nursing home in its functional area, there is a failure to comply with the regulations, it may, with the consent of the registered proprietor of the home or in pursuance of an order of the District Court under *subsection (2)*, take charge of and manage the home and may, for that purpose appoint a person to take charge of and manage the home on its behalf during such period as the health board or the District Court, as may be appropriate, may determine.

(*b*) A person appointed under *paragraph (a)* shall have all such powers as are reasonably required for the purposes of his functions under that paragraph.

(*c*) The registered proprietor of a nursing home and any person in charge of or managing it shall not be in charge of or take part in the management of the home during a period in which a health board or a person appointed by it, is in charge of and managing the home under this section.

(*d*) The amount paid by a health board to a person appointed to it under *paragraph (a)* in respect of the salary of the person payable by the board under the terms of the appointment may, if the board so thinks fit, be recovered by the board from the registered proprietor of the nursing home concerned as a simple contract debt in any court of competent jurisdiction.

(2) (*a*) Where, on application to it in that behalf by a health board, the District Court is satisfied that, in relation to a nursing home in the functional area of the board, there is a failure to comply with the regulations, that Court may make an order (in this subsection referred to subsequently as "a management order") authorising the health board to take charge of and manage the home, and, for that purpose, to appoint such person as the board may determine to manage and take charge of the home on its behalf, during such period, not exceeding three months, as may be specified in the order.

(*b*) An application under *paragraph (a)* may be made either on notice to the registered proprietor of the nursing home concerned or ex parte, but the period specified in a management order made pursuant to an application made ex parte shall not exceed two weeks.

(*c*) A management order may be made from time to time in respect of a particular nursing home.

(*d*) The jurisdiction conferred on the District Court by this subsection shall be exercised by the justice of the District Court for the time being assigned to the District Court district in which the nursing home concerned is situated.

PENALTIES

[11.20] When the person to whom the certificate has issued commits an offence under the Act, s 11 provides:

11 A person guilty of an offence under this Act shall be liable-

(*a*) on summary conviction, to a fine not exceeding £1,000 or to imprisonment for a term not exceeding three months or to both,

(*b*) on conviction on indictment of an offence under section 3, to a fine not exceeding £50,000 or to imprisonment for a term not exceeding two years or to both.

SUMMARY

[11.21] Care of the elderly in Ireland has been neglected over a number of years. The elderly relied on voluntary nursing homes and those who did not have the financial means usually ended up in what were known as the "poorhouses". The Incapacitated Persons Act 1964 went some way towards regulating the standard of care to which they were entitled. The 1990 Act has updated the law on nursing homes and aims to ensure a high standard of care. The Nursing Home Regulations 1993 place a particular emphasis on a range of new responsibilities for nurses employed in nursing homes. An Bord Altranais in their recent report *The Future of Nurse Education and Training in Ireland,*[12] in the light of the evolving patterns of caring for the elderly people, recommends that a greater level of nurse education in the care of the elderly be provided.

---

[12] Published by An Bord Altranais July 1994, see pp. 47-48.

CHAPTER 12

ASSOCIATIONS AND TRADE UNIONS

INTRODUCTION

[12.01] The nursing profession traditionally has been known as the caring profession. However in order to exist within a democratic society, it has been necessary for nurses to form associations and unions to protect their terms and conditions of employment. The following is a list of some of the associations and trade unions pertaining to nurses outlining their history, objectives and aims.[1]

IRISH MATRONS' ASSOCIATION

[12.02] The Irish Matrons' Association enables its members to meet regularly to discuss matters of professional interest. The objectives of the Association are:

(1) To uphold the authority/responsibility of the matron's role within the changing environment of health care.

(2) (a) To study all nurse education programmes and advise An Bord Altranais, the Department of Health and other related bodies, and (b) to ensure continuous dialogue and Tutor colleagues.

(3) (a) To encourage and support nursing colleagues in upholding Christian ethical values and the formation of ethical Committees, and (b) to promote effective nursing/medical liaison in the best interests of patient care.

(4) To ensure effective participation in the planning of any new legislation relevant to the health services generally and nursing in particular.

(5) To influence the direction of the nursing profession within the context of the health care services and to encourage research into nursing practice.

[12.03] The rules regarding membership include the following:

1. The Association shall be formed by hospital matrons, superintendent public health nurses in post, and honorary members, who are registered general trained nurses.

2. On retirement from post, membership will cease and the Secretary should be notified.

---

[1]This information has kindly been submitted by the various associations.

3. The annual subscription is payable at the beginning of each calendar year. The Annual General Meeting is to be held in October each year. Individual members should receive at least 14 days notice of the Annual General Meeting from the Honorary Secretary.

4. Meetings take place on the first Thursday of every alternate month; February, April, June, December. The Annual General Meeting is held in October.

5. The President, Honorary Secretary, Honorary Treasurer shall be elected every two years. The Vice-President shall be invited to serve for the same two year period by the incoming Executive/President. Nominations for officers for election to be sent into the Honorary Secretary one month before the Annual General Meeting. Voting shall take place at the Annual General Meeting.

6. A Standing Committee should be formed to act with the officers for 2 years as observers and spokesmen on matters of interest to the nursing profession, as they arise, and to support colleagues in time of stress and prepare for Conference.

7. Applications for membership shall be made to the Honorary Secretary, for submission to the next meeting. Associate membership will be open to people who are in an acting capacity for at least 6 months.

8. No new rule may be made, nor any standing rule to be rescinded or amended at the Association's Annual General Meeting, and not unless full notice of such proposed alteration, addition or omission shall have been given to every member with the notice convening the meeting.

9. Officers and five members shall form a quorum.

10. Papers may be read, or problems discussed at each meeting subject to be notified to members by the Honorary Secretary.

IRISH NURSING RESEARCH INTEREST GROUP (I.N.R.I.G.)

[12.04] The Irish Nursing Research Interest Group (I.N.R.I.G.) is a voluntary organisation of nurses in Ireland which provides a means by which nurses interested in research in nursing can share their knowledge, ideas and experiences. It provides a forum for the dissemination of research findings and for the discussion of issues concerning nursing, nursing research and related matters. The group also offers resources for nurses undertaking research through the provision of an annual research bursary as well as through the availability of committee members for consultation. I.N.R.I.G. is also concerned with the changes and trends in Irish and international nursing. The group is alert to such changes and trends and frequently contributes through formal submissions to debates on issues relating to ongoing national and international developments.

[12.05] I.N.R.I.G.'s aims are:-

1. To foster an interest in research in nursing in Ireland.
2. To bring together any nurses who are actively engaged in research.
3. To discuss studies published and their application to nursing practice.
4. To provide a forum where nursing is discussed scientifically and experiences and problems can be shared.

[12.06] The group holds 'Research evenings' each month, in which a nursing research paper (research report or literature review) is presented and discussed. The group also organises an annual conference in the Autumn of each year, attracting a country-wide audience to hear papers by national and international speakers. I.N.R.I.G. also publishes a quarterly newsletter (free of charge to members) which contain a chairperson's report, book reviews, conference reports, notices of forthcoming events, a letter page and editorial comment on current and important issues.

IMPACT: THE PUBLIC SECTOR UNION

[12.07] IMPACT the public sector union represents 26,000 members employed in the public and civil service. Members are organised in five divisions - Civil Service, Health, Local Government, Semi-State and Municipal. The largest is the Health and Welfare Division. IMPACT's membership in the health services covers the full range of health professionals, including nurses, and gives IMPACT a special expertise and puts the union in a unique position of influence. A nurses' professional group exists within the union and the union is active in representing the interests of general nurses, midwives and public health nurses. The basic function of IMPACT is to protect and promote the interests of members in accordance with the rules, policies and procedures of the crucial to the role and effectiveness of the union. IMPACT aims to:

1. Protect and improve wages and conditions.
2. Safeguard the interests of members.
3. Ensure receipt of whatever services which are provided for members.
4. Provide information about matters affecting the members and general union matters.
5. Provide for effective participatory and democratic procedures. Nurses, like other members have access to the Union's legal assistance scheme and other benefits.

As a specialist trade union IMPACT has a deep understanding of the needs and problems of the health service and its nursing and professional staff.

THE IRISH NURSES ORGANISATION (I.N.O.)

[12.08] The Irish Nurses Organisation was formed in 1919 by a small group of nurses and midwives. In 1941 they were granted an Excepted Body Licence under the 1941 Trade Union Act, which enabled them to carry on negotiations on behalf of their members. In 1978 their Annual Conference decided that the Organisation should become affiliated to the Irish Congress of Trade Unions. The process of affiliation included the formation of a Union called the Nurses Union of Ireland and the affiliation was completed in January, 1990.

[12.09] Following the affiliation of the union a formal legal process saw the Union change its name to the original Irish Nurses Organisation, which, in effect, means that the Irish Nurses Organisation is now a registered trade union affiliated to the Irish Congress of Trade Unions. The Organisation represents some 14,000 members in all categories of nurses and midwives and in all grades from student nurse to director of nursing. It is well regarded both nationally and internationally as the representative voice of Irish nursing and this is confirmed by the status in which its journal, *The World of Irish Nursing*, is held - the journal is a copyright journal to be found in all copyright libraries of Ireland and the UK. The Organisation is affiliated to the International Council of Nurses, as the sole national nursing association in Ireland (only one Organisation per country may affiliate to I.C.N.) and to the standing committee of nurses of the EU (P.C.N.). The Irish Nurses Organisation has representatives on a wide range of international, European and national committees and actively pursues research and education for its members and the profession generally.

[12.10] Policy is determined at the Annual Delegate Conference and developed and implemented by a twenty-five member executive council which meets monthly (except August). The executive council and membership are serviced by a secretariat which includes a general secretary, deputy general secretary, assistant general secretary, five industrial relations officers, an education and research officer and a recruitment and promotions officer, each of whom is a registered nurse and between all of whom every division of nursing is represented. They in turn are supported by eleven clerical and administrative staff. The Organisation is committed to the advancement of nursing as a profession and a science, and continually up-dates policies and offers members an opportunity to up-date their skills and knowledge with a view to ensuring that the next century will see a more informed, better trained profession which continues to serve a public out of a philosophy of compassion and caring.

S.I.P.T.U. - NURSING

[12.11] The Services Industrial Professional and Technical Union (S.I.P.T.U.) was born in 1990 as the result of a merger of Ireland's largest and oldest unions, the I.T.G.W.U. and the F.W.U.I. The I.T.G.W.U. has represented health care workers since 1917 and both unions have represented nurses for many years. The current nursing membership of SIPTU is 6000. The traditional base of the Union was in the psychiatric services but this changed from the 1970's onwards, notably since the abolition of the marriage bar. Now although SIPTU still represents a majority of psychiatric nurses, they constitute a minority within the overall nursing membership of the Union. Despite the fact that at 200,000 members, SIPTU represents one in three of all Irish workers, nurses have a distinct identity and decision-making structure within the Union. Known as the National Nursing Council, a series of national committees backed-up by a staff of four at national level, guide and support the activities of the thirty nursing branches throughout the Republic of Ireland. Apart from the full range of trade union, professional and legal services to members, the Union also offer scholarships to members and their children, education and training services, specialist advice on equality matters and other benefits. The Union's membership is represented on many trade union and professional bodies, including An Bord Altranais and it holds the Irish seat on the European Committee on Nurse Training.

SUMMARY

[12.12] The above is a short list of unions to which nurses have affiliated themselves. It must be said that these associations have shown over the years that they have sought to work in the best interests of the nursing profession in regards to the upgrading of terms and conditions of employment and in negotiating wage agreements on their behalf. Membership of a trade union will protect a nurse in her workplace.

APPENDIX

SAMPLE CONSENT FORM

I..of ....

.... hereby consent to

(undergo
*

(the submission of my   *(child .... to undergo)

                             (ward   )

the operation of ....

the nature and purpose of which have been explained to me by

Dr./*Mr ....

I also consent to such further or alternative operative measures as may be found necessary during the course of the above-mentioned operation and to the administration of general, local or other anaesthetics for any of these purposes.

No assurance has been given to me that the operation will be performed by any particular practitioner.

Date.. Signed...

                                    (PATIENT/PARENT/GUARDIAN/NEXT OF KIN)*

                          Witness..

I confirm that I have explained the nature and purpose of this operation to the patient/parent/ guardian/next of kin.*

Date.. Signed...
                                     (MEDICAL PRACTITIONER)

*DELETE AS APPROPRIATE

<u>ANY DELETIONS, INSERTIONS OR AMENDMENTS TO THE FORM ARE TO BE MADE BEFORE THE EXPLANATION IS GIVEN AND THE FORM SUBMITTED FOR SIGNATURE.</u>

NURSES ACT 1985

PART V

Inquiry by the Fitness to Practise Committee into the conduct of a nurse

38 (1) The Board or any person may apply to the Fitness to Practise Committee for an inquiry into the fitness of a nurse to practise nursing on the grounds of-

(a) alleged professional misconduct, or

(b) alleged unfitness to engage in such practice by reason of physical or mental disability,

and the application shall, subject to the provisions of this Act, be considered by the Fitness to Practise Committee.

(2) Where an application is made under this section and the Fitness to Practise Committee, after consideration of the application, is of opinion that there is not sufficient cause to warrant the holding of an inquiry, it shall so inform the Board and the Board, having considered the matter, may decide that no further action shall be taken in relation to the matter and shall so inform the Committee and the applicant, or it may direct the Committee to hold an inquiry into the matter in accordance with the provisions of this section.

(3)Where an application for an inquiry is made under this section and the Fitness to Practise Committee, after consideration of the application, is either of opinion that there is a prima facie case for holding the inquiry or has been given a direction by the Board pursuant to *subsection (2)* of this section to hold the inquiry, the following shall have effect-

(a) the Committee shall proceed to hold the inquiry,

(b) the Chief Executive Officer, or any other person with the leave of the Fitness to Practise Committee, shall present to the Committee the evidence of alleged professional misconduct or unfitness to practise by reason of physical or mental disability, as the case may be,

(c) on completion of the inquiry, the Fitness to Practise Committee shall embody its findings in a report to the Board specifying therein the nature of the application and the evidence laid before it and any other matters in relation to the nurse which it may think fit to report including its opinion, having regard to the contents of the report, as to-

(i) the alleged professional misconduct of the nurse, or

(ii) the fitness or otherwise of that nurse to engage in the practice of nursing by reason of alleged physical or mental disability,

as the case may be

(4) When it is proposed to hold an inquiry under *subsection (3)* of this section the person who is the subject of the inquiry shall be given notice in writing by the Chief Executive Officer sent by pre-paid post to the address of that person as stated in the register of the nature of the evidence proposed to be considered at the inquiry and that person and any person representing him shall be given the opportunity of being present at the hearing.

(5) The findings of the Fitness to Practise Committee on any matter referred to it and the decision of the Board on any report made to it by the Fitness to Practise Committee shall not be made public without the consent of the person who has been the subject of the inquiry before the Fitness to Practise Committee unless such person has been found, as a result of such inquiry to be:

(*a*) guilty of professional misconduct, or

(*b*) unfit to engage in the practice of nursing because of physical or mental disability,

as the case may be.

(6) The Fitness to Practise Committee shall be for the purpose of an inquiry held under *subsection (3)* of this section have the powers, rights and privileges vested in the High Court or a judge thereof on the hearing of an action in respect of-

(*a*) the enforcement of the attendance of witnesses and their examination on oath or otherwise, and

(*b*) the compelling of the production of documents,

and a summons signed by the Chairman of the Committee or by such other member of the Committee as may be authorised by the Committee for that purpose may be substituted for and shall be equivalent to any formal procedure capable of being issued in an action for enforcing the attendance of witnesses and compelling the production of documents.

(7) Where-

(*a*) a person on being duly summoned to attend before the Fitness to Practise Committee makes default in attending, or

(*b*) a person, being in attendance as a witness before the Fitness to Practise Committee, refuses to take an oath lawfully required by the Fitness to Practise Committee to be taken, or to produce any document in his power or control lawfully required by the Fitness to Practise Committee to be produced by him or to answer any question to which the Fitness to Practise Committee may lawfully require an answer, or

(*c*) a person, being in attendance before the Fitness to Practise Committee, does anything which, if the Fitness to Practise Committee were a court of law having power to commit for contempt, would be contempt of court,

such person shall be guilty of an offence and shall be liable on summary conviction to a fine not exceeding £1,000.

(8) A witness before the Fitness to Practise Committee shall be entitled to the same immunities and privileges as if he were a witness before the High Court.

Erasure or suspension of registration from register for professional misconduct, unfitness to practise or failure to pay retention fee

39(1) Where a nurse-

(*a*) has been found, by the Fitness to Practise Committee, on the basis of an inquiry and report pursuant to *section 38* of this Act, to be guilty of professional misconduct or to be unfit to engage in the practice of nursing because of physical or mental disability, or

(*b*) has failed to pay a retention fee charged by the Board after the Board had, not less than two months previously by notice in writing sent by pre-paid post to the person, at his address as stated in the register, requested payment of the fee on more than one occasion,

the Board may decide that the name of such person should be erased from the register or that, during a period of specified duration, registration of the person's name in the register should not have effect.

(2) On making a decision under this section, the Board shall forthwith send by pre-paid post to the person to whom the decision relates, at his address as stated in the register, a notice in writing stating the decision, the date thereof and the reasons therefor.

(3) A person to whom a decision under this section relates may, within the period of 21 days beginning on the date of the decision, apply to the High Court for cancellation of the decision and if he so applies-

(*a*) the High Court, on the hearing of the application, may-

(i) cancel the decision, or

(ii) declare that it was proper for the Board to make a decision under this section in relation to such person and either (as the Court may consider proper) direct the Board to erase such person's name from the register or direct that during a specified period (beginning not earlier than 7 days after the decision of the Court) registration of the person's name in the register shall not have effect, or

(iii) give such other directions to the Board as the Court thinks proper,

(b) if at any time the Board satisfies that such person has delayed unduly in proceeding with the application, the High Court shall, unless it sees good reason to the contrary, declare that it was proper for the Board to make a decision under this section in relation to such person and either (as the Court may consider proper) direct the Board to erase the person's name from the register or direct that during a specified period (beginning not earlier than 7 days after the decision of the Court) registration of the person's name in the register shall not have effect,

(c) the High Court may direct how the costs of the application are to be borne.

(4) Where a person to whom a decision of the Board under this section relates does not, within the period of 21 days beginning on the date of the decision, apply to the High Court for confirmation of the decision, the Board may apply *ex parte* to the High Court for confirmation of the decision, and, if the Board so applies, the High Court, on the hearing of the application shall, unless it see good reason to the contrary, declare accordingly and either (as the Court may consider proper) direct the Board to erase the name of such person from the register or direct that during a specified period (beginning not earlier than 7 days after the decision of the Court) registration of the person's name in the register shall not have effect.

(5) The decision of the High Court on an application under this section shall be final, save that, by leave of that Court or the Supreme Court, an appeal, by the Board or the person concerned, from the decision shall lie to the Supreme Court on a specified question of law.

(6)
  (*a*) On erasing the name of a person from the register under this section, the Board shall forthwith send by pre-paid post to such person, at his address as stated in the register, notice in writing of the erasure.

  (*b*) Where a direction is given under this section that during a specified period registration of the name of a person in the register shall not have effect, the Board shall, before the commencement of that period, send by pre-paid post to such person, at his address as stated in the register, notice in writing of such direction.

(7) The name of any person which has been erased from the register under this section may at any time be restored to that register by direction of the Board but not otherwise, and when a person's name is so restored to that register, the Board may attach to the restoration such conditions (including the payment of a fee not exceeding the fee which would be payable by such person for registration if he was then being registered for the first time) as the Board thinks fit.

(8) Where the registration of a person in the register has ceased to have effect under this section for a period of specified duration, the Board may, if it so thinks fit, on application made to it by such person, by direction terminate the suspension.

(9) On the hearing of an application under this section, the High Court may, if it thinks proper to do so, admit and have regard to evidence of any person of standing in the nursing profession as to what is professional misconduct.

Attaching of conditions to retention on register

40 (1) The Board, following an inquiry and report by the Fitness to Practise Committee pursuant to *section 38* of this Act, may decide to attach such conditions as it thinks fit to the retention in the register of a person whose name is entered in the register.

(2) On making a decision under this section, the Board shall forthwith send by pre-paid post to the person to whom the decision relates, at his address as stated in the register, a notice in writing stating the decision, the date thereof and the reasons therefor.

(3) A person to whom a decision under this section relates may, within the period of 21 days beginning on the date of the decision, apply to the High Court for cancellation of the decision and if he so applies -

(*a*) the High Court, on the hearing of the application, may-

(i) cancel the decision, or

(ii) declare that it was proper for the Board to make a decision under this section in relation to such person and either (as the Court may consider proper) direct the Board to attach such conditions as the Court thinks fit to the retention of the name of such person in the register, or

(iii) give such other directions to the Board as the Court thinks proper,

(*b*) if at any time the Board satisfies the High Court that such person has delayed unduly in proceeding with application, the High Court shall, unless it sees good reason to the contrary, declare that it was proper for the Board to make a decision under this section in relation to such person and (as the Court may consider proper) direct the Board to attach such conditions as the Court may specify to the retention of the name of such person in the register,

(*c*) the High Court may direct how the costs of the application are to be borne.

(4) Where a person to whom a decision of the Board under this section relates does not within the period of 21 days beginning on the date of the decision, apply *ex parte* to the High Court for confirmation of the decision and, if the Board so applies, the High Court, on the hearing of the application shall, unless it sees good reason to the contrary, declare accordingly and as the Court may consider proper) direct the Board to attach such conditions as the Court may specify to the retention of the name of such person on the register.

(5) The decision of the High Court on an application under this section shall be final save that, by leave of the Court or the Supreme Court, an appeal by the Board or the person concerned from the decision shall lie to the Supreme Court on a specified question of law.

(6) On attaching conditions under this section to the retention of the name of a person on the register, the Board shall forthwith send by pre-paid post to such person, at his address as stated in the register, notice in writing of the conditions.

(7) The Board may at any time remove in whole or in part the conditions attached to the retention of the name of any person on the register.

Powers of the Board to advise, admonish, etc.

41 (1) The Board, following an inquiry and report by the Fitness to Practise Committee pursuant to *section 38* of this Act into the conduct of a person whose name is entered in the register may, on receipt of the report of the Committee, if it so thinks fit, advise, admonish or censure such person in relation to his professional conduct.

(2) The powers conferred by *subsection (1)* of this section may be exercised either in addition to or in substitution for any of the powers conferred by *sections 39, 40 and 42* of this Act.

Erasure from register of persons convicted of indictable offences

42 (1) Where a nurse is convicted in the State of an offence triable on indictment or is convicted outside the State of an offence consisting of acts or omissions which would constitute an offence triable on indictment if done or made in the State, the Board may decide that the name of such person should be erased from the register.

(2) On making a decision under this section, the Board shall forthwith send by pre-paid post to the person to whom the decision relates, at his address as stated in the register, a notice in writing stating the decision, the date thereof and the reasons therefor.

(3) A person to whom a decision under this section relates may, within the period of twenty-one days, beginning on the date of the decision, apply to the High Court for cancellation of the decision and if such person so applies-

(*a*) the High Court, on the hearing of the application, may-

(i) cancel the decision, or

(ii) confirm the decision and direct the Board to erase the name of such person from the register, or

(iii) give such other directions to the Board as the Court thinks proper,

(*b*) if at any time the Board satisfies the High Court that such person has delayed unduly in proceeding with the application, the High Court shall, unless it sees

good reason to the contrary, confirm the decision and direct the Board to erase the name of such person from the register,

(*c*) the High Court may direct how the costs of the application are to be borne.

(4) Where a person to whom a decision of the Board under this section relates does not within the period of twenty-one days, beginning on the date of the decision, apply to the High Court for cancellation of the decision, the Board may apply *ex parte* to the High Court for confirmation of the decision and, if the Board so applies, the High Court, on the hearing of the application, shall, unless it sees good reason to the contrary, confirm the decision and direct the Board to erase the name of such person from the register.

(5) The decision of the High Court on an application under this section shall be final, save that by leave of that Court or the Supreme Court, an appeal, by the Board or the person concerned, from the decision shall lie to the Supreme Court on a specified question of law.

(6) On erasing the name of a person from the register under this section, the Board shall forthwith send by pre-paid post to such person, at his address as stated in the register, notice in writing of the erasure.

(7) The name of any person which has been erased from the register under this section may at any time be restored to the register by direction of the Board but not otherwise, and when a person's name is so restored to the register, the Board may attach to the restoration such conditions (including the payment of a fee not exceeding the fee which would be payable by such person if he was then being registered for the first time) as the Board thinks fit.

Continuance of existing inquiry

43 Where the former Board has decided to hold, or has appointed any member or members of that Board to hold, an inquiry pursuant to the Nurses Act, 1950, and that inquiry has not been completed before the commencement of this Act, the inquiry shall be discontinued and shall be recommenced by the Fitness to Practise Committee as if this Act had been in force at the time at which such decision was taken or such member or members were appointed and the provisions of this Part of this Act shall apply to any inquiry discontinued and recommenced pursuant to this section.

Application by Board for order suspending registration

44 (1) Whenever the Board is satisfied that it is in the public interest so to do, the Board may apply to the High Court for an order in relation to any person registered in the register that, during the period specified in the order, registration of that person's name in the register shall not have effect.

(2) An application under this section may be made in a summary manner and shall be heard otherwise than in public.

(3) The High Court may make, in any application under this section, such interim or interlocutory order (if any) as it considers appropriate.

Privilege in respect of certain matters

45 Proceedings under *section 38* of this Act, proceedings of or communications to or by the Board pursuant to *sections 39, 40, 41* and *42* of this Act, reports made by the Fitness to Practise Committee to the Board under this Part of this Act and any other communications between the Committee and the Board made in the exercise or performance of the powers, duties or functions of the Committee or the Board, as the case may be, shall in any action for defamation, be absolutely privileged.

Notification to Minister of name erased or restored and of suspensions imposed and terminated

46 The Board shall notify the Minister, and, in the case of a person the name of whose employer is known to the Board, such employer, on the occasion of-

(*a*) the erasure of the name of a person from the register,

(*b*) the restoration of the name of a person to the register,

(*c*) the suspension of the name of a person from the register,

(*d*) the termination of a period of suspension from the register, or

(*e*) the attachment of conditions to the retention of the name of a person on the register,

of the erasure, restoration, suspension, termination of suspension or attachment of conditions, as the case may be.

Restoration to register of name removed or termination of suspension for non-payment of retention fee

47 (1) The Board shall, on the payment of a special fee to the Board by any person whose name was erased or whose registration was suspended pursuant to *section 39(1)(b)* of this Act from the register for non-payment of a retention fee (and for no other reason) restore the person's name to the register or terminate the suspension, as the case may be.

(2) In this section "special fee" means a fee of such amount as may be fixed from time to time by the Board with the consent of the Minister.

THE CODE OF PROFESSIONAL CONDUCT FOR EACH NURSE AND MIDWIFE

(An Bord Altranais, January 1988)

Definition

"**Patient**" - the use of the word patient in the code is to be broadly interpreted as individuals or groups who have contact with the nurse in his/her capacity and does not necessarily denote or imply ill health.

"**Nurse**"- where used in the code, the word nurse shall have the meaning assigned to it in the Nurses Act 1985. The word "nurse" means a person registered in the Live Register of Nurses as provided for in section 27 of the Nurses Act 1985 and includes a midwife and nursing includes midwifery

An Bord Altranais is the statutory body which provides for the registration, control and education of nurses and for other matters relating to nurses and the practise of nursing. It sees its overall responsibility to be in the interest of the public.

The purpose of this code is to provide a framework to assist the nurse to make professional decisions, to carry out his/her responsibilities, and to promote high standards of professional conduct.

This code provides guidelines. Specific issues will be considered, when they arise or may be the subject of interpretative statements to be issued from time to time by An Bord. An Bord shall take appropriate action as defined in Part V of the Nurses Act 1985 where nurses fail to meet the following requirements.

The nursing profession demands a high standard of professional behaviour from its members and each registered nurse is accountable for his or her practice.

The aim of the nursing profession is to give the highest standard of care possible to patients. Any circumstances which could place patients/clients in jeopardy or which militate against safe standards of practice, should be made known to appropriate persons or authorities.

Information regarding a patient's history, treatment and state of health is privileged and confidential. It is accepted nursing practice that nursing care is communicated and recorded as part of the patient's care and treatment. Professional judgment and responsibility should be exercised in the sharing of such information with professional colleagues. The confidentiality of patients' records must be safeguarded. In certain circumstances, the nurse may be required by a court of law to divulge information held. A nurse called to give evidence in court should seek in advance legal and/or professional advice as to the response to be made if required by the court to divulge confidential information.

The nurse must uphold the trust of those who allow him/her privileged access to their property, home or workplace.

It is appropriate to highlight the potential dangers to confidentiality of computers and electronic processing in the field of health services administration.

It is necessary for patients to have appropriate information for making an informed judgment. Every effort should be made to ensure that a patient understands the nature and purpose of their care and treatment. In certain circumstances there may be a doubt whether certain information should be given to a patient and special care should be taken in such cases.

Any form of sexual advance to a patient with whom there exists a professional relationship will be regarded as professional misconduct.

The nurse must acknowledge any limitations of competence and refuse in such cases to accept delegated functions without first having received instruction in regard to those functions and having been assessed as competent.

A nurse shall be entitled to make known at the earliest possible opportunity to an appropriate person or authority any conscientious objection which may be relevant to professional practice.

The nurse shares the responsibility of care with colleagues and must have regard to the workload of and the pressures on professional colleagues and subordinates and take appropriate action if these are seen to be such as to constitute abuse of the individual practitioner and/or to jeopardise safe standards of practice.

Each nurse has a continuing responsibility to junior colleagues. He/she is obliged to transmit acquired professional knowledge, skills and attitudes both by word and example. The nurse must not delegate to junior colleagues tasks and responsibilities beyond their skill and experience.

The nurse is responsible for the overall care provided by students. The nurse's responsibility in transmitting knowledge, skills and attitudes and in maintaining standards of care extends to student nurses wherever their learning activity occurs.

The nurse shall work in close co-operation with members of the health professions and others in promoting community and national efforts to meet the health needs of the public.

The nurse must at all times maintain the principle that every effort should be made to preserve human life, both born and unborn. When death is imminent, care should be taken to ensure that the patient dies with dignity.

When making public statements, the nurse shall make it clear whether he/she is acting in a personal capacity on or behalf of the profession.

The nurse should avoid the use of professional qualifications in the promotion of commercial products in order not to compromise the independence of professional judgment.

The nurse should not accept any gifts or favours from patients/relatives which could reasonably be interpreted as seeking to exert undue influence or to obtain preferential treatment.

The nurse must at all times take reasonable precautions to ensure that from the point of view of his/her health, he/she is competent to carry out his/her duties. Abuse of alcohol or other drugs adversely affects that competence.

In taking part in research, the principles of confidentiality and the provision of appropriate information to enable an informed judgment to be made by the patient, must be safeguarded. The nurse has an obligation to ascertain that the research is sanctioned by the appropriate body and to ensure that the rights of the patient are protected at all times. The nurse should be aware of ethical policies and procedures in his/her area of practice.

NURSES RULES 1988

(An Bord Altranais)

Made under the Nurses Act 1985

An Bord Altranais in exercise of the powers conferred on it by sections 26, 27, 28, 31, 32 and 33 of the Nurses Act 1985, hereby makes the following rules:-

PART 1 - PRELIMINARY

Citation

1. These rules may be cited as the Nurses Rules, 1988.

2. In these rules, unless the context otherwise requires, the following expressions have the meanings respectively assigned to them-

"The Act" means the Nurses Act 1985 (No. 18 of 1985).
"The Board" means An Bord Altranais established under the Act.
"Chief Executive Officer" means the person who is for the time being acting as Chief Executive Officer of the Board and includes any person duly authorised to act and acting on his behalf.
"The Minister" means the Minister for Health.
"The register" means the register of nurses maintained by the Board pursuant to the provisions of s 27 of the Act.
" Registered nurse" means a person whose name is entered in the register and includes a midwife.
"registered general nurse", or
"registered psychiatric nurse", or
"registered sick children's nurse", or
"registered mental handicap nurse", or
"registered midwife", or
"registered public health nurse", or
"registered nurse tutor"
means a person whose name is entered in the relevant division of the register as provided for in *Rule 3*.

PART II – THE REGISTER

3.1 The Nurses (Registration) Rules 1988 are hereby revoked.

3.2 Subject to the provisions of *Rule 11* the Register of nurses maintained by the Board in accordance with *section 27* of the Act shall be divided into the following divisions:

(i) The General Nurses Division containing the names of persons admitted to the

Register as qualified and competent to practise as Registered General Nurses (Abbreviation R.G.N.)

(ii) The Psychiatric Nurses Division containing the names of persons admitted to the Register as qualified and competent to practise as Registered Psychiatric Nurses (Abbreviation R.P.N.)

(iii) The Sick Children's Nurses Division containing the names of persons admitted to the Register as qualified and competent to practise as Registered Children's Nurses (Abbreviation R.S.C.N.)

(iv) The Mental Handicap Nurses Division containing the names of persons admitted to the Register as qualified and competent to practise as Registered Mental Handicap Nurses (Abbreviation R.M.H.N.)

(v) The Midwives Division containing the names of persons admitted to the Register as qualified and competent to practise as Registered Midwives (Abbreviation R.M.)

(vi) The Public Health Nurse Division containing the names of persons admitted to the Register as qualified and competent to practise as Registered Public Health Nurses (Abbreviation R.P.H.N.)

(vii) The Nurse Tutors Division containing the names of persons admitted to the Register as qualified and competent to practise as Registered Nurse Tutors (Abbreviation R.N.T.)

3.3 The Board may register a person in more than one division of the register if such person applies and satisfies the prescribed conditions for registration in each such division.

3.4 The abbreviations shown in *paragraph 2* of this rule shall be used to designate nurses registered in such divisions.

3.5 The Board shall register in the appropriate division of the register the name of every person who has applied for registration, has paid the appropriate registration fee and who has satisfied the Board that such person complies with the prescribed conditions for registration.

3.6 Before admission to any division of the register an applicant, unless entitled to be registered under any Directive adopted by the Council of the European Communities, shall:

(a) have completed to the satisfaction of the Board the prescribed course of training for that division in a hospital or institution approved by the Board under section 34 of the Act for that purpose and have passed the examinations prescribed by the Board, or

(b) notwithstanding the provisions of *Rule 4* if the training of the person applying for registration took place outside the State, satisfy the Board that such training was adequate and that she is competent to practise in the discipline of nursing in which registration is being sought.

3.7 Subject to *paragraph 6* of this rule the Board may grant temporary registration for periods of specific duration.

3.8 In considering an application for registration the Board shall be entitled to require such evidence as it sees fit in relation to the applicant's training, character, age, health or any other matter relevant to the application as will enable the Board to determine the application, always provided that in the case of an application from a national of a Member State of the European Communities whose training took place in a Member State other than the State the application is dealt with in accordance with any relevant Directive of the European Communities and is accompanied by an appropriate certificate from the competent authority in the State in which training took place and the fee from time to time determined by the Board with the consent of the Minister in accordance with section 25(*a*) and (*d*) of the Act.

3.9 Each division of the register shall show in respect of each person admitted to that division the following particulars-

(a) date of registration;

(b) a personal identification number which will be assigned to each registered nurse;

(c) full names;

(d) address;

(e) nursing qualifications other than those required for registration in that division and which are recognised by the Board as appropriate for entry in the register;

(f) details of training leading to registration in that division.

3.10 (a) Continued registration of each person admitted to the register shall be subject to the payment of the appropriate retention fee.

(b) The retention fee shall become payable on the 1st day of January in respect of each calendar year following the year in which the initial registration takes place except that in cases where initial registration takes place between 1st September and 31st December the retention fee shall not be payable in respect of the calendar year immediately following such registration.

PART III – TRAINING AND EDUCATION

4. Training courses leading to registration

4.1 Subject to *paragraph 5* of this Rule the period of training required for admission to the General Nurses Division of the Register shall be not less than three years training in accordance with the syllabus of training approved by the Board for that purpose and the training shall be carried out in a hospital or institution approved by the Board for the training of General Nurses.

4.2 Subject to *paragraph 5* of this Rule the period of training required for admission to the Psychiatric Nurses Division of the Register shall be not less than three years training in accordance with the syllabus of training approved by the Board for that purpose and the training shall be carried out in a hospital or institution approved by the Board for the training of Psychiatric Nurses.

4.3 Subject to *paragraph 5* of this Rule the period of training required for admission to the Sick Children's Nurses Division of the Register shall be not less than three years training in accordance with the syllabus of training approved by the Board for that purpose and the training shall be carried out in a hospital or institution approved by the Board for the training of Sick Children's Nurses.

4.4 Subject to *paragraph 5* of this Rule the period of training required for admission to the Mental Handicap Nurses Division of the Register shall be not less than three years training in accordance with the syllabus of training approved by the Board for that purpose and the training shall be carried out in a hospital or institution approved by the Board for the training of Mental Handicap Nurses.

4.5 In the case of a person whose name is already entered in one of the Divisions referred to in *paragraphs 1, 2, 3 and 4* of this Rule and who wishes to be registered in one of the other Divisions referred to in those paragraphs, the period of training shall be not less than eighteen months in accordance with the syllabus approved by the Board for such shortened period of training for that other Division and the training shall be carried out in a hospital or institution approved by the Board for that purpose.

4.6 The period of training required for admission to the Midwives Division of the Register shall be not less than two years training in accordance with the syllabus of training approved by the Board for that purpose and the training shall be carried out in a hospital or institution approved by the Board for that purpose.

4.7 The period of training required for admission to the Public Health Nurses Division of the Register shall be not less than one year's training in accordance with the syllabus of training approved by the Board for that purpose and the training shall be carried out in a hospital or institution approved by the Board for that purpose.

4.8 The period of training required for admission to the Tutors Division of the Register shall be not less than two years training in accordance with the syllabus of training approved by the Board for that purpose and the training shall be carried out in a hospital or institution approved by the Board for that purpose.

4.9 Notwithstanding the foregoing provisions of this Rule the Board may approve proposals from approved hospitals or institutions to provide an integrated course of training of not less than four years' duration leading to registration in the General Nurses Division and the Psychiatric Nurses Division or the Sick Children's Division.

5. Requirements for admission to training

5.1 Before admission to the courses of training of not less than three years duration leading to the registration in either

(i) the General Nurses Division, or

(ii) the Psychiatric Nurses Division, or

(iii) the Sick Children's Nurses Division, or

(iv) the Mental Handicap Nurses Division

the candidates for registration must

(a) in the Post-Primary Leaving Certificate Examination have obtained -

- a minimum of two C's in higher papers and four D's in ordinary papers in the following subjects:

- Irish (unless exempted by the Department of Education)

- English

- Mathematics

- a Science subject - as listed by the Department of Education in its Science and Applied Science list

- two other subjects. In the case of a candidate exempted from Irish three other subjects

or

have achieved equivalent educational attainments to the foregoing, such equivalents to be adjudicated on by the Higher Education Authority (established under the Higher Education Authority Act 1971)

or

in the case of a candidate, who is twenty four years of age or over on the 15th of October of the year of application, satisfy the approved hospital or institution concerned of her suitability for nurse training;

(b) be at least seventeen years of age on the 1st day of June of the year of application.

5.2 The Leaving Certificate or equivalent results referred to in the previous paragraph may be accumulated over not more than two sittings of the Leaving Certificate Examination or equivalent.

5.3 Before admission to the course of training leading to registration in the Midwives

Division of the Register the name of the candidate for registration must already be entered in the General Nurses Division of the Register.

5.4 Before admission to the course of training leading to registration in the Public Health Nurses Division of the Register the name of the candidate for registration must already be entered in the General Nurses Division of the Register and in the Midwives Register and the candidate must have two years experience in General nursing or Midwifery practice.

5.5 Before admission to the course of training leading to registration in the Tutors Division of the Register the applicant's name must already be entered in one of the other Divisions of the Register.

6. Approval of hospitals and institutions for training purposes

6.1 A hospital or institution proposing to provide a course of training leading to registration in any Division of the Register shall apply to the Board for approval and in this connection shall supply to the Board full details of how it is proposed to implement it. Such details shall include:

- a full description of its training facilities,

- the amount of experience each nurse in training is assured,

- details of training to be provided in other hospitals, institutions, or community services,

- particulars of teachers and lecturers including their qualifications,

- details of educational facilities available at all centres where training will take place,

- evidence of systematic arrangements whereby the attendance of each nurse in training at a series of lectures as required under the Board's syllabus for such training is assured.

6.2 Before granting approval to a hospital or institution the Board shall satisfy itself both in regard to the hospital or institution and its associated bodies in which training is to be carried out

(a) that an adequate quantity and quality of clinical material is available;

(b) that the educational facilities for the nurses in training are adequate;

(c) that the levels of teaching staff and lecturers and their qualifications are adequate;

(d) that the practice of Nursing is of such a standard as to satisfy the Board;

(e) that the accommodation is of a satisfactory standard.

6.3 Before a hospital or institution is granted approval it will be inspected by representatives of the Board.

6.4 The Matron or Director of Nursing or Chief Nursing Officer in a training hospital or institution shall supply to the Board such details, as may be required by the Board, of any person accepted for training.

EXAMINATIONS

7. Registration

7.1 The Board shall hold examinations for the purpose of determining whether candidates are qualified for registration in the General Nurses Division, the Psychiatric Nurses Division, the Sick Children's Nurses Division or the Mental Handicap Nurses Division of the Register. Such examinations may consist of:-

• Continuous assessment to establish proficiency in clinical nursing skills;

• Written examinations;

• Oral examinations.

7.2 Not earlier than 11 calendar months after entry to training, the Board shall hold the Registration (Part 1) Examination (written) which must be successfully completed before the candidate may proceed to the second year of training. A period of two years must elapse between the successful completion of the Registration (Part 1) Examination (written) and the candidate's first attempt at the written part of the Registration examination.

7.3 Before entry to the written examinations, the candidates shall be required to:-

(i) apply to the Board on the appropriate entry form for entry to the examination;

(ii) pay the appropriate entry fee to the Board;

(iii) submit a certificate signed by the Matron or Director of Nursing or Chief Nursing Officer and the Principal Tutor or Tutor of the approved hospital or institution concerned certifying that the candidate is proficient in the relevant clinical nursing skills;

(iv) submit a certificate signed by the Matron or Director of Nursing or Chief Nursing Officer and the Principal Tutor or Tutor of the approved hospital or institution concerned certifying that the candidate has received the theoretical, technical and clinical instruction required by the syllabus for entry to the written part of the relevant examination.

7.4 Registration (Part 1) Examinations and Registration Examinations will normally be held once a year and may be held more frequently if training courses commence at different times in the same year or for the purpose of repeat examinations.

7.5 In the case of a Registration (Part 1) Examination

(i) a candidate who fails to obtain a Certificate of Proficiency in Clinical Nursing Skills will be allowed a second attempt before the next successive Registration (Part 1) Examination and failure at the second attempt will result in training being discontinued and the candidate may not proceed to the written examination;

(ii) a candidate who is not successful at the written examination will be allowed one further attempt which must, except in cases of hardship, be made at the next Registration (Part 1) Examination (written). Failure at the second attempt will result in training being discontinued.

7.5 In the case of a Registration Examination

(i) a candidate who fails to obtain a Certificate of Proficiency in Clinical Nursing Skills required for a Registration Examination shall be permitted two further successive attempts to obtain such certificate for subsequent Registration Examinations, and if still unsuccessful after three attempts, training will be discontinued and the candidate shall not proceed to any further such Examination;

(ii) a candidate who is unsuccessful in the written/oral examination shall be allowed two further attempts at successive written/oral Registration examinations, and if still unsuccessful after three attempts, training will be discontinued and the candidate shall not proceed to any further such Examination.

7.7 Candidates who are considered proficient in clinical nursing skills shall receive their certificates not later than eight weeks before the written element of the Registration (Part 1) or Registration Examinations as the case may be, and a candidate who is refused a certificate can appeal against such refusal in writing by registered post to reach the Board not later than six weeks before the written part of the examination. On consideration of such appeal, the Board shall convey its decision to the candidate and the hospital or institution concerned and the Board's decision will be final.

7.8 A candidate, who considers that the result of the written element of the Registration (Part 1) or Registration Examination does not accurately reflect her performance in such Examination, may appeal to the Board for a re-examination of one or more of the papers involved. An application for re-examination of any of papers, accompanied by the appropriate fee, must be forwarded by the candidate concerned by registered post to reach the Board not later than fourteen days after the issue of the examination result.

7.9 In order to be successful in any examination, a candidate must obtain at least 50% of the marks allotted for each subject of the examination, and where an oral examination forms part of an examination, a candidate must obtain at least 50% of the aggregate marks allotted for both the written and the oral elements of each subject of the examination. With effect from the 1st day of January 1989 the aggregation of marks between the written and oral elements will be subject to the candidate having obtained a minimum of 45% in each element of the examination. Honours shall he awarded to candidates achieving an overall mark of 70%.

7.10 A person whose name is already registered in one of the divisions of the Register and who is a candidate for registration in one of the other divisions referred to in paragraph 1 of this rule shall not be required to take the Registration (Part 1) Examination.

8. Registration in the Midwives Division

8.1 The Board shall hold examinations for the purpose of determining whether candidates are qualified for registration in the Midwives Division of the Register and such examinations shall consist of:-

- Continuous assessment to establish proficiency in clinical midwifery skills;
- a written examination;
- an oral examination.

8.2 In the eighth calendar month after commencement of training, the candidate shall be required to:-

(i) apply to the Board on the appropriate entry form for entry to the examination;

(ii) pay the appropriate entry fee to the Board.

8.3 (i) When a period of nine calendar months training has been completed, the candidate shall be required to obtain and submit a certificate (First Certificate) signed by the Matron or Director of Nursing and Principal Tutor or Tutor of the approved hospital or institution concerned, certifying that the candidate is proficient in clinical midwifery skills.

(ii) A candidate who fails to obtain the First Certificate of Proficiency in Clinical Midwifery Skills, after the completion of nine calendar months training, shall be allowed a second attempt before the completion of twelve calendar months training. Failure to obtain the First Certificate at the second attempt will result in training being discontinued.

8.4 (i) When a period of eighteen calendar months training has been completed, the candidate shall be required to obtain and submit a certificate (Final Certificate) signed by the Matron or Director of Nursing and Principal Tutor or Tutor of the approved hospital or institution concerned, certifying that the candidate is proficient in clinical midwifery skills.

(ii) A candidate who fails to obtain the First Certificate of Proficiency in Clinical Midwifery Skills, after the completion of eighteen calendar months training, shall be allowed a second attempt at the end of a further two calendar months training. Failure to obtain the First Certificate at the second attempt will result in training being discontinued.

8.5 (i) After completion of the two year training programme, the Board shall hold the written and oral elements of the Registration Examination. Such examinations will normally be held on four occasions each year.

8.6 Before entry to the written or oral examination, the candidate shall be required to:-

(i) Have submitted the First and Final Certificates of Proficiency in Clinical Midwifery skills;

(ii) Submit a certificate signed by the Matron or Director of Nursing and Principal Tutor or Tutor of the approved hospital or institution concerned, certifying that the candidate has received the theoretical and technical instruction required by the syllabus for entry to the written and oral examinations.

8.7 A candidate who is refused either the First or Final Certificate of Proficiency in Clinical Midwifery Skills may appeal against such refusal in writing by registered post to reach the Board not later than two weeks after obtaining the result. On consideration of such appeal, the Board shall convey its decision to the candidate and the hospital or institution concerned and the Board's decision in such matters shall be final.

8.8
(i) A candidate, who considers that the result of the written element of the Examination does not accurately reflect her performance in such Examination, may appeal to the Board for a re-examination of the paper. An application for re-examination, accompanied by the appropriate fee, must be forwarded by the candidate concerned by registered post to reach the Board not later than fourteen days after the issue of the examination result.

(ii) A candidate who is unsuccessful in the written or oral examination shall be allowed two further attempts at successive written and oral examinations and if still unsuccessful after three attempts, training will be discontinued and the candidate shall not proceed to any further such Examination.

8.9 In order to be successful in the written and oral examinations, a candidate must obtain at least 50% in each element. Honours shall be awarded to candidates achieving a mark of 70% in the aggregated results.

9. General Provisions

9.1 The Board shall set out in the syllabus for each training programme details of theoretical, technical and clinical instruction and experience required for completion of such programme and may, with the consent of the Minister, include criteria in relation to the duration of theoretical instruction, the extent of night duty and the manner in which breaks in training - including sick leave and maternity leave - shall be treated for the purpose of completion of such programmes.

9.2 The Board shall inform candidates as soon as possible after their examination as to the results of the examinations.

PART IV - CANDIDATE REGISTER

10.1 The Board shall establish and maintain a Register of Candidates admitted for training on which the name of every such candidate shall be entered.

10.2 Not later than fourteen days after the commencement of training a student shall apply to the Board on the appropriate form to have her name entered on the Candidate Register.

10.3 The student's training shall be taken to have commenced on the date certified in the appropriate form by the Matron or Director of Nursing and Principal Tutor or Tutor of the approved hospital or institution concerned.

10.4 Each student whose name is entered on the Candidate Register shall be issued with a personal identification number and shall be supplied with a student card bearing such identification number, title of course of training for which she is registered and date of commencement of training together with a copy of the syllabus for such training course.

10.5 A candidate shall apply to have her name entered separately on the Candidate Register for each registration course undertaken.

10.6 A fee in accordance with section 25(*e*) of the Act shall be payable by a student in respect of each application for entry in the Candidate Register.

10.7 The Matron or Director of Nursing and Principal Tutor or Tutor or other appropriate person shall inform the Board when a student ceases training before completion of the course and the reason therefor.

PART V - TRANSITIONAL

11.1 A person whose name was entered in the Clinical Teachers Supplementary Division of the former Register shall have the qualification of "Clinical Teacher" entered after her name where entered in any division of the new Register and shall be entitled to use the abbreviation "C.T." after her name.

11.2 A person whose name was entered in the Advanced Psychiatric Nurses Supplementary Division of the former Register shall have the qualification of "Advanced Psychiatric Nurse" entered after her name where entered in the Psychiatric Nurses Register.

11.3 Persons whose names were entered in the Supplementary Division of the former Register containing names of General nurses who had passed the examination for the Post-Registration Qualification in Tuberculosis shall have the qualification "Qualified Tuberculosis Nurse" entered after her name in the new Register.

11.4 Persons whose names were entered in the Supplementary Division of the former Register containing names of General nurses who had passed the examination for the Post-registration Qualification in Orthopaedic Nursing shall have the qualification "Qualified Orthopaedic Nurse" entered after her name in the new Register.

11.5 (a) A person whose name was entered in the Infectious Diseases Nurses Division of the former register and who is entitled to be registered in one or more of the Divisions of the new register shall have the qualification "Infectious Diseases Nurse" entered after her name in the new Register;

(b) a person whose name was entered in the Infectious Diseases Nurses Division of the former register and who is not entitled to be registered in one or more of the Divisions of the new Register shall have her name entered on a Supplementary division of the new register entitled "Supplementary Infectious Diseases Nurses Division" and shall be entitled to use the initials "R.I.D.N." after her name.

11.6 (a) A person whose name was entered in the Sanatorium Nurses Division of the former register and who is entitled to be registered in one or more of the Divisions of the new register shall have the qualification "Sanatorium Nurse" entered after her name in the new Register;

(b) a person whose name was entered in the Sanatorium Nurses Division of the former register and who is not entitled to be registered in one or more of the Divisions of the new Register shall have her name entered on a Supplementary division of the new register entitled "Supplementary Sanatorium Nurses Division" and shall be entitled to use the initials "R.S.N." after her name.

COUNCIL DIRECTIVE (77/452/EEC)

Council Directive of 27 June 1977 concerning the mutual recognition of diplomas, certificates and other evidence of the formal qualifications of nurses responsible for general care, including measures to facilitate the effective exercise of the right of establishment and freedom to provide services.

CHAPTER 1

SCOPE

Article 1

1. This Directive shall apply to the activities of nurses responsible for general care.

2. For the purposes of this Directive "activities of nurses responsible for general care" shall mean activities pursued by persons holding the following titles:

in Germany: "Krankenschwester", "Krankenpfleger";
in Belgium: "hospitalier(ère)/verpleegassistent(e)", "infirmier(ère)
    hospitalier(ère)/ziekenhuisverpleger (-verpleegster)";
in Denmark: "sygeplejerske";
in France: "infirmier ((ère)";
in Ireland: Registered General Nurse;
in Italy: "infermiere professionale";
in Luxembourg: "infirmier";
in the Netherlands: "verpleegkundige":
in the United Kingdom:
England, Wales and Northern Ireland: "State Registered Nurse);
Scotland: Registered General Nurse.

CHAPTER II

DIPLOMAS, CERTIFICATES AND OTHER EVIDENCE OF FORMAL QUALIFICATIONS OF NURSES RESPONSIBLE FOR GENERAL CARE

Article 2

Each Member State shall recognise the diplomas, certificates and other evidence of formal qualifications awarded to nationals of Member States by other Member States in accordance with Article 1 of Directive 77/453/EEC and which are listed in Article 3, by giving such qualifications, as far as the right to take up and pursue the activities of a nurse responsible for general care in a self-employed capacity is concerned, the same effect in its territory as those which the Member State itself awards.

Article 3

The diplomas, certificates and other evidence of formal qualifications referred to in Article 2 are the following:

(a) *in Germany:*

- the certificates awarded by the competent authorities as a result of the "staatliche Prüfung in der Krankenpflege" (State nursing examination),

- the certificates from the competent authorities of the Federal Republic of Germany stating that the diplomas awarded after 8 May 1945 by the competent authorities of the German Democratic Republic are recognised as equivalent to those listed in the first indent;

(b) *In Belgium:*

- the certificate of "hospitalier(ère)/verpleegassistent(e)" awarded by the State or by schools established or recognised by the State,

- the certificate of "infirmier(ère) hospitalier(ère)/ziekenhuisverpleger (-verpleegster)" awarded by the State or by schools established or recognised by the State,

- the diploma of "infirmier(ère) gradué(e) hospitalier(ère)/ gegradueerd ziekenhuisverpleger (-verpleegster)" awarded by the State or by higher paramedical colleges established or recognised by the State;

(c) *in Denmark:*

- the diploma of "sygeplejerske" awarded by nursing schools recognised by the "Sundhedsstyrelsen" (State board of health);

(d) *in France:*

- the State diploma of "infirmier (ère)" awarded by the Ministry of Health;

(e) *in Ireland:*

- the certificate of "Registered General Nurse" awarded by "An Bord Altranais" (the Nursing Board);

(f) *in Italy:*

- the "diploma di abilitazione professionale per infermiere professionale" awarded by State recognised schools;

(g) *in Luxembourg:*

- the State diploma of "infirmier"

- the State diploma of "infirmier hospitalier gradué"
awarded by the Ministry of Public Health on the strength of an examining board decision;

(h) *in the Netherlands:*

- the diplomas of "verpleger A", "verpleegster A" or "verpleegkundige A",

- the diploma of "verpleegkundige MBOV (Middelbare Beroepsopleiding Verpleegkundige)" (intermediate nursing training),

- the diploma of "verpleekundige HBOV (Hogere Beroepsopleiding Verpleegkundige)" (higher nursing training),

awarded by one of the examining boards appointed by the public authorities;

(i) *in the United Kingdom*:

- the certificate of admission to the general part of the Register, awarded in England and Wales by the General Nursing Council for England and Wales, in Scotland by the General Nursing Council for Scotland and in Northern Ireland by the Northern Ireland Council for Nurses and Midwives.

CHAPTER III
EXISTING CIRCUMSTANCES

Article 4

In the case of nationals of Member States whose diplomas, certificates and other evidence of formal qualifications do not satisfy all the minimum training requirements laid down in Article 1 of Directive 77/453/EEC, each Member State shall recognise as being sufficient proof, the diplomas, certificates and other evidence of formal qualifications of nurses responsible for general care awarded by those Member State before the implementation of Directive 77/453/EEC, accompanied by a certificate stating that those nationals have effectively and lawfully been engaged in the activities of nurses responsible for general care for at least three years during the five years prior to the date of issue of the certificate.

These activities must have included taking full responsibility for the planning, organisation and carrying out of the nursing care of the patient.

CHAPTER IV
USE OF ACADEMIC TITLE

Article 5

1. Without prejudice to Article 13, host Member States shall ensure that nationals of Member States who fulfil the conditions laid down in Articles 2 and 4 have the right to use

185

the lawful academic title, inasmuch as it is not identical to the professional title, or, where appropriate, the abbreviation thereof of their Member State of origin or of the Member State from which they come, in the language or languages of that State. Host Member States may require this title to be followed by the name and location of the establishment or examining board which awarded it.

2. If the academic title used in the Member State of origin, or in the Member State from which a foreign national comes, can be confused in the host Member State with a title requiring, in that State, additional training which the person concerned has not undergone, the host Member State may require such a person to use the title employed in the Member State of origin or the Member State from which he comes, in suitable wording to be indicated by the host Member State.

CHAPTER V
PROVISIONS TO FACILITATE THE EFFECTIVE EXERCISE OF THE RIGHT OF ESTABLISHMENT AND FREEDOM TO PROVIDE SERVICES IN RESPECT OF THE ACTIVITIES OF NURSES RESPONSIBLE FOR GENERAL CARE

A. Provisions specifically relating to the right of establishment

Article 6

1. A host Member State which requires of its nationals proof of good character or good repute when they take up for the first time any activity referred to in Article 1 shall accept as sufficient evidence, in respect of nationals of other Member States, a certificate issued by a competent authority in the Member State of origin or in the Member State from which the foreign national comes from attesting that the requirements of the Member State as to good character or good repute for taking up the activity in question have been met.

2. Where the Member State of origin or the Member State from which the foreign national comes from does not require proof of good character or good repute of persons wishing to take up the activity in question for the first time, the host Member State may require of nationals of the Member State of origin or the Member State from which the foreign national comes an extract from the "judicial record" or, failing this, an equivalent document issued by a competent authority in the Member State of origin or the Member State from which the foreign national comes.

3. If the host Member State has detailed knowledge of a serious matter which has occurred outside its territory and which is likely to affect the taking up within its territory of the activity concerned, it may inform the Member State of origin or the Member State from which the foreign national comes.

The Member State of origin or the Member State from which the foreign national comes shall verify the accuracy of the facts if they are likely to affect in that Member State the taking up of the activity in question. The authorities in that State shall decide on the nature and extent of the investigation to be made and shall inform the host Member State of any consequential action which they take with regard to the certificates or documents they have issued.

Member States shall ensure the confidentiality of the information which is forwarded.

Article 7

1. Where, in a host Member State, provisions laid down by law, regulation or administrative action are in force laying down requirements as to good character or good repute, including provisions for disciplinary action in respect of serious professional misconduct or conviction for criminal offences and relating to the pursuit of any of the activities referred to in Article 1, the Member State of origin or the Member State from which the foreign national comes shall forward to the host Member State all necessary information regarding measures or disciplinary action of a professional or administrative nature taken in respect of the person concerned, or criminal penalties imposed on him when pursuing his profession in the Member State of origin or the Member State from which he came.

2. If the host Member State has detailed knowledge of a serious matter which has occurred outside its territory and which is likely to affect the pursuit within its territory of the activity, it may inform the Member State of origin or the Member State from which the foreign national comes.

The Member State of origin or the Member State from which the foreign national comes shall verify the accuracy of the facts if they are likely to affect in that Member State the pursuit of the activity in question. The authorities in that State shall decide on the nature and extent of the investigation to be made and shall inform the host Member State of any consequential action which they take with regard to the information they have forwarded in accordance with paragraph 1.

3. Member States shall ensure the confidentiality of the information which is forwarded.

Article 8

When a host Member State requires of its own nationals wishing to take up or pursue any of the activities referred to in Article 1 a certificate of physical or mental health, that State shall accept as sufficient evidence thereof the presentation of the document required in the Member State of origin or the Member State from which the foreign national comes.

Where the Member State of origin or the Member State from which the foreign national comes does not impose any requirements of this nature on those wishing to take up or pursue the activity in question, the host Member State shall accept from such national a certificate issued by a competent authority in that State corresponding to the certificates issued in the host Member State.

Article 9

Documents issued in accordance with Articles 6, 7 and 8 may not be presented more than three months after their date of issue.

Article 10

1. The procedure for authorising the person concerned to take up any activity referred to in Article 1, pursuant to Articles 6, 7 and 8, must be completed as soon as possible and not later than three months after presentation of all the documents relating to such person, without prejudice to delays resulting from any appeal that may be made upon the termination of this procedure.

2 In the cases referred to in Articles 6 (3) and 7(2), a request for re-examination shall suspend the period stipulated in paragraph 1.

The Member State consulted shall give its reply within three months.

On receipt of the reply or at the end of the period the host Member State shall continue with the procedure referred to in paragraph 1.

B. Special provisions relating to the provision of services

Article 11

1. Where a Member State requires of its own nationals wishing to take up or pursue any of the activities referred to in Article 1 an authorisation, or membership of or registration with a professional organisation or body, that Member State shall in the case of the provision of services exempt the nationals of Member States from that requirement.

The person concerned shall provided services with the same rights and obligations as the nationals of the host Member State; in particular he shall be subject to the rules of conduct of a professional or administrative nature which apply in that Member State.

Where a host Member State adopts a measure pursuant to the second subparagraph or becomes aware of facts which run counter to these provisions, it shall forthwith inform the Member States where the person concerned is established.

2. The host Member State may require the person concerned to make a prior declaration to the competent authorities concerning the provision of its services where they involve a temporary stay in its territory.

In urgent cases this declaration may be made as soon as possible after the services have been provided.

3. Pursuant to paragraphs 1 and 2, the host Member State may require the person concerned to supply one or more documents containing the following particulars :

- the declaration referred to in paragraph 2,

- a certificate stating that the person concerned is lawfully pursing the activities in question in the Member State where he is established,

- a certificate that the person concerned hold one or other of the diplomas, certificates or other evidence of formal qualifications appropriate for the provision of the services in question and referred to in this Directive.

4. The document or documents specified in paragraph 3 may not be produced more than 12 months after their date of issue.

5. Where a Member State temporarily or permanently deprives, in whole or in part, one of its nationals or a national of another Member State established in its territory of the right to pursue one of the activities referred to in Article 1, it shall, as appropriate, ensure the temporary or permanent withdrawal of the certificate referred to in the second indent of paragraph 3.

Article 12
Where registration with a public social security body is required in a host Member State for the settlement with insurance bodies of accounts relating to services rendered to persons insured under social security schemes, that Member State shall exempt nationals of Member States established in another Member State from this requirement in cases of provision of services entailing travel on the part of the person concerned. However, the persons concerned shall supply information to this body in advance or, in urgent cases, subsequently, concerning the services provided.

C. Provisions common to the right of establishment and freedom to provide services

Article 13
Where in a host Member State the use of the professional title relating to one of the activities referred to in Article 1 is subject to rules, nationals of other Member States who fulfil the conditions laid down in Articles 2 and 4 shall use the professional title of the host Member State which, in that State, corresponds to those conditions of qualification, and shall use the abbreviated title.

Article 14
Where a host Member State requires its own nationals wishing to take up or pursue one of the activities referred to in Article 1 to take an oath or make a solemn declaration and where the form of such oath or declaration cannot be used by nationals of other Member States, that Member State shall ensure that an appropriate and equivalent form of oath or declaration is offered to the person concerned.

Article 15
1. Member States shall take the necessary measures to enable the persons concerned to obtain information on the health and social security laws and, where applicable, on the professional ethics of the host Member State.

For this purpose, Member States may set up information centres from which such persons may obtain the necessary information. In the case of establishment, the host Member States may require the persons concerned to contact these centres.

2. Member States may set up the centres referred to in paragraph 1 within the competent authorities and bodies which they must designate within the period laid down in Article 19(1).

3. Member States shall see to it that, where appropriate, the persons concerned acquire, in their own interest and in that of their patients, the linguistic knowledge necessary for the exercise of their profession in the host Member State.

CHAPTER VI
FINAL PROVISIONS

Article 16

In the event of justified doubts, the host Member State may require of the competent authorities of another Member State confirmation of the authenticity of the diplomas, certificates and other evidence of formal qualifications issued in that other Member State and referred to in Chapters II and III, and also confirmation of the fact that the person concerned has fulfilled all the training requirements laid down in Directive 77/453/ EEC.

Article 17

Within the time limit laid down in Article 19(1), Member States shall designate the authorities and bodies competent to issue or receive the diplomas, certificates and other evidence of formal qualifications as well as the documents and information referred to in this Directive and shall forthwith inform the other Member States and the Commission thereof.

Article 18

This Directive shall also apply to nationals of Member States who, in accordance with Regulation (EEC) No 1612/68, are pursuing or will pursue as employed persons one of the activities referred to in Article 1.

Article 19

1. Member States shall bring into force the measures necessary to comply with this Directive within two years of its notification and shall forthwith inform the Commission thereof.

2. Member States shall communicate to the Commission the texts of the main provisions of national law which they adopt in the field covered by this Directive.

Article 20

Where a Member State encounters major difficulties in certain fields when applying this Directive, the Commission shall examine these difficulties in conjunction with the State and shall request the opinion of the Committee of Senior Officials on Public Health set up under Decision 75/365/EEC as amended by Decision 77/455/EEC.

Where necessary, the Commission shall submit appropriate proposals to the Council.

Article 21

This Directive is addressed to the Member States.

COUNCIL DIRECTIVE (77/453/EEC)

Council Directive of 27 June 1977 concerning the co-ordination of provisions laid down by law, regulation or administrative action in respect of the activities of nurses responsible for general care.

Article 1

1. Member states shall make the award of diplomas, certificates and other evidence of formal qualifications of nurses responsible for general care as specified in Article 3 of Directive 77/452/EEC subject to passing an examination which guarantees that during his training period the person concerned has acquired:

   (a) adequate knowledge of the sciences on which general nursing is based, including sufficient understanding of the structure, physiological functions and behaviour of healthy and sick persons, and of the relationship between the state of health and the physical and social environment of the human being;

   (b) sufficient knowledge of the nature and ethics of the profession and of the general principles of health and nursing;

   (c) adequate clinical experience; such experience, which would be selected for its training value, should be gained under the supervision of qualified nursing staff and in places where the number of qualified staff and in places where the number of qualified staff and equipment are appropriate for the nursing care of the patients;

   (d) the ability to participate in the practical training of health personnel and experience of working with such personnel;

   (e) experience of working with members of other professions in the health sector.

2. The training referred to in paragraph 1 shall include at least:

   (a) a general school education of 10 years' duration attested by a diploma, certificate or other formal qualification awarded by the competent authorities or bodies in a Member State, or a certificate resulting from a qualifying examination of an equivalent standard for entrance to a nurses' training school;

   (b) full-time training, of a specifically vocational nature, which must cover the subjects of the training programme set out in the Annex to this Directive and comprise a three-year course or 4600 hours of theoretical and practical instruction.

3. Member States shall ensure that the institution training nurses is responsible for the co-ordination of theory and practice throughout the programme.

The theoretical and technical training mentioned in part A of the Annex shall be balanced and co-ordinated with the clinical training of nurses mentioned in part B of the same

Annex in such a way that the knowledge and experience listed in paragraph 1 may be acquired in an adequate manner.

Clinical instruction in nursing shall take the form of supervised in-service training in hospital departments or other heath services, including home nursing services, approved by the competent authorities or bodies. During this training student nurses shall participate in the activities of the departments concerned in so far as those activities contribute to their training. They shall be informed of the responsibilities of nursing care.

4. Five years at the least after notification of this Directive and in the light of a review of the situation, the Council, acting on a proposal from the Commission, shall decide whether the provisions of paragraph 3 on the balance between theoretical and technical training on the one hand and clinical training of nurses on the other should be retained or amended.

5. Member States may grant partial exemption to persons who have undergone part of the training referred to in paragraph 2 (b) in the form of other training which is of at least equivalent standard.

Article 2

Notwithstanding the provisions of Article 1, Member States may permit part-time training under conditions approved by the competent national authorities.

The total period of part-time training may not be shorter than that of full-time training. The standard of the training may not be impaired by its part-time nature.

Article 3

This Directive shall also apply to nationals of Member States who, in accordance with Council Regulation (EEC) No. 1612/68 of 15 October 1968 of freedom of movement for workers within the Community, are pursuing or will pursue, as employed persons, one of the activities referred to in Article 1 of Directive 77/452/EEC.

Article 4

1. Member States shall bring into force the measures necessary to comply with this Directive within two years of its notification and shall forthwith inform the Commission thereof.

2. Member States shall communicate to the Commission the texts of the main provisions of national law which they adopt in the field covered by this Directive.

Article 5

Where a Member State encounters major difficulties in certain fields when applying this Directive, the Commission shall examine these difficulties in conjunction with the State and shall request the opinion of the Committee of Senior Officials on Public Health set up under Decision 75/365/EEC as amended by Decision 77/455/EEC.

Where necessary, the Commission shall submit appropriate proposals to the Council.

Article 6

This Directive is addressed to the Member States.

TRAINING PROGRAMME FOR NURSES RESPONSIBLE FOR GENERAL CARE

The training leading to the award of a diploma, certificate or other formal qualification of nurses responsible for general care shall consist of the following two parts:

A. Theoretical and technical instruction:

(a) nursing:

nature and ethics of the profession, general principles of health and nursing, nursing principles in relation to:
- general and specialist medicine,
- general and specialist surgery,
- child care and paediatrics,
- maternity care,
- mental health an psychiatry,
- care of the old and geriatrics;

(b) basic sciences:

anatomy and physiology,

pathology,

bacteriology, virology and parasitology,

biophysics, biochemistry and radiology,

dietetics,

hygiene:
- preventative medicine,
- health education,

pharmacology;

(c) social sciences:

sociology,

psychology,

principles of administration,

principles of teaching,

social and health legislation, legal aspects of nursing.

B. Clinical instruction:

Nursing in relation to:

- general and specialist medicine,

- general and specialist surgery,

- child care and paediatrics,

- maternity care,

- mental health an psychiatry,

- care of the old and geriatrics;

- home nursing.

COUNCIL DIRECTIVE (92/85/EEC)

Council Directive of 19 October 1992 on the introduction of measures to encourage improvements in the safety and health at work of pregnant workers and workers who have recently given birth or are breastfeeding (tenth individual Directive within the meaning of Article 16 (1) of Directive 89/391/EEC).

(Articles 1-12 and Annex I-II)

SECTION I
PURPOSE AND DEFINITIONS

Article 1: Purpose

1. The purpose of this Directive, which is the tenth individual Directive within the meaning of Article 16(1) of Directive 89/391/EEC, is to implement measures to encourage improvements in the safety and health at work of pregnant workers and workers who have recently given birth or who are breastfeeding.

2. The provisions of Directive 89/391/EEC, except for Article 2(2) thereof, shall apply in full to the whole area covered by paragraph 1, without prejudice to any more stringent and/or specific provisions contained in this Directive.

3. This Directive may not have the effect of reducing the level of protection afforded to pregnant workers, workers who have recently given birth or who are breastfeeding as compared with the situation which exists in each Member State on the date on which the Directive is adopted.

Article 2: Definitions

For the purposes of this Directive:

(a) "pregnant worker" shall mean a pregnant worker who informs her employer of her condition, in accordance with national legislation and/or national practice;

(b) "worker who recently gave birth" shall mean a worker who has recently given birth within the meaning of the national legislation and/or national practice and who informs her employer of her condition, in accordance with that legislation and/or practice;

(c) "worker who is breastfeeding" shall mean a worker who is breastfeeding within the meaning of the national legislation and/or national practice and who informs her employer of her condition, in accordance with that legislation and/or practice.

SECTION II: GENERAL PROVISIONS

Article 3: Guidelines

1. In consultation with the Member States and assisted by the Advisory Committee on Safety, Hygiene and Health Protection at Work, the Commission shall draw up guidelines

195

on the assessment of the chemical, physical and biological agents and industrial processes considered hazardous for the safety or health of workers within the meaning of Article 2.

The guidelines referred to in the first subparagraph shall also cover movements and postures, mental and physical fatigue and other types of physical and mental stress connected with the work done by workers within the meaning of Article 2.

2. The purpose of the guidelines referred to in paragraph 1 is to serve as a basis for the assessment referred to in Article 4(1).

To this end, Member States shall bring these guidelines to the attention of all employers and all female workers and/or their representatives in the respective Member States.

Article 4: Assessment and information

1. For all activities liable to involve a specific risk of exposure to the agents, processes or working conditions of which a non-exhaustive list is given in Annex I, the employer shall assess the nature, degree and duration of exposure, in the undertaking and/or establishment concerned, of workers within the meaning of Article 2, either directly or by way of the protective and preventive services referred to in Article 7 of Directive 89/391/EEC, in order to:

- assess any risks to the safety or health or any possible effect on the pregnancies or breastfeeding of workers within the meaning of Article 2,

- decide what measures should be taken.

2. Without prejudice to Article 10 of Directive 89/391/EEC, workers within the meaning of Article 2 and workers likely to be in one of the situations referred to in Article 2 in the undertaking and/or establishment concerned and/or their representatives shall be informed of the results of the assessment referred to in paragraph 1 and of all measures to be taken concerning health and safety at work.

Article 5: Action further to the results of the assessment

1. Without prejudice to Article 6 of Directive 89/391/EEC, if the results of the assessment referred to in Article 4(1) reveal a risk to the safety or health or an effect on the pregnancy or breastfeeding of a worker within the meaning of Article 2, the employer shall take the necessary measures to ensure that, by temporarily adjusting the working conditions and/or the working hours of the worker concerned, the exposure of that worker to such risks is avoided.

2. If the adjustment of her working conditions and/or the working hours is not technically and/or objectively feasible, or cannot reasonably be required on duly substantiated grounds, the employer shall take the necessary measures to move the worker concerned to another job.

3. If moving her to another job is not technically and/or objectively feasible or cannot reasonably be required on duly substantiated grounds, the worker concerned shall be

granted leave in accordance with national legislation and/or national practice for the whole of the period necessary to protect her safety or health.

4. The provisions of this Article shall apply mutatis mutandis to the case where a worker pursuing an activity which is forbidden pursuant to Article 6 becomes pregnant or starts breastfeeding and informs her employer thereof.

Article 6: Cases in which exposure is prohibited

In addition to the general provisions concerning the protection of workers, in particular those relating to the limit values for occupational exposure:

1. pregnant workers within the meaning of Article 2(a) may under no circumstances be obliged to perform duties for which the assessment has revealed a risk of exposure, which would jeopardise safety or health, to the agents and working conditions listed in Annex II, Section A;

2. workers who are breastfeeding, within the meaning of Article 2(c) may under no circumstances be obliged to perform duties for which the assessment has revealed a risk of exposure, which would jeopardise safety or health, to the agents and working conditions listed in Annex II, Section B.

Article 7: Night work

1. Member States shall take the necessary measures to ensure that workers referred to in Article 2 are not obliged to perform night work during their pregnancy and for a period following childbirth which shall be determined by the national authority competent for safety and health, subject to submission, in accordance with the procedures laid down by the Member States, of a medical certificate stating that this is necessary for the safety or health of the worker concerned.

2. The measures referred to in paragraph 1 must entail the possibility, in accordance with national legislation and/or national practice, of:

(a) transfer to daytime work; or

(b) leave from work or extension of maternity leave where such a transfer technically and/or objectively feasible, or cannot reasonably be required on duly substantiated grounds.

Article 8: Maternity leave

1. Member States shall take the necessary measures to ensure that workers within the meaning of Article 2 are entitled to a continuous period of maternity leave of at least 14 weeks allocated before and/or after confinement in accordance with national legislation and/or national practice.

2. The maternity leave stipulated in paragraph 1 must include compulsory maternity leave of at least two weeks allocated before and/or after confinement in accordance with national legislation and/or national practice.

Article 9: Time off for ante-natal examinations

Member States shall take the necessary measures to ensure that workers within the meaning of Article 2(a) are entitled to, in accordance with national legislation and/or national practice, time off, without loss of pay, in order to attend ante-natal examinations, if such examinations have to take place during working hours.

Article 10: Prohibition of dismissal

In order to guarantee workers within the meaning of Article 2, the exercise of their health and safety protection rights as recognised under this Article, it shall be provided that:

1. Member States shall take the measures to prohibit the dismissal of workers, within the meaning of Article 2, during the period from the beginning of their pregnancy to the end of the maternity leave referred to in Article 8(1), save in exceptional cases not connected with their condition which are permitted under national legislation and/or national practice and, where applicable provided that the competent authority has given its consent;

2. If a worker, within the meaning of Article 2, is dismissed during the period referred to in point 1, the employer must cite duly substantiated grounds for her dismissal in writing;

3. Member States shall take the necessary measures to protect workers, within the meaning of Article 2, from consequences of dismissal which is unlawful by virtue of point 1.

Article 11: Employment rights

In order to guarantee workers within the meaning of Article 2 the exercise of their health and safety protection rights as recognised in this Article, it shall be provided that:

1. in the cases referred to in Articles 5, 6 and 7, the employment rights relating to the employment contract, including the maintenance of a payment to, and/or entitlement to an adequate allowance for, workers within the meaning of Article 2, must be ensured in accordance national legislation and/or national practice;

2. in the case referred to in Article 8, the following must be ensured:

   (a) the rights connected with the employment contract of workers within the meaning of Article 2, other than those referred to in point (b) below;

   (b) maintenance of a payment to, and/or entitlement to an adequate allowance for, workers within the meaning of Article 2;

3. the allowance referred to in point 2(b) shall be deemed adequate if it guarantees income at least equivalent to that which the worker concerned would receive in the event of a break in her activities on grounds connected with her state of health, subject to any ceiling laid down under national legislation;

4. Member States may make entitlement to pay or the allowance referred to in points 1 and 2(b) conditional upon the worker concerned fulfilling the conditions of eligibility for such benefits laid down under national legislation. These conditions may under no circumstances provided of previous employment in excess of 12 months immediately prior to the presumed date of confinement.

Article 12: Defence of rights

Member States shall introduce into their national legal systems such measures as are necessary to enable all workers who should themselves wronged by failure to comply with the obligations arising from this Directive to pursue their claims by judicial process (and/or, in accordance with national laws and/or practices) by recourse to other competent authorities.

ANNEX 1

NON-EXHAUSTIVE LIST OF AGENTS, PROCESSES AND WORKING CONDITIONS REFERRED TO IN ARTICLE 4(1)

A. Agents

1. Physical agents where these are regarded as agents causing foetal lesions and/or likely to disrupt placental attachment, and in particular:

(a) shocks, vibration or movement;

(b) handling of loads entailing risks, particularly of a dorsolumbar nature;

(c) noise;

(d) ionising radiation;[1]

(e) non-ionising radiation;

(f) extremes of cold or heat;

(g) movements and postures, travelling - either inside or outside the establishment - mental and physical burdens connected with the activity of the worker within the meaning of Article 2 of this Directive.

2. Biological agents

Biological agents of risk groups 2, 3 and 4 within the meaning of Article 2(d) numbers 2, 3 and 4 of Directive 90/679/EEC,[2] in so far as it is known that these agents or the therapeutic measures necessitated by such agents endanger the heath of pregnant women and the unborn child and in so far as they do not yet appear in Annex II.

3. Chemical agents

The following chemical agents in so far as it is known that they endanger the health of pregnant women and the unborn child and in so far as they do not yet appear in Annex II:

(a) substances labelled R 40, R 45, R 46, and R 47 under Directive 67/548/EEC[3] in so far as they do not yet appear in Annex II;

---

[1] See Directive 80/836/Euratom (OJ No. L 246, 17.9.1980, p.1.)

[2] OJ No L 374, 31.12.1990, p. 1.

[3] OJ No L 196, 16.8.1967, p. 1. Directive as last amended by Directive 90/517/EEC)OJ No L 287, 19.10.1990, p.37.

(b) chemical agents in Annex I to Directive 90/394/EEC;[4]

(c) mercury and mercury derivatives;

(d) antimitotic drugs;

(e) carbon monoxide;

(f) chemical agents of known and dangerous percutaneous absorption.

B. Processes

Industrial processes listed in Annex 1 to Directive 90/394/EEC.

C. Working conditions.

Underground mining work.

---

[4] OJ No L 196, 26.7.1990, p.1.

ANNEX II

NON-EXHAUSTIVE LIST OF AGENTS AND WORKING CONDITIONS REFERRED TO IN ARTICLE 6

A. Pregnant workers within the meaning of Article 2(a)

1. Agents.

(a) Physical agents.

Work in hyperbaric atmosphere, e.g., pressurised enclosures and underwater diving.

(b) Biological agents.

The following biological agents:

- toxoplasma,

- rubella virus,

unless the pregnant workers are proved to be adequately protected against such agents by immunisation.

(c) Chemical agents.

Lead and lead derivatives in so far as these agents are capable of being absorbed by the human organism.

2. Working conditions.
Underground mining work.

B. Workers who are breastfeeding within the meaning of Article 2(c)

1. Agents.

(a) Chemical agents

Lead and lead derivatives in so far as these agents are capable of being absorbed by the human organism.

2. Working conditions.

Underground mining work.

INDEX